Among
the Healers

Among the Healers

Stories of Spiritual and Ritual Healing around the World

Edith Turner

RELIGION, HEALTH, AND HEALING
Susan S. Sered and Linda L. Barnes, Series Editors

PRAEGER

Westport, Connecticut
London

Library of Congress Cataloging-in-Publication Data

Turner, Edith L. B., 1921–
    Among the healers : stories of spiritual and ritual healing around the world /
Edith Turner.
       p.   cm.—(Religion, health, and healing, ISSN 1556–262X)
    Includes bibliographical references and index.
    ISBN 0–275–98729–9 (alk. paper)
    1. Spiritual healing.   2. Alternative medicine.   3. Medicine, Magic, mystic,
and spagiric.   I. Title.   II. Series.
    BL65.M4T87   2006
    615.8'52'09—dc22   2005019268

British Library Cataloguing in Publication Data is available.

Library of Congress Catalog Card Number: 2005019268
ISBN: 0–275–98729–9
ISSN: 1556–262X

First published in 2006

Praeger Publishers, 88 Post Road West, Westport, CT 06881
An imprint of Greenwood Publishing Group, Inc.
www.praeger.com

Printed in the United States of America

∞™

The paper used in this book complies with the
Permanent Paper Standard issued by the National
Information Standards Organization (Z39.48–1984).

10 9 8 7 6 5 4 3 2 1

Copyright Acknowledgments

Contents

Series Foreword

The Religion, Health, and Healing series brings together authors from a variety of academic disciplines and cultural settings in order to foster understandings of the ways in which religious traditions, concepts, and practices frame health and healing experiences both in the United States and around the world. The books in this series offer examples of the meanings associated with religion, spirituality, curing, and healing, in diverse historical and social contexts.

The word *healing* in and of itself is multidimensional and multifunctional, especially in religious settings. It can mean the direct, unequivocal, and scientifically measurable cure of physical illnesses. It can mean the alleviation of pain or other symptoms. It can also mean coping, coming to terms with, or learning to live with that which one cannot change (including physical illness and emotional trauma). Healing can mean integration and connection among all the elements of one's being, the reestablishment of self-worth, connection with one's tradition, or personal empowerment. Healing can be about repairing one's relationships with friends, relations, ancestors, the community, the world, the Earth, and/or God. It can refer to developing a sense of well-being or wholeness, whether emotional, social, spiritual, physical, or in relation to other aspects of being that are valued by a particular group. Healing can be about purification; repenting from sin; the cleaning up of one's negative karma; entry into a path of "purer," abstinent, or more moral daily living; eternal salvation; or submission to God's will.

Healing can concern the individual, the family, the community, the nation, the world, or the cosmos as a whole. We think here of healing acts that range from personal spiritual awakenings to the national healing that went on in the United States after September 11, as well as the notion of *tikkun olam* (repairing the world) as it is used in Jewish mystical writings. Perhaps the most common theme in religious accounts of healing is the enactment of change, whether understood as restoration to an earlier state or as transformation to a new one, in relation to the experience of affliction or suffering.[1]

The transformation that comes about in the healing process implies movement from one, less desirable state, to another, more desirable state. Thus, the study of religion and healing includes looking at how individuals, communities, and religious traditions diagnose and interpret causes of illness and the sources of affliction, as well as notions of what constitutes health, both ideally and pragmatically.

Exploring ways in which biomedicine—the biologically based system that many people identify simply as "medicine"—converges with different religions in the United States today is another central concern of this series. Some of these interactions are synergistic, while others are antagonistic. As examples of the first, we think of hospital chaplains, of interdisciplinary teams on hospital ethics committees, of faith-based clinics, and of the many health care providers who draw upon their personal spiritual resources in order to provide compassionate care to their patients. As examples of the second, we think of public disputes regarding abortion and the end of life, and of the disdain expressed by some members of the medical community for the traditional healing practices of some immigrant groups or some spiritually related healing practices included under the broad heading of *complementary and alternative medicine*.

While the series focuses primarily upon the United States, the historical underpinnings and global contexts in which these practices and ideas unfold are an important part of the landscape that the series will explore as well. Thus, we are especially delighted to begin this series with Edith Turner's broadly painted picture of the religious and spiritual healers whom she has known over the course of her long career as an anthropologist. Turner has also selected many accounts of healing from other anthropological writings to substantiate the general picture. In *Among the Healers*, Turner shares the experiential approach to understanding cultures developed together with her late husband Victor Turner during the years they conducted fieldwork together in Africa and Europe, and refined further as she continued to work in Ireland, the United States, and among the Iñupiat. Turner's depiction of her growing conviction that healing is *real* allows her to delve deeply into the meanings, and not only the forms, of religious healing. Moving from her observations of healers in her adopted home state of Virginia to her visits and revisits in Africa, Turner's work is an extraordinary example of the anthropologist's commitment to "make the exotic familiar and to make the familiar exotic."

That commitment encapsulates the aim of this series. We hope that through facilitating the publication of studies of diverse healers, healing communities, and healing practices, we will offer readers tools to uncover both the common and the uncommon ways in which Americans engage with, find meaning in, and seek to embrace, transcend, or overcome individual and communal suffering.

Susan S. Sered and Linda L. Barnes
Boston, MA
March, 2005

NOTE

1. For more on this, see Linda Barnes and Susan Sered, eds., *Religion and Healing in America* (New York: Oxford University Press, 2005).

Preface

My life reaches far back. There were already many decades behind me when I saw healing for the first time. When I was a teenager I loved the Romantic poets, a fact that has a bearing on this story. Later, when I married, my husband, Victor Turner, I read Margaret Mead and became an anthropologist. As for me, I began a life of child rearing. I knew that Central Africa was going to be our special area. Although I was the mother of three children, I too was fascinated with the science of human behavior, and was determined to do fieldwork too and to work on the rituals for young girls.

We went out to Zambia—then known as Northern Rhodesia. I immersed myself in fieldwork, finding that I was often drawn into the Africans' drum rituals. The drum rituals—actually healing rituals—also involved a great array of physical material: special meaningful objects, medicines, face marks, arrows, and beads, with meanings to which we began to pay close attention. The rituals were acts of great sensitivity and skill, directed toward mysterious spirits, *akishi*.

After we came back home, with the drums still echoing in our heads and making us long for Africa, both of us suddenly joined the Catholic Church, a religion full of ritual. The date was 1958, before Vatican II. We were now plunged into yet another mass of symbols, in our own society.

In the 1960s we moved to the United States, and from there we conducted research on religious pilgrimages in Mexico and Europe. We went to Israel and studied the Hasidim and Arabs and their different religions; we were in Brazil for a time, working on Umbanda spirit rites and impressed by their power. Back in the United States, we worked intensively on symbolism, especially the symbols of Africa, and saw the complexity, subtlety, and power in them. Their rituals were what they actually *did* to reach the spirits. Africans cried aloud to the spirits—"Come out! *Fuma!*" The medicine people drummed and sang, making a loud and beautiful noise to arouse the spirit. They danced to invite the spirit. They showed their love and longing for their ancestors by making small gifts and sacrifices to them. They seemed to be able to "get on the spirituality wavelength" and knew how to do it. They knew how to attract a spirit and bring about its presence, and they went about it with the most serious purpose—the healing and fruitfulness of the people.

In the 1970s, after much thinking about how people experienced their religions, Vic and I stumbled on an idea that we named *communitas*, the fellowship between person and person on the simplest level. I was stirred to the core and began to explore it. In 1983 Vic died of a heart attack and I sorely missed him. I was now on my own with the consciousness of communitas still on me, creating a hunger in me. Where could I find this full human being, this sociable "I"? By 1985 I was feeling the tug of Africa badly. I wanted to go back and be among the dancing and mocking women, I wanted to hear those great bursts of delighted laughter, join in the triumph of the mother-power, witness the amazing discovery of these women—that they were stronger than the men. So I went back to Africa. Good things happened on that trip: an assistant came with me, a student named Bill Blodgett, and he and I met Fideli, a practicing medicine man, and before we knew where we were we found ourselves in Fideli's ritual, fully in it, and I saw the religion of Africa for myself. One day in the village, around a little African shrine—just a forked pole— holy things were being done. Drums played. The old medicine men sang and I sang too, caught up in the friendship that suddenly flowered. The crowd was intent on "singing out" a harmful spirit from the body of a sick woman. I was plunged in the African spirit milieu in spite of myself. At the climax I saw the harmful spirit come out of the sick woman. I saw it, a large gray sphere, a ghost-spirit.

After this revelation the only thing to do was to follow up on what happened. I began to search—in Africa, the Arctic, Ireland, anywhere on the map—following clues. The search took its own form. Inside myself I felt the scientific obligation to reduce religion to logic beginning to melt away. Now I had another obligation, to go to countries where people said they had experienced spirit events, and listen to what they were talking about—let *them* missionize *me*. I was not going to missionize them. It was time for a reversal.

A plan began to form. I would live with ordinary people in countries where spiritual healing was still practiced, where people habitually experienced their religion, or where God was all around. Opportunities came my way. I spent a year among the healers of the Iñupiat in northern Alaska; after that I lived with the dairy farmers of southwestern Ireland. I found confirmation of my guess: both communities had real spirit experiences. This was what I was after. The quest drew me even farther afield—and I found more: among the Yupik of St. Lawrence Island in the Bering Straits; with Saami healers in the Kola peninsula of Russia; at a Maori *marae* festival in New Zealand; then back home to experience a curious healing, with myself as subject, in the Hilton Hotel in San Francisco; then to learn from American suburban healers; and afterwards to join in the praying in American black healing churches. All these cases gave me confirmation. Meanwhile I remembered what I had seen in Africa in earlier decades and began to reinterpret it. Way back in 1953 during my two years in Zambia, there were a number of times when I felt hints of the presence of African ancestors and even powers, but I had let them pass unrecorded. Now these experiences had a different meaning. I also remembered witnessing a deer dance in the 1970s among the Yaqui of Arizona, when the dancer *became* the deer; I remembered participating in Umbanda spirit gatherings in Brazil; then in the 1980s when I was with the shamans of Korea. One could sense the attention in the shamans' voices and feel the presence of those whom they were calling. It was true. Now that my eyes had been opened, I noticed what I had overlooked before: spirits were present and they were real. This was a matter far removed from medical or psychological understanding.

My disbelief was willingly suspended. Some might say I had become a neo-Romantic, happy in the imaginary expansion of my horizon. It was not the case with the experiences portrayed in this book. The revelations were not illusions that took place inside people's heads. For instance, when the Maoris called on the presence of the ancestors at their *marae* ritual, the ancestors were indeed present; and the same kind of truth applied to countless other experiencers in different parts of the world.

Accordingly, from that time onward I participated wherever I could. I not only sang and danced along with the people but I also prayed with them, submitted to their healing, and tried to do the healing myself.

Material of this kind, then, drawn from my work and that of many similar anthropologists in twenty-four cultures, is the source of the stories in this book. They are stories that open up a world of forces and spirits; this kind of world is what religion is about. It even looks to be our human birthright. Everyone has the right to these experiences, whether in the form of drumming, healing, prayers, visions, giving oneself to God, or a strange sense of energy. The realization of what happened, there at the ritual in Zambia, changed my personal direction in life.

Acknowledgments

My principal debt is to the numerous authors and recorders of the passages that I have used in the stories about healing in this book. I thank these authors and attribute the strength of the book to them: Julia Megan Webb, David Eisenberg, Richard Katz, Stephen Friedson, Meredith McGuire, Suchitra Samanta, Thomas Csordas, Francis MacNutt, Richard Erdoes and Lame Deer, William Powers, Joan Metge, Janice Reid, James Dow, John Neihardt, Yoram Bilu, Douglas Reinhardt, Ruel Tyson, Michael Walsh, Janice Boddy, Roy Willis, Froelich Rainey, Larry Peters, Shaykh Hakim Chishti, Jacob Moreno, and Michael Harner.

I owe a special debt of gratitude to friends and discussants in my own fields of research who have helped me understand the healing of their countries: Fideli Benwa of Zambia and the healer I am calling Claire, both of whom showed me the greatest kindness in my researches. The healers of Charlottesville, Virginia, who attended our monthly gatherings did wonders to enlighten me on many types of healing, and I thank them here, especially Janet Holmes and Sue Jansen. The church and its small groups gave more than friendship—they taught me spirituality. St. Patrick's Purgatory in Ireland made me humble—or it tried to. During the years of experience, my daughter Irene Wellman became in a sense the mother of this book and welcomed it with delight. I specially thank Reed Malcolm, Tom Grady, Suzanne Staszak-Silva, and Cheryl Adam for their help with the manuscript. Furthermore, I am more grateful than certain folks in academia will ever know—those who gave me encouragement and the nerve to do what I needed to do—Susan Starr Sered, Linda L. Barnes, Matthew Engelke, Roy Wagner, Benjamin Ray, Pamela Frese, Rory Turner, and many others. Students who learned shamanism and healing in my class brought many as-yet-undiscovered aspects of healing to my notice, particularly Justin Shaffner, Tatiana Tchoudakova, and Jessica Freeman. Native Americans have constantly spoken their words of wonder about the spirits and told me of healings and visions. I thank them all, and I thank the many dead who gave life to my work— first and foremost, Victor Turner, trailblazer into the forests of mystical participation, and secondly, my own father, George Davis, M.D., who taught me biology and knowledge of the world in which we live, and aroused in me a profound respect for healing.

The research of my own that has gone into the book was funded by the Carter-Woodson Institute for African and African American Research, the Wenner-Gren Foundation for Anthropological Research, the University of Virginia, and James and Mary McConnell. I am most grateful for their support.

Finally, I owe the existence of the book to the great-spirit-energy-power-communitas of the universe. Thank you.

Introduction: Coming to Recognize Spiritual Healing

When nonmedical healing happens in this world, we usually welcome it. We wonder whether it has a spiritual origin. Does a miracle occur? What is happening when nonmedical healers work on people and they get better? Can we ever know what is going on at the spiritual level? Does something pass between healer and sufferer?

Spiritual healing is almost beyond words and definitions. When we venture into this shadowy area we cannot find words to describe it, and yet somehow we have found the location where healing dwells. We haltingly say what we think, and then to our surprise we find that our listeners recognize what we are trying to say. Their eyes shine, and they come out with strange stories of their own that exactly catch the drift of it. Some folk try to put the incommunicable nature of spiritual healing into long words such as *ineffability*, but this leads to a swamp of jargon, which is not what healing is about. Healing is known in the actual experience that the healer goes through and the experience of the person being healed. The simplest way to put the matter is that the sufferer is no longer in pain. Some mysterious path to power has opened up, to the betterment of the person's body, soul, and mind.

Many stories affirm that healing is provided by a power or spirit helper coming to assist a willing person who has the gift from the power or spirit. It is this power or spirit that works through the healer for the sufferer and takes away pain and the source of the trouble. Healing is done by

paying close attention to what is going on in the body of the sick person, giving love, and letting go any idea that "you can't know another
person's feelings."

The longing for healing is central at the depth of human consciousness—at the depth of its human pole; and the work of the healer takes
effect just where that deep consciousness of healer joins with the sufferer
and latches onto the powers or conscious spirits that dwell around and
through them both. Looked at rightly, healing, like the miraculous loss
of self in sex, or the act of feeding the hungry, or the giving of one's life
for another, is a supremely good physical act on behalf of a human being.
Of all religious acts, healing is the most innocent, the most often miraculous, the most desired.

In the twenty-first century there are many thousands of healers of
different kinds across the world, and millions are interested in the oc-
currence of healing. One can see the interest everywhere. A little bunch
of black kids watch an ancient African healer chase a bad spirit up and
down inside the body of a sick woman. They are fascinated. The grown-
ups all around are watching critically, and nod when the woman shakes,
for it is the spirit shaking her. They all know. In America, my psychic
friend, Sue, listens intently to her patient describing her previous incar-
nation. Sue's face is twisted and odd, drawing the patient on, relieving
her of her tensions.

The Inuit healer is aware through her fingers of a large cyst in the
stomach of an old lady. The healer bends her head to touch the woman's
head while both her hands are on the body, bringing the fleeting soul
back and back, drawing it back into the woman's body through the top
of her head. At last the healer relaxes, exhausted. She has made it, and
the woman recovers. The healer loves her work, she knows the soul, she
is familiar with it. She feels through her fingers how the tissues ache, and
she draws out the ache like a throbbing bird into her hands.

I go to an Inuit healer. She spreads her hands over my head, just once,
collects the headache right out of it, and tosses it away. I immediately
feel great.

Why don't the doctors do this? Not only is it fascinating, but also one
would like to know exactly what is going on when the headache stops.

The present book on healing came about from a number of people
self-selected from the circles of modern cultural anthropology, who went
out to the field across the globe to see what they could make of the mysteries of religion and ritual. They went, not to grab back healing meth-
ods for themselves, nor to acquire Buddhist enlightenment, nor for

spiritual ecstasy, but to honor those countries outside of ours for their wisdom, their prophets, their healers, and their openness to the sacred. These fieldworkers were anthropologists of religion—of what we may now call spirituality. They have revealed extraordinary close-up accounts of healing, given in their various settings, and these show the live action of the healing itself.

The material in this book is presented so that by honoring other healers, we may approach the sacred ourselves. The book does not have the single aim of teaching how to experience. It plays between, on the one hand, the extraordinary variations in healing all over the world, often linked to local religious systems and further enriched by the oddities of human individuality; and, on the other hand, an underlying universal that seems to appear with blinding truth on the occasions of healing. In this regard one learns a great deal when encountering similar traits occurring in widely separated groups. The cases in this book are gathered together under the heads of the traits because in this way the reader can look at the stories side by side with their "sister" cases and see their relationship to one another. Once this commonality is understood, we see that, with regard to the aspect of healing as a general feature of life, all have a human right to it. The key is in the hands of anyone. Once readers have assimilated something of the grand partnership in healing that is secretly joined throughout the world, with all its idiosyncrasies much loved, with the diversities in their turn empowering one's hopes to try healing, then the idea of actually doing it will come to readers and they will realize that it is quite possible. Simple helps in this matter are found in the text.

STORYTELLING

There is no better way to start learning about spiritual healing than with a story. A story can bring the past to the present, open people up for the experience of being healed, and prepare them to do the work of healing themselves. The telling of the story of a spiritual experience—whether transmitted by speech or in print—is the means whereby a spiritual fact can be conveyed to another person whole and entire, be received by listeners as an actual experience of their own, and be counted as such in the memory of the hearer.

I am only one of many who tell stories. On my trip to Africa I found that spirits were real, for I saw one with my own eyes at the height of an Ihamba healing ritual. My curiosity was hooked, and I told the story. I realized how much a story of the remembered facts matters. Many others on the track of healing have told their stories or transcribed the stories of the subjects of the experience. A story, told by the experiencer with the event alive in his or her mind, is the completion of the gift of the experience. True storytelling is the opening to another person, the communication of breath that is the physical side of the spirit, and the connection of the soul with other souls. The human being with its soul can reach another, and this is part of the connectedness that runs through the universe. There has always been a connection of all things with all things. Our biologies grew up in primeval times to know this, just as our eyes developed to see light. This is the recognition of what has been called the law of mystical participation. Carl Jung put it well, divining that each individual is deeply connected with everyone else, down in regions of the unconscious we do not much explore. Somehow our actions are imbued with knowledge derived from connectedness, whether we know it or not.

ENERGY, POWER, AND SPIRITS

The stories in this book represent but a few of the multitudinous occasions when spiritual healing has occurred. Each case is different. Even so, in each of the cases the experience of both sufferer and healer has come through as a local variation on certain commonalities. Three major traits across the globe have appeared: healing with energy, healing with power, or healing with spirits—to use our translations of the terms that the various societies themselves have used in their own languages.

The *energy* section shows how individuals avail themselves of a cloudy but real gift that they may actually feel in the hands, hands that may sometimes develop such heat that the whole body experiences a boiling sensation. Usually the hands are the instruments of healing. Disease is felt as a spiritual substance that the hands often have to pull out, sometimes with a great effort and with a shout of agony. This is the emphasis on energy, whereas there exists a somewhat different perception when it comes to power.

Power is a phenomenon mightily arriving, sometimes unexpectedly, even overriding the healer's will. It is bigger than energy, taking control, overwhelming, flooding out from the gods or God. Occasionally people get a sense of a reservoir of power that is available to us all, that is always there (like the earth's oxygen). The conditions for this are unpredictable, and people recognize each manifestation of power as special.

Where human interconnectedness is most strong—bringing a vivid awareness of its healing power—this is when people start talking about some force or spirit that intervenes. "The music is playing itself: something else is creating it," band members have been known to say. Youngsters with their guitars repeatedly resort to this time of joy, this source of bliss—being in the "Zone."

Spirits tend to be insistent: they take the initiative, they take one by the scruff of one's neck and deposit one in an unfamiliar vocation. They are sometimes visible, they often speak; they choose a person, and a person does not choose them. These are beings who are felt to be very near. What stands out in the spirit category are episodes when a budding healer finds a spirit battering on his or her door, demanding to have its headquarters there for the sake of the sick and for the sake of the survival of the human faculty of spirituality. One sees great drama in the willingness of a healer to take on a spirit to help with healing, agreeing even to possession rites if these will only help the healing. For the sake of the sick, healers will undertake tricky shamanic adventures with dangerous flights and struggles with evil spirits.

Spiritual experiences can be distinguished from energy experiences. They often represent a purposeful visitation of a discernable visual entity, with a mysterious consciousness intent on communicating something and claiming a place in one's life.

COMMUNITAS

We know of sacred events when people heal in church. The healers touch the sick, while standing behind them are others who are touching them, and so on throughout the whole congregation, in collective prayer. This collective element is *communitas*, fellowship, or friendship—the best and key element of healing, love between many, a form of the "social" of a different order from the "social" implied in the "socializing" that children are supposed to undergo. One is aware of this different social sense, communitas, arising in times of illness, danger, or change; when new and exciting things are going on; and during sacred events. One can recognize it as fellow feeling when simply working in tandem with others, or when thrown together under hard circumstances—especially drastically changed circumstances. In these circumstances odd things happen. People are somehow freed not to be simply the result of social norms and their childhood conditioning. In these circumstances, they know each other as full human beings. People recognize the feeling and *like* it. Communitas is in no way "society" governed. Government and opinion are rarely in the picture here.

This "healing of society" is also what happens in collective music. It is the communitas of joining in harmonic sound, and it develops the sense of something outside of the people doing the work. Music is a power today in small bands among teenagers, at a time in life when communitas is often missing due to our pathologically individualistic Western society. Teenagers tell me that being in a band is an initiation for them—they now have a reason to live, they have become adult.

This kind of religious experience may change a person's life. People to whom the gift comes may find themselves unable to devote their lives to anything else.

ABOUT THE STORIES

The twenty-three clusters of stories are organized into five groups: energy, the experience of power, the transmission of power, spirits, and communitas. These chapters, from 2 to 6, serve as a road map, assisting the reader as she or he navigates through the wild country of religion. Here one receives the ability to see through the eyes of other cultures. One understands that the bonding of spirit and matter is a general feature of existence, a natural working state of affairs. One becomes familiar with the personal changes that seem so terrible to some young healer who has just been called to the mystery.

Chapter 1 tells the story of the village cure in Zambia. A real spirit is present. In the account one may trace how details of people's earthly life may be gathered up and focused in a spiritual event, in our day and age, in circumstances far from Christianity, far from high school science teaching, far from the television idea of the occult, and far from the spirit-starved daily life of a modern American. Chapter 1 shows how a revelation slowly develops during a ritual.

The next chapters give stories dealing with the five questions: "What is this thing called 'energy'?" "What does healing power do to people?" "How is healing power transmitted?" "What are people's experiences of spirits?" and "What is the experience of communitas?" They are very human stories. They convey the sense of a healer at work, as well as the spiritual processes through which both patient and healer must pass, and they give actual events with their higher implications.

This book hands to the reader the knowledge gained from the healing stories told by people across the world, and lays out the main features of the healing experience. I contribute eight stories from my own field research. As regards the stories of others, in order that the reader may come closer to the actual experience, the stories will be given much as they were told by the ones who experienced them. The accounts are very individual and very personal. On the one side, they reveal the strangeness and peculiarities of the different experiences, and on the other, they give us a curious conviction that they are all of a piece—that there are common features all over the world.

All the stories contain firsthand accounts either of being healed or of healing, whether they are written by the different authors or transcribed from the tapes or notes they recorded. Fifteen of the accounts are by the healing practitioners themselves. The array demonstrates the psychic unity of humankind, and it confirms that the forces through which healers communicate their benefits are real powers and real spirits.

Perhaps the most moving of the cases involved anthropologists who themselves experienced the same spiritual events as the people among whom they were doing research. The reader then hears the thoughts of highly sophisticated scholars, overcome because the people in the field were right. Because of their testimony, radiant with the power of the spiritual healing, the stories of these researchers have a special capacity to bring to life those spirit events for us.

There seems to be a chain of living power, originating in the spirits and brought into play in healing events. The spirits first endow the healers with experience, the events follow, and the events eventually become transmuted into stories that convey that experience. The power thus takes on a second life, that of stories that have power in them. The heart of each story contains a moment-by-moment close-up account of healing—one feels one is "there," in spirit parlance. The stories deal with the facts of a mysterious connection between conscious beings everywhere. This very connection is the theme of the book.

CHAPTER 1

———— ✠ ————

Breakthrough to Healing:
The Sighting of an African Spirit

One day in the fields between two villages in what is now Zambia, in the year around 1910, there took place a terrible act of violence. A man in one of the villages found a man from the neighboring village consorting with his wife, and he rushed at the adulterer with an axe and killed him. Many troubles resulted from this act. A village court convened and, in keeping with the law, the judges separated two of the murderer's family from him, a boy and a girl, and gave them in compensation to the victim's family. The children were thus "pawns," used to settle the dispute. Such pawns were termed "slaves" by the white administration. Years passed and the girl pawn married an important headman in the dead man's family and seemed to settle down, bringing a sister of hers from home to stay with her. But the boy pawn, their brother Sakutoha, grew up to be a hunter and won his freedom. Now he was determined to get the girls back into his own family to help him form a new village. He had a hunter brother too, Kashinakaji, and Kashinakaji continually argued with the sisters to join them—and to bring in their own children as well, they would all be in the family. But the sisters refused; they would not budge. Both Sakutoha and Kashinakaji were very angry. Meanwhile the eldest sister had a son, Singleton, and later a young grandson, Fideli, and the second sister had a family of three, Meru, Liza, and Mulandu. After a time the two hunters grew old and died, and as was the custom, the people took out a tooth from the jaw of one of the dead men to use as a valuable hunting charm. But the tooth was lost. This was bad news.

In 1985 Meru got sick.

Now, in this hunting society, the spirit of a dead hunter is of major importance for a person's health and for friendly relations with the ancestors. If a hunter spirit were angry in any way, he might enter a living relative and make him or her sick. Meru was feeling a tooth gnawing inside her body. It continually wandered about inside, making her life a misery so that she could not eat, sleep, or work. Something must be done. Meru was feeling the reality of this spirit.

By 1985, what everyone suspected was that an Ihamba, a spirit in the form of a hunter's tooth, had indeed entered Meru; but whose tooth it was, after all this time, no one was exactly sure. It so happened that Singleton and his nephew Fideli knew the rituals for persuading the tooth to come out of Meru. Their dead forefathers in their spiritual state could help them do it, and had often taught them the herbal medicines for the rites. Meru was in a nervous, depressed condition and begged the medicine men to go ahead.

Singleton and Fideli decided to help her, using their curious craft. The first task would be to identify who the spirit was, talk to it personally, and offer it what it wanted. Personal confrontation was essential. The ritual then aimed to locate the Ihamba tooth in her body and extract it by sucking it out with cupping horns. To do this properly as spirit doctors, they needed an understanding of the three kinds of beings involved in the case: the woman herself, the dead hunter in the form of his vengeful tooth, and the dead hunter in his all-too-conscious spirit existence. The ritual curers were going to have to talk with them all in the course of the ritual. The doctors invariably found the tooth to be a very difficult customer, intransigent and angry, to be treated with respect. It had no intention of coming out. Because of this, Meru would have to change her own attitude to that of a "coming-out" attitude, that is, she would have to come out with her grievances—come out with her "words," called *mazu*—so as to loosen up the trouble and get it to show itself. This would open communication between the doctor and the spirit. "Come out, *twaya*" was to become a frequent call in this ritual.

It so happened that in that same year, in November 1985, I arrived in Mwinilunga District in Zambia to do four months' fieldwork in my old field area among the Ndembu, known through the publications of my husband, Victor Turner,[1] who died in 1983. I was accompanied by a young student friend, Bill Blodgett. On this return visit I was growing interested in the spiritual nature of ritual and wanted to participate as deeply as possible in the religious side of it. Bill arranged for us to meet with Singleton and Fideli, and they agreed to let us attend the Ihamba ritual they were planning. I did not know at the time what might be involved in making a close-up study—I did not know what I was in for.

The ritual took place on Wednesday, November 27, 1985, on the outskirts of the village that was called Kahona. At first Singleton and Fideli had decided to schedule the ritual on Thursday, November 28, and began to send out messages to the villagers. Then the news came through that Princess Anne of England was due to visit the Ndembu on that day on behalf of the Save the Children Fund. So the date for the Ihamba was rescheduled one day earlier, on Wednesday, November 27, at dawn, thus adding a factor that became important during the actual proceedings.

The village was cool and quiet that Wednesday in the predawn twilight. Bill and I found our way to the main plaza down a slippery path of red clay that wound between mud brick walls. When we emerged into the open, we saw in the dim light a circle of eight thatch-roofed houses under the spreading arms of banana trees.

As yet there was no sun; all was damp with a hint of rain. In the dim light we peered around. Was anything going to happen? The night before I had had a curious dream. I dreamed I saw a long hill. Running from the top to the bottom of the hill I saw a high wall, dividing it. My side was all dull, and the far side was sunny and fertile. Halfway down the wall was a door, a very heavy door—something I had seen in former dreams, so I thought, and it had always been closed. I wanted to open it. Now it stood slightly ajar—that solid oaken door, smelling peppery, as oak wood does. I pushed hard, and it opened a little more, so I was able to slip through to the pleasant hillside beyond. That was good. Curiously, it was not until decades afterward that I realized I had been called to a quest for openings and breakthroughs, deep matters inside me that were to do with my own soul.

Bill had brought his tape-recording equipment with him. In the twilight village an Ihamba apprentice named Vesa approached, followed by Fideli, and the two gave us a courteous greeting: "*Shikenu mwani,*" "Well met, friends." Vesa set the ritual in motion by bringing out his drum, *ngoma*, a tall African bongo, which he set upright. He fetched a flat basket containing the equipment, a musical rasp, an axe, and a hoe, and with a serious gesture placed the basket on the top of the drum. The basket's contact with the drum dedicated it to the coming ritual of healing, also called an *ngoma*, like the drum. Then he and Fideli between them raised the basket high in the air: its raising was its honoring.

In this ritual, symbolism was actual effect. The touch of the basket on the drum did not merely *symbolize* that the basket was sacred. Sacredness, a kind of energy, had connected between them; the basket now *was* sacred.

Singleton joined us. He was 70 years old, a tall man, spare, with a long lined face—a conscious face, capable of unearthly flashes of irony and mischief, a man who said what he thought, an elder. He had touches of gray in his hair. He wore old blue overalls and moved with limber ease in spite of his age. Our friend Fideli was his nephew. Fideli's face shone with the health of early middle age—an able man, a thinker, with a knowledge of science the origin of which I could not trace. He carried himself this morning with the buoyant air of one who was looking forward to a procedure in which he was well versed. His religion was Baha'i, a religion with its missioners in many parts of the world, including a small center in his own neighborhood. Baha'i is remarkable because it is nonexclusive, tolerant toward other religions. Fideli rested confidently in his faith, and I thank the Baha'i for it.

Both men agreed to let me number as one of the doctors, because I had brought writings on their ceremony based on previous visits. With Singleton in the lead we set off into the low scrub to look for herbs— that is, medicines, *yitumbu*, bits of special tree and plant that had powerful effects, spiritually as much as biochemically. In this mass of vegetable stuff, although it seemed to be merely a collection of unfamiliar botanical specimens, there was something more. We began to see into the mystical participation of people and plants as the Africans knew it.

We started off in a line through last year's elephant grass until we reached the fields. In front walked Singleton, playing rhythmically on the wooden rasp, singing a plaintive little ditty in which we all joined:

Mukongu, katu-katu ye—
Mukongu, katu-katu ye—
Hunter-doctor, let's go—o.
Hunter-doctor, let's go—o.

We sang the second line a note below the first, in falling tones, with Fideli's light bass continually sounding the fourth harmonic below and Singleton's rasp softly sussurating like the shivers of cold chills. We were tuning and repeating and all the time gradually approaching and focusing on the first medicine tree.

We reached an area blighted by the planting of the same crop over and over again. Singleton walked swiftly now, weaving toward a low tree he spotted among the old garden mounds. It was an African oak, the "greeting" tree, the "mother" of the ritual. Inherent in this living thing, this oak, was a power, the power to bring together a herd of animals. Singleton hunkered down before the bole and took out a lump of red chalk from his mongoose skin bag. He drew a red line down the west side of the trunk, then a line from the foot of the tree to himself, and then a line down the east side of the tree. Tree, line, medicine man. The power of the oak was connected with Singleton to work the cure. Singleton told us, "Ihamba knows. He says, 'I'm soon going to be out of the patient.'" So the tooth-spirit, Ihamba, was a conscious being.

Singleton addressed the spirits in the tree. These entities were Singleton's dead ancestors who had previously practiced the Ihamba ritual. From that moment onward in the ritual, Singleton was informed in his task by the spirits of his father, Sambumba, and others. They would guide him to the herbal trees and send him discernment during the ritual.

Singing "*Mukongu*" to the gentle rasp of Singleton's reed as it swished over the ridged bar, we went on to collect a variety of medicines to fill the basket. We had bark from the blessing tree to give us the ancestors' blessings; roots from the Congo pepper to kill the germs inside the patient; thorn tree twigs to catch the Ihamba spirit; a broom branch to sweep witchcraft substances from the blood; a chip off another African oak to gather a crowd of people; the coco plum, so sweet that it would draw people to it; and a double-leaf plant to kill Ihamba's brood that might be left inside the body after the mother Ihamba came out. Also the double-leaf would bring out the afterbirth. There was the sighting tree, to make Ihamba come in sight quickly; a piece of the strong smelling soap root bark as a lid to stop Ihamba from escaping out of the can once it was caught; a bitterwood forked sapling to make the shrine post that would be planted in the middle of the sacred ground—bitter enough to make the teeth drop out; ironwood for the sacred fire with no stringiness in it to tie up the hunting power; a small hard termites' nest as a house and grave for Ihamba after it had come out; a no-reason plant, which just jumped out from the soil for no reason; a leaf from the falling-leaf tree— the Ihamba would fall off the patient; and finally, an herb used for expelling placentas in childbirth, to expel the Ihamba. All these, some flaming yellow-orange roots, others rosy red inside, some vivid black, the

tangle of roots of the double-leaf—sweet and lemon-smelling, the bitterwood pole, the prickles of the thorn, and all the rest made a telling
collection, more telling than color, scent, or prickles when one included
the coming-out effect of drinking the mixture (whose exact properties
were unknown to me) and, most of all, its spiritual power to cure.

"There are medicines for the below and the above and inside, every
medicine to make Ihamba come out," said Singleton, gazing on the bush
country. Then he said, "Let's go back to the road."

We returned to Meru's hut. We found a shaded spot behind her open-
air kitchen to establish a shrine and set up herbal treatments. First Fideli planted the shrine pole, the forked pole of bitter wood sharpened
into horns to attract the hunter's spirit, and he set the squared-off spirit
house in front of it. The woman assistant, Etina, got busy and pounded
the leaves to make leaf tea. Goats' horns for cupping lay ready in the
medicine basket. A boy went to fetch the drums, and people began to
assemble.

Now Singleton medicated the five doctors. He, Fideli, Vesa, Luka (the
second apprentice), and I drank some of the leaf tea. For a moment my
head swam, then after a minute my senses cleared. Singleton announced
to the crowd, "If there're any pregnant women here, go away." The concentrated coming-out effect of medicines and objects was so strong that
there was real danger of a woman having a miscarriage.

Singleton inspected the shrine, then said, "Look, we've made a mistake. We should have had Meru facing east, where the sun comes up from
under the earth, not west, the way we've got it."

"We did it like that because of the shade," said Fideli. "But it doesn't
matter; we'll leave it as it is." But it did matter.

A small procession was approaching—Vesa leading Meru, the sick
woman with the Ihamba tooth in her body. Vesa seated her on an antelope skin in front of the pole. She scowled at the sight of the medicines
around her, especially the razor blade lying in the basket. This was a miserable, proud, haughty, suffering woman. They proceeded to wash her
with spongy masses of wet leaf medicine, squeezing all the pounded and
focused coming-out plants into her body until she was drenched with the
speaking and penetrating way-opening stuff. The medicines now began
telling the Ihamba inside her, "Come out." The doctors gave her some
of the drinking medicine so that the opening effect would get to work
inside her body as well.

The ritual power was accumulating. The drums began with their rapid
threefold beat. The men called for a couple of axe heads, and soon the

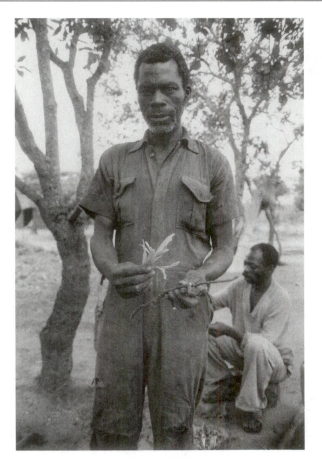

Singleton uses Ihamba medicine leaves.

iron's deafening syncopated clink compelled our hands to clap, starting an effect like strobe lights in my brain. We all responded in plangent woodland harmony.

To begin with, the doctors were watching the actions and statements of the patient in order to discern the tooth's name. The identity of the spirit was vital to the success of the healing. Singleton put his urgent question to the tooth wandering and biting inside her: "Do you come from your grandfather Nkomba? Shake, shake, if it's you, Nkomba." He was commanding both her body and the spirit inside it. She twitched one shoulder, then the other; her body rocked imperceptibly in time to the music as she sat with her palms turned up and legs outstretched.

An apprentice drinks an Ihamba medicinal potion.

Fideli applies medicine to an Ihamba patient's arm.

"Are you Kadochi? Shake if you are. Quick now!" Singleton danced the antelope mating dance before her.

Singleton put these questions to the unknown spirit in Meru's body because if the doctors found the right spirit, the call would make her shake. Singleton also put the question by proposing two alternatives: "If you want to come out, shake, but if you refuse, die down, don't shake." It was a kind of divination: her body was becoming an oracle, responding by swinging from side to side in time with the drumming, or by simply staying still. Singleton often spoke directly to the spirit while at the same time looking for an answer in the patient's body. It was her body that would shake, the spirit shaking her. From time to time Singleton spoke to the patient herself about her troubles, going from spirit to patient to spirit again.

Already the group had increased to a crowd of about thirty people, at least half of whom were children. The doctors were saying, "Maybe it's Kashinakaji's tooth. If you're Kashinakaji the hunter, shake. Come quick!" Singleton drove off the crowding children to make room, and then he danced the antelope, speeding back and forth, bent forward with his arms stretched in front like forelegs, belling his song; then he danced all around the assembly in a clockwise direction, holding the people together and sacralizing them. Now the onlookers danced forward and put pennies in the basket. Meru was in the middle of them, and sure enough, she was shaking well, swaying deeply from side to side.

"If you want the cupping horns, shake," Singleton told the spirit. Meru shook. Now Fideli got to work; he dipped the horn in hot medicine, then unwrapped the razor blade. Meru looked sourly at it: she was afraid of the pain.

Singleton assured her, "We'll only make one cut." Accordingly Fideli gave one tiny stab at her back, and as the blood ran down her skin he set up the horn over it. He sucked hard at the open end and blocked it up with solid beeswax. They acquired two other horns, which they sucked on lower down her back, pulling at them really hard so that they stood up from the suction.

Singleton came close to Meru and shouted, "Twaya! Come out!"—directing his call into her body. Meru was entering the stage of *mazu*, coming-out-with-grudges—literally, *words*. Words were of prime importance to the success of Ihamba. An outburst of words was the coming out of whatever was secretly bothering the patient about her life in the village. It was as if dark stuff ought to come out of the soul in this ritual. An almost perfect translation of the process would be the actual etymology of the word *psychoanalysis*, which means "spirit-un-loosen."

An Ihamba patient trembles under the stimulus of Singleton's antelope dance.

Suddenly, in a high voice, Meru unburdened herself: "I don't agree. I have something on my liver, my heart. It's my children; all my children have died. I just want to die because there's no one to look after me." These were her words. The people heard her frankness and were pleased, and they sang aloud.

But Singleton was watching Meru. He addressed the spirit in a matter-of-fact, argumentative voice, "There's a difficulty here. You said your *words*, just a few of them, and now you seem to be aggrieved when you shake. You quiver like you're not a gun hunter at all. What's worrying you when you quiver like that?" His voice rose. "What's up? I told you your brother Mulandu and I could help you with your worries. You spoke the truth when you said you might as well die because all your children are dead. You said, how can you stay the same and walk about when your children are dead? Sure, you had worries, and we were happy when you came out with them. But I haven't seen you shake well yet. You did when we began, but now you're stiff with worries. What's the matter? There must be something else."

They applied the horns again and resumed. There was something recalcitrant inside her body that did not want to be dragged out. Meru herself was not helping at all.

Bill and I could sense the diviner's knowledge of the spirit condition of the patient, his concern that there was a blockage. The doctor's way to deal with it was to clear the way. He was tempting and tempting Ihamba to come out. This was equivalent to taking a fellow to a bar to get him to talk, to let out all his grievances—or somehow induce tears.

Instead, Meru's brother, Mulandu, the head of the farm beside the village, a man with an elderly face and concerned look, said to her, "You're annoyed about money, aren't you?" She listened, her head drooping to the left. Then he announced, "It was all because of her younger sister Liza. They had a bad quarrel about money. Meru brewed a calabash of millet beer and Liza took it away to sell it for her. Afterwards Meru—she's the older of the two—said, 'Where's the money?' The younger sister said, 'Mika bought it and hasn't given me the money.' Actually Liza had the dollar in her pocket all the time. Liza said to herself, 'I'll see if my older sister will make a fuss.' Of course the older sister began to get annoyed, real angry. I was sitting there at the time. She and her younger sister started shouting at each other. Then the younger sister said, 'All right, elder sister, I've been fooling you. Here's your 80 cents,' and she handed her 80 cents, just 80 cents. The older sister refused the money. 'I'm not going to take it, because you're *cheating* me. I made the beer. Why do you cheat me? I say no, bring the full amount here. And quit being so quarrelsome, Liza.' Later Liza told me, 'That's right. I did it just to see what she'd do.' There you have it," concluded Mulandu.

Now, with the drums all around, Mulandu addressed Meru's body. "If you're aggrieved because your sister cheated you, shake. If not, keep still." Meru shook immediately, her body almost falling on the ground from side to side to the drum rhythm.

I was thinking that most of this sounded like a family quarrel, even a legal disposition. Yet it could not be just that, nor was it psychoanalytic case material either. It was a case of a tooth inside, stoppered up by the stopping up of words or grudges. The flow of human interconnection was the concern. One might envisage the flow as the traffic flow of human intercourse, either moving smoothly the way it was intended, or snarled and dangerous. To cope with the snarl the Ndembu did not use psychological terms, such as *psychosis*, *cathexis*, and such, which are imponderables, to explain individuals' behavior. They saw something concrete amiss in the physical and social body, a tooth—and they also saw it as spiritual.

After eight weary attempts, Fideli turned around and said, "It's so difficult to make Ihamba come out if the people don't sing."

Singleton stood in front of Meru with his eyes shut, quiet. He was listening to something, then sang loud, above the other voices.

"It must be Kashinakaji," he said.

Kashinakaji was Meru's great-uncle. Now, in his form as a dead hunter, he had come back to afflict her. They began to remember Kashinakaji's anger. The shadowy past was taking expression in present woes. The power and character of the Ihamba tooth were spreading to us all, while the power of the medicines dominated the circle of ground where the crowd gathered. I shivered, tracing the effect of ritual, tracing its delicate tuning in those sensitive psyches who, being kin, knew one another so well. The importance of tuning was seen in the simple statement, "It's so difficult to make Ihamba come out if the people don't sing"—and its opposite, "It's easy when they do." I realized that choral harmonized singing was of the essence in this ritual.

Now Mulandu, Meru's brother, addressed the spirit: "If you're annoyed because your cousin the elder Paulos isn't around, shake hard; if not and it's something else, stop shaking."

The participants began a heated discussion on the subject of Meru's cousin-brother Paulos, who was unaccountably absent. Mulandu was irritated because Paulos was not there. Meru looked grim—resigned but grim. The drums sounded and she began to shake; Paulos's absence was a glitch in the proceedings, but at least the problem was coming to the surface. They put a query to the Ihamba spirit: "if you want Paulos to come, shake." Meru's body did shake, so they sent the apprentice on a long trip to Paulos with a message asking him to come as soon as he could. Meru's face relaxed. The whole procedure was a technique of opening up, the unclenching of the soul of a person.

Meru, with her back stuck with two horns, suddenly said her words. They poured out in a high oratorical tone: "I say as soon as someone brings me honey to make beer and I've just managed to get it brewed, a certain somebody takes the beer away from me. Then Ihamba comes. But I say no, no, no. If you don't sing for me, I'll die. I'm old, and all I've got left is hardship, with my little children dying. And see what happens? I brew honey to make beer to sell, and then what happens? My younger sister sells it. It's my understanding that right up to today, I'm still the elder and a certain someone's still the junior. As for me, all I want to do is die, but I don't die. As you say, I've struggled in vain against my sister, and it's a sad thing. The way things are, I'll die."

Singleton was still for a moment, attentive. He said, "I've seen him. It's Ihamba, so he's got to come out of her. It's come. We may now say we're very happy. This is it, we're saying *words*. Ihamba, you'll soon find you've fallen down, and we've given money for you to come out. See, here's the money." Then, to the body of the patient: "If that's not true, keep quiet and don't shake; if that's the way it really is, let the bad spirit come out. Our forefathers in the grave have heard my *words*."

He continued, "The man who's turning up any minute is your brother, the brother you wanted to come. He meant to come on Thursday: now at last he's arrived. He's here right now and he'll find us."

Paulos had indeed arrived, creating quite a stir—Paulos, the revered headman, wearing a hat. He was welcomed by many. He went to the medicine basket and put down the biggest village contribution yet, 20 cents. He had his own complaints.

"When I was living with my wife at Luanshya on the Copperbelt, people treated us with respect and didn't let us down by changing the date of an Ihamba without telling us. Why wasn't I told?"

"It's all because there's a visit from a big notable tomorrow," explained Singleton, and he patiently sorted out the misunderstanding having to do with Princess Anne's visit. Having heard Singleton out, Paulos went to stand to the west of the crowd amid a little knot of clients.

Then, as the drums began again, Singleton savagely addressed the horns on Meru's back, "*Twaya! Fuma!* Get out!" as if he were shouting at a thieving dog.

Now the heat was drawing up black clouds above us; Meru fell shaking in the midst of the singing, in the dim light under the shade branches, just as Singleton was saying, "What trouble it's giving us!" He bent over and tried to draw out the tooth.

A gabble of voices broke in, "Yes, she's fallen—look, she's half dead."

"Is that what you want—witchcraft dancing in her?"

"Yes, that's what you want."

They wanted the spirit to show itself so that they could bring it out. Even so, there was a tone of horror in the voices. Singleton darted with his skin bag to catch the tooth. He worked on the horn, but when he took it off it was empty: another disappointment.

So much was coming out, but the tooth resisted. It was a long ritual.

Meru sat up and the horns were reset. Meru spoke from her ritual position: "I feel resentment."

"We've seen Ihamba," said Fideli. "And you have put on your *words*."

Meru's pain got to us all; we stood with bitter expressions, gazing at her. Fideli took a leaf poke and dripped medicine on Meru's head. Singleton held his mongoose hunter's bag in front of her face, then brushed

The singing increases to bring the Ihamba spirit out of the patient.

her face with it. But Meru would not shake. All were thinking of hunting, *wuyanga*. While the percussion thundered, they sang keeningly,

> Where does *wuyanga* come from?
> Where does the elephant come from?
> The chief has come.

In the midst of the heady rhythm Meru keeled over in trance, her
body twitching in the dust.

"She's fallen!" Singleton sprang to her side. "*Twaya*, come out!" he
shouted as he bent over her body and worked on her back with his horn
and bag. "We'll show 'em hunting! We'll show 'em *wuyanga*!" and the
song took up the refrain:

> *Wuyanga, wuyanga, wuyanga, wuyanga, wuyanga, wuyanga—*

hypnotically, endlessly, in which we all joined—

> *wuyanga, wuyanga—*

calling, calling the ancient hunters.

The status of Meru's mother was now being questioned. It was all coming out that her mother had actually been a slave. The position of a pawn was nothing better than that. Even Meru's children and grandchildren had no rights and were called slaves. Meru suffered from her low unsupported status, particularly from being deprived of her grandchildren. Her own shadowy maternal uncle, Kashinakaji, who would have needed her family in his own village, was angry.

Singleton called to the spirit, "Kashinakaji, if you really are in there trying to eat this person, come out!" Then he begged and bludgeoned the spirit: "I'm following exactly what Paulos said; I've said all my *words*. You need only listen to what I've been saying. Haven't I shouted loud enough? We want this thing to come out; let's beat the drums, let the drums touch the earth—you've been refusing, I tell you. Now! We want this thing to come out! Just that. If there's somebody in there, come out! Kashinakaji, you're dead, you must keep quiet. But if you're alive, come out! We're not happy."

Singleton was straddling in his dance beside Meru, bending over her and shouting into her body. Her long face looked straight ahead with an inner fury. She was shaking sporadically, sometimes with jerks, sometimes falling over, dropping bloody but useless horns; the sun burned hot, and frustration was high. Something was wrong, yet at this point many things began to change and jell, and now arose a matter that hurt me too.

It so happened that as midday approached, our ritual site became very hot and I sought shade on the opposite side of the circle. This brought me near Paulos. Paulos and my assistant, Bill, were talking with my African assistant, Morie, a man who had turned out to be an alcoholic. Now, while I watched Meru's shaking, I became conscious of Morie's harsh voice in my ear.

"Paulos complains you never came to his house last Saturday as you said you would. He waited all day for nothing." I sat rigid, feeling guilty as I often did with Morie. Why did he have to interrupt the fascinating process before my eyes?

I muttered, "Our calendar must have got mixed up." Morie promptly turned to Paulos and translated this as "She forgot! *Wunajimbiri.*" I was furious with Morie for making me out to be rude, but it was true. I had forgotten.

I started around, now remembering that on Saturday we had had to go to the funeral of Line, the old African carpenter of the 1950s who had long been senile. How could I have gone to Paulos's village that day? But

was it auspicious to mention death and burial at an Ihamba ritual? Everyone around me quieted, and I felt they were reading my mind. The silence grew total: why, they were waiting for me to say my words. The
matter of Morie's lifestyle was involved, and, what made it difficult, it
would mean shame for his father if I came out with it. Deeply embarrassed, I looked down and gestured that it did not matter, then rose to
get away from Morie and went off around the men to where Bill stood.
They had wanted me to come out with my words: it was part of Ihamba.
My heart was full of rage against Morie. What could I do? He was my old
friend's son, and, what was even trickier, my landlady's son. I sat trying
to resolve my mind about Morie and Paulos. After a second I again rose
and went back around to Paulos, and there I grasped him by the hand
and told him about the Saturday burial; he seemed to understand. I
arranged to visit him on Monday morning instead—but where did he
live? I asked.

"Morie will bring you," said Paulos.

Morie was still standing nearby. I shrugged and said, "Possibly"—then
returned to Bill and stood clapping to the drums that were beating out
the next round. I felt miserable.

Meru came right back to the primary cause, Liza's deception over the
beer. "Liza cheated me. She's not even here at the Ihamba. I'm annoyed:
Liza, my younger sister."

It was stalemate.

What followed happened quicker than I could write it. Into Singleton's mind came the memory of the mistake they had made in orienting
the ritual scene at the beginning: Meru had been seated facing west, and
she still was. Singleton's intention became clear to me as I was pushed
back to make room for the drums. We all moved back, and a lot of shifting took place. Meru was helped up, and the antelope skin moved, then
they seated her on the other side of the shrine pole. Spirit house, basket,
pans, mortar, and receiving can were moved, and Singleton took up his
new station as well, so that at last Meru was relocated in the right position, east of the shrine pole, facing the dawning direction of the sun,
where it first comes out. She was now headed into the epitome of emer-
gence, into the coming out of the sun itself. The scene was exactly the
same, only in reverse.

"E-eyo!" said Mulandu with great satisfaction. "That's right." Meru
looked outward, her face very serious; this was the position of frankness
and revelation. I was gazing northwest across the shrine at Morie sitting
south of it. The sky had grown dark and a wind came up. "This is about

Morie and me," I realized, "at least as much as some of the other complaints." My thoughts pained me again, whilst beyond, the drums thundered and Singleton hopped rapidly, foot after foot, in front of Meru. My
thoughts went on.

"They wanted my *words*. They're to do with me and Morie. I'm annoyed about Morie, and must bring it out. But I can't confess publicly as
it involves his father, who's Christian, and who's jealous, yet a friend—
and it's about his drunken son. But how I want to join in, right here, and
can't because of loyalty!—And these great people, waiting for my *words*."
So I had to accept the impossibility, and accepting it, tears came to my
eyes. They hurt me, hurt me.

"Okay, okay, okay, that's how it *is*—and its woe. That's it, then!"

And just then, through my tears, I saw the central figure sway deeply:
all leaned forward—this was indeed going to be it. I realized along with
them that the barriers were breaking—just as I let go in tears. Something
that wanted to be born was now going to be born. Then a kind of palpable social integument broke and something calved along with me. I
felt the spiritual motion, a tangible feeling of breakthrough going through
the whole group. Then it was that Meru fell—the spirit event first and
the action afterwards. Singleton was very agile amid the bellow of the
drums, swooping rhythmically over Meru with finger horn and skin bag
ready to catch the tooth, Bill beating the side of the mortar with a stick
in time with the drum, and as for me, I had just found out how to clap.
You simply clap along with the rhythm of the drum, *and clap hard*. All
the rest falls into place. Your own body becomes deeply involved in the
rhythm, and everyone reaches a unity.

Clap clap clap—Mulandu was leaning forward and all the others were
on their feet—this was it. Quite an interval of struggle elapsed while I
clapped like one possessed, crouching beside Bill amid the singing and a
lot of urgent talk, while Singleton pressed Meru's back, guiding and leading out the tooth—Meru's face in a grin of tranced passion, her back
quivering rapidly. Suddenly Meru raised her arm, stretched it in liberation, and I saw with my own eyes a giant thing emerging out of the flesh
of her back. This thing was a large gray sphere about six inches across,
something between solid and smoke, a kind of globular ghost. I was
amazed—delighted. I still laugh with glee at the realization of having
seen it, the Ihamba, and so big! We were all just one in triumph. The
gray thing was actually out there, visible, and you could see Singleton's
hands working and scrabbling on the back and the thing was there no
more. Singleton had it in his pouch, pressing it in with his other hand

as well. The receiving can was ready; he transferred whatever it was into the can and capped the bark lid over it. It was done.

I sat back breathless. Meru was quiet. At once there was a huge flash of lightning—the light of a clap of thunder that exploded simultaneously overhead. Meru sat up panting. The longed-for rain poured down, and we all rushed into the kitchen shelter.

"Go to the house you two," said Fideli, and Bill and I rushed on through the curtain of rain to the house door. Bill stumbled before he entered, fell into the mud, and then came in out of breath. Singleton entered with his blue shirt dark with water, carrying the receiving can which he set down on the floor. I wore a big smile.

Singleton held up his hands to us, then squatted down and dredged a long time in the bloody mixture. At length he drew out an old tooth, a molar, natural size, ordinary and concrete, with a dark root and one side sheared off as if by an ax. It was the Ihamba.

On the evening of the same day, November 27, Singleton and Fideli visited our hut to explain what was coming next in Ihamba and discuss Meru's ritual. Bill and I were extremely pleased to see them. The first thing that Singleton said was, literally, "The thing we saw, we were five." This was his statement that the doctors too had seen a "thing." Singleton was counting the five doctors, of which I was one.

On December 6 at 6:00 in the morning, Singleton fed the Ihamba with meat from an antelope. The winnowing basket lay ready on the dirt floor, with Singleton's mongoose skin pouch on it, also a clean Vaseline jar with a lid, now half full of maize meal made from the grain that is hard "like a tooth." Singleton put a disk made of antelope liver and a sac of blood in the basket. Now he removed from the pouch some red clay, which he crushed with the end of his finger horn, smearing it over his fingers for protection; after this, he took up the liver ring and carefully removed the Ihamba tooth from his pouch, then chose a tiny piece of red clay. Holding the tooth and clay together he inserted them into the hole in the liver disk. He put the disk containing the Ihamba into the Vaseline jar, stuffing it in and positioning it with his thumb at the center of the surface of the corn meal. Then he poured over it the blood from the sac, and screwed on the lid. The bottle was now colored brilliant red above and white below, a union of blood and meal. "Marvelous," I wrote in my notes. Bill wrote later, "Subjectively, I felt very strange. Images flashed through my mind . . . bread and wine . . . semen and menstrual blood . . . solid and liquid . . . yin and yang . . . a boulder in the stream and the water . . . time flowing past . . . life itself." We both felt that what had been done was an act of goodness—of real justice. Singleton said that when the Ihamba was fed with blood it was satisfied, and we could see that it was.

Now that the feeding was done, Singleton called Meru into the house. She came running, radiant and smiling all over her middle-aged face. Singleton took the blood sac and marked her on her shoulders and beside her eyes. She was now cured and protected.

COMMENTARY

For this I start with the comments of Singleton and Fideli as they are of major importance, conveying as they do the people's own assessment of the group's activities that day. I stand behind their statements in the most positive way. The passages derive from the conversation we had with Singleton and Fideli in our hut after Meru's ritual.

We settled down to talk and I respectfully described what I had seen. I was still in a state of amazement. When the keystone of the bridge is put into position and everything holds, you tend to just look on with your mouth hanging open. This is what happened to me.

Fideli's voice was rich and generous, while Singleton's was urgent and precise. A rapid swinging flow developed in the conversation, and as it went on it became deeply personal and interconnected.

Singleton began, "We'll explain it to you, you personally, our own friends who went into the bush with us, so people may know what the hunters' medicine against Ihamba is like and so we can be compared to many others. It's something very important. We've a right to tell you so we can be seen to be different, because now's the time, now while you're living in Africa. We need to tell you these things exactly as they are. This is the first time you'll know what the hunters' drum really is."

Bill said, "I want to ask about the Ihamba itself."

"Yes," said Fideli with great tenderness. "You can ask me, Billy, anything you want. Even if you have to break the night and go on till morning, I'll do it. It's like this. There's a problem with Ihamba, a strange one. Ihamba always runs like an air. Get me?"

Bill said, "An air? Can it fly?"

"Yes, it's always flying about. The medicine we collect in the bush prevents Ihamba from getting into Meru's legs. See?"

"And the dripping medicine?"

"Yes, I'll tell you, Bill. Write the things I'm telling you, don't write on your own, just write what I'm telling you. It comes from him"—indicating Singleton—"and it comes from my father. We get the dripping medicine from a plant called 'leaping out quickly.' It prevents the Ihamba from hiding in the fingernails. Every medicine is for that, so Ihamba won't escape. It's a passing air, get me? The medicine is to stop Ihamba coming out of her body and going into someone standing around." Both of the doctors grew excited. "We have to catch it in the can. I'll give you a good example. Ihamba can touch you when you don't know it—touch you, exactly that. So you give the patient a horn tucked into the front of her hair, and also between her toes. It makes Ihamba stay inside the body so you can catch it in the cupping horn."

The talk turned to the tests, *makunyi*, to see whether Meru really had an Ihamba. This word also meant the divining process, such as when Meru shook. I said to Singleton, "I saw you make the *makunyi* again and again. And I was going to ask you questions about that. It's a test, isn't it, to see if your question is right or not—?"

Fideli interrupted me very solemnly. "Mrs. Turner, let me explain that. Mrs. Turner, here you are with Billy and I'm here with Mr. Singleton Kahona. We're different from you, Mr. Kahona and I. You know everything."

"Well . . ." I said, "I know some stuff from the old times, some."

Singleton took it up. "My father handed down to me the responsibility of the medicines. Now I possess the right to cure someone and not fail in it. On my honor, it's true before God and my father and my uncle, because the thing is from my father. How can I fail to cure a person? I know things from my father. I can't fail with my cures; there's no question about it. You know things from your husband, Edie, your late husband Mr. Turner. He told you things. Have you failed? Have I failed?"

"No way," I assured him.

I went back to the topic of the test, the divination. "So you're divining all the time, aren't you? At every stage the Ihamba itself is telling you what to do. Like—inside her it's telling her to shake, to answer the question. 'If it's so-and-so, shake. If it isn't, don't.' So you're learning from the Ihamba inside."

Fideli looked from me to Bill in wonder. "She knows; she's onto it. Yes. I think, Mrs. Turner, we've come to the end." And Fideli was going to wrap up the evening then and there.

Bill broke in, "Can I ask some more questions? I've loads of questions about Liza's grudge."

Singleton said, "Yes: Liza. Meru wanted Liza, that sister of hers, to be at the Ihamba. But it seemed she was someplace else. She sure was someplace else. Before we took the Ihamba out of Meru and before it actually bit her, it heard the sisters and said to itself, 'Oho, the older and younger sisters are quarreling.' So we gave her the test, remember? It was while they were backbiting that the Ihamba started to get into action. It was listening to them."

Bill said, "Why doesn't Ihamba want to come out of the patient when there are quarrels? Why won't it come out until everyone's heart is at peace?"

"Because Ihamba is an air person."

"Supposing," said Bill, "the Ihamba ritual takes a long long time and the patient doesn't shake, say, for sixteen hours. Do you give up?"

Singleton said, "You mean there's no sign of Ihamba? But the Ihamba *will* appear. The patient simply has a lot on her liver." (He meant what we call "in her heart.")

Fideli added, "The patient has thoughts inside her body. They may be hard thoughts, or her thoughts may be rotten like Meru's about Liza; if she explains the thoughts exactly as they are, the Ihamba will in fact come out . . . Ihamba came out! We called you into the house to come and see what Ihamba looked like. It was very important."

GENERAL COMMENTS

The question of most people about the events would be "What's actually going on in Ihamba?" Singleton and Fideli answered this question, as was their right. How Ihamba affected me afterward was that in my research, I began to participate in an interesting new field in healing studies along with a few others who had had similar experiences. I was aiming to build up a reliable archive of documented accounts and spot interesting regularities. Now, increasing numbers of researchers are doing the same thing, writing—much as I have done here—from within the belief of the people among whom they work. This is real reportage on that other world, that other level where the spirits and powers are known.

Once people become accustomed to accept this kind of material for discussion, everything falls into place, as I saw when the implications of my Ihamba experience dawned on me: "the keystone fell into place." So the Ndembu perform ritual because spirits exist. The medicines do talk to the Ihamba in their mystic way and say, "Come out." Singleton *was* speaking to the spirit of Kashinakaji inside Meru's body, and so on.

Later in my reading I came across a chapter entitled "Extracting Harmful Intrusions" in *The Way of a Shaman* by Michael Harner, a laughing, bushy-bearded anthropologist who often experienced shamanism himself.[2] His book contains one of the few descriptions that does not ascribe an extraction to trickery:

> Illness due to power intrusion is manifested by such symptoms as localized pain or discomfort, often together with an increase in temperature, which (from a shamanic point of view) is connected with the energy from a harmful power intrusion. . . . The shamanic removal of harmful power intrusions is difficult work, for the shaman sucks them out of a patient physically as well as mentally and emotionally. This technique is widely used in shamanic cultures in such distant areas as Australia, North and South America, and Siberia.
>
> If you ever viewed the film *Sucking Doctor*, which shows the healing work of the famous California Indian shaman Essie Parrish, you saw a shaman pulling out intrusive power. But Western skeptics say that the shaman is just pretending to suck something out of the person, an object that the shaman had already secreted in his mouth. Such skeptics have apparently not taken up shamanism themselves to discover what is happening.
>
> What is happening goes back to the fact that the shaman is aware of two realities, as among the Jívaro. The shaman is pulling out an intrusive power that in the shamanic state of consciousness has the appearance of a particular [entity, such as a gray spirit form] which he also knows is the hidden nature of a particular [material object, such as a tooth]. When a shaman sucks out that power, he captures its spiritual essence in [the object] that is its ordinary material home. That . . . is, in other words, a power object. The fact that the shaman may then bring out the power object from his mouth and show it to a patient and audience as the ordinary-state-of-consciousness evidence does not negate the nonordinary reality of what is going on for him in the shamanic state of consciousness.[3]

In the same way, the Ndembu were right to see in what have been called *symbols* actual powers and spirits. We can trace spirit processes going on in an important object that is more than just a metaphor for a social situation. It is the actual path of the power of a spirit. So when I consider the Ihamba tooth, which was the resultant, the trophy, the material prize gained from the long morning of ritual, and wonder about its appearing at the end—after what I saw, and after what the doctors said about its journeys in the body—what then? The tooth did become present; I do not know how. I have to say that by the year 2005, I have seen so many material things alter under the circumstances of power and spirit that I grant the Ndembu doctors the truth of what they say. Singleton used the same word, *Ihamba*, about the thing that was inside—that is, the spirit form I saw coming out, and the tooth. The doctors could "dissolve" from one to the other, that is, they regarded the two things: Ihamba, and the tooth; as the same thing.

That little hard tooth, which in its manifestation in the body was bubbled into a big shadowy spirit form invading the veins and arteries, visible, audible, palpable, reminds me of a similar report made by Essie Parrish, the Pomo Indian shaman referred to above:

> When that sick man is lying there, I usually see the power. These things seem unbelievable but I, myself, I know, because it is in me. . . . Way inside of the sick person lying there, there is something. It is just like seeing through something—if you put tissue over something, you could see through it. That is just the way I see it inside. I see what happens there and can feel it with my hand—my middle finger is the one with the power. The pain sitting somewhere inside the person feels like it is pulling your hand towards itself—you can't miss it.[4]

Essie Parrish was dealing with a similar power under the skin as Singleton in Africa. The skill of Singleton appears to correspond to hers. She was an articulate, English-speaking woman from an entirely different culture area. Benwa, Fideli's uncle, told us that sufferers could see the Ihamba moving through the veins of the body—"I am telling you the truth," he added. He did not use the "tissue" image, but there are many references in the Ihamba proceedings to seeing and sensing the Ihamba. Singleton said, "I've seen that it's the Ihamba, so he must come out of her." "We've seen the Ihamba," said Fideli. I myself saw how Singleton drew many lines with his small horn around the cupping horn on Meru's back. Also, Fideli said, "When an Ihamba goes into a horn, you feel it vibrating." As far as I was concerned, everything they said was vindicated by the actual sight of the spirit form, gray, quite definite, and fuzzy, like a thick cloud of guck. As we have seen, it is this object that is central to my account, not the concrete tooth. The tooth is vital insofar as it can be transmuted and drawn out in this gray spherical form; and afterwards, in the hard form, it can be pampered and fed. The fuzzy object is somehow Kashinakaji in a shapeless malevolent state. So we go back and forth.

What Ihamba itself consists of is the biting inside, that hard spirit who cannot come out without a sudden transformation. Therefore the villagers beg and plead with the spirits to release the sick one, keening out the song, caught up in the drum music with their clapping hands, and all agog to catch the event when it happens. What is important in Ihamba is the moment when Singleton clutches the "thing" in his skin pouch. This is the moment of translation of the Ihamba that was within into its outward form, following its exit from Meru's body. Singleton then puts it into the receiving can, and later in the house its form is visible to everyday sight as a tooth somehow deriving from the spirit form.

CHAPTER 2

———— ❖ ————

Energy Healing

After years of being curious about healing, following up clues, and traveling from one major culture area to another, I gradually found the evidence piling up. There is a real power among humans, and the power to heal is a human faculty. Various types of healing have links to our biology; energy gives power to our bodies, even to our brains and endocrine systems, and we are healed. Although I mention the body here, this is not a reductionist notion aimed at explaining away healing as merely neurobiological or psychological. Rather, our bodies, our biology, and especially our brains are also spiritual, and we have a human/spiritual faculty like a radio receiver involved in our whole makeup. We can recognize and understand these processes for what they are. The African ritual described in chapter 1 shows people who are able to transmit or broadcast spirituality in this way.

The high moments of healing derive from sources beyond the mundane, either from spirit or power. *Spirit* and *power*, here, are very like the way physicists describe light. Light can be either a particle, called a *photon*, or a wave, depending on the viewpoint and context. Obviously, light travels in a straight line, much like a beam of particles. But if it is passed through a minute hole and it falls on a screen, diffusion rings are obtained, much like the rings on a still pond when a stone is thrown in. These rings are waves. One might compare a *spirit*, a separate thing that travels, to a particle, an object here. And healing *power* is like a wave, a strong force or a vibration, and then one feels it as an overpowering effect setting one ashiver, and people call it *energy* or *vibrations*. Many things in nature have two ways of existing and can switch from one to another, such as a chrysalis turning into a butterfly, or the way two quiescent bodily cells, when united, become an embryo that suddenly develops and takes on food, having been nothing before but a couple of blueprints of genes. A baby switches from sharing its mother's blood to becoming an independent, air-breathing individual. Similarly, energy can quiver into particularity and become a person, or a person can under pressure flow into pure energy and then heal. This is hard to think about but it happens.

The term *energy* itself is interesting. A word analogous to energy is used in many cultures. What we know as energy approximates what many people experience in healing across the globe, and they have their own traditional words for it. It is known as *chi* or *qi* in China, or *ki* in Japan, and this term has caught on among Western healers. The bushmen of the Kalahari call it *num*, something that can get boiling hot. In Malaysia it is known as *wind* (*angin*), and it is similarly known in Nepal. In Malawi, east Africa, it is known as *vimbuza* (which is also a kind of spirit), an energy that becomes very hot before it is able to heal. These peoples and many others are adept in the craft of dealing with energy.

However, way back in the early 1980s I myself had no understanding of energy at all. At last, in 1996, I experienced it most dramatically as a kind of electricity that healed me. The first case in this chapter gives this electricity event and how I began to inquire into the mystery of energy. Next I give a range of other people's living stories of energy healing. The reader may find a quality in the stories that sets the scalp tingling. I recommend giving such sensations respect.

ENERGY HEALING AT AN ANTHROPOLOGY MEETING

I could never understand how healers used energy. *Energy?* They put energy into the body to heal? It was impossible. What was the stuff called energy? On November 22, 1996, when I myself experienced energy healing, I changed my tune.

I was attending the American Anthropological Association annual meetings at the Hilton Hotel, sharing a bedroom with my longtime friend and colleague in the anthropology of ritual, Pam Frese, she of the strong intellect and great warmth of soul, and the possessor of a wonderful gift

of golden hair. In my bedroom that night of the 22nd, while I was trying to sleep, I contracted a most severe attack of giddiness (which turned
into vomiting), so much so that when I got out of bed I had to hold onto
the furniture. Pam woke up and tenderly gave me assistance, but it was
of no avail. All night long the trouble became worse so that I could not
even lift up my head without the room swimming around. I was going to
miss the day's sessions. All the next morning I lay there in misery. A little
after noon Pam burst into the room. She was excited about something.

"Edie, I met that man called—" I seemed to hear, "Daar An."

"Whoozat?"

"Look, I told him you were sick. He's just an ordinary white sociologist, he was in the panel on communitas and humanism with you yesterday. Then—he put his hands on my shoulders. He said, 'Go back to
Edie and put your hands on *her*, right?' So I've come straight to you. I
don't know what this is all about, but here goes. Sit up."

I reared up miserably and Pam placed her hands on my shoulders.

Then she cried out, "My arms! My arms!" She was wearing short
sleeves, and all along her arms I could see goose bumps pricking up everywhere. "It feels strange!" she said. At that moment I felt a sensation going
up my own back like an extremely strong cold chill, right up my spine
and over the top of my head. These were no ordinary goose bumps. I felt
I was being turned inside out with one immense bodily shudder. We
stared at each other.

I said, "Pam! I feel quite all right!" I gave my head a shake. "I'm not
dizzy anymore. I'm fine. Who was that man?" She told me, but I have to
be discreet about his name.

I was delighted. "A healing!" Both of us grinned.

Pam said, bustling about, "Look, you have a rest. I'm going to hear
Roy Wagner's paper."

"Wait, I'm coming with you." I put on my clothes feeling perfectly
well, and we went to hear Roy Wagner's paper.

***

Now I saw. This was the energy that American healers had been talking about all the time, and I blamed myself for not believing them. I had
thought it must be spirits the healers were talking about and that, being
Americans, they were afraid to say so because Christians might not ap-
prove—after all, those spirits did not necessarily come from the Christian God. Therefore the healers felt safer calling the healing agency
energy, which was acceptable—for instance, energy was the stuff in elec-

tric light, and that was safe enough. So I thought. One may gauge the depth of my misunderstanding when the startling Hilton event occurred. I *felt* the energy. It was hard to swallow at the time. Now I had to try to understand something very primal. For instance, energy, real spiritual energy, *might* be the prevailing condition of the universe. Possibly this healing was given to teach me. I had believed neither in energy healing nor, to tell the truth, in what I had seen of Christian laying on of hands. I thought the subjects of such healings were kidding themselves. Healers could take out harmful intrusions, yes, I could see that. Spirits could work miracles. Yes, I was enough of a Catholic to admit that. And I had actually seen a spirit figure in Africa. But considering the highly mundane context of my 1996 energy event, anyone would think I was in an environment sufficiently sanitized against any belief in nonlogical powers. Now it seemed that healing was invading the halls of academe. Furthermore, here was a case of energy healing—and it was my own case. I was going to have to admit that energy healing was real and one could feel it.

I began to ponder the implications of the event. It would seem to constitute some kind of datum at the very least, something impinging itself—it seemed purposefully—on our discipline; and I had a feeling it would not be good etiquette to ignore it. It would not even be good anthropology. Worse, it would be rude and ungracious. Subsequently I inquired of other people and did some reading, and found I was not alone in having the experience. I had felt it: it had set me on my feet. I began to wonder if there were some "ether," some medium, through which healing flows like a jolt of electricity, because that was how I experienced it.

I wrote thanking the healer, and this is what he replied:

Just a few ruminations regarding healing. . . . I have given thought to what happened and why it happened that day in San Francisco, and my most current theory is that I may have a "power," but more importantly that day something special happened. At that moment in time there was a very fortuitous alignment of souls and psyches: you, me, and your female roommate who acted as the "messenger." I "sensed" this special alignment that day. I knew you were not well because it had been mentioned in the board meeting that morning, and I know I must have been thinking about you on some level. When I ran into your roommate later in the book display section and she too told me about how you were doing, the connection became more palpable, and—of crucial importance—I sensed that your roommate was of deep and beautiful soul and would be a good conduit of my good wishes. The touch I gave her (to give to you) was a reflex action born in the deeper, less linear parts of my mind/psyche and could not have felt more sincere and natural. I did not dwell on the act and was frankly very surprised to hear from you later that you were feeling much better.

My insight is simply that for the "power" to happen it must exist simultaneously in at least two or more people. Too frequently in our culture there are those with the power but who are around no other kindred souls (or, probably more likely the case, people who have the power or could be good conduits but simply suppress this dimension of themselves in the service of the gods of capitalism, narcissism, and self-doubt). We were very fortunate that day.

I replied to the healer,

We need a world where that sort of healing would be natural, and people would indeed use the reflex actions born in the deeper, less linear parts of their minds/psyches. That is what those reflexes are there for. Also one does need the community bond to nurture the gift.

※

The healer's word, *reflex*, was the exact word for what I felt, a natural reflex. I was also touched by the healer's "surprise" at what he had done, his strong sense of social connection, and the way his words expressed something of the deeper levels of his mind/psyche. Perhaps one factor was that the day before, the healer and I had spoken at the same session on fellow feeling, the magic times of communitas. He was a pleasant, unassuming person.

Still, what was this agency, this parcel of magic power that was passed from hand to hand and delivered to me in my bedroom? It certainly fitted with what energy healers were saying. Many of those they healed said that they felt the healers' power; felt their hands to be "real hot, oven hot"; "felt a shock"; and the like. Yet the Hilton healer, the sociologist, was just an ordinary guy. So was Pam, my roommate. What I had felt had truly passed through these two. People are permeable, for one thing. There is something around that can suddenly be given to a person and then be passed on. After all, I had learned in Africa that my "seeing" was not limited to material things. Now I had learned more: that energy too could travel, energy could heal. What else could energy do?

CHINESE HEALING: CHI

At that time I was running a monthly gathering of a group of local Charlottesville, Virginia, healers, in which one of our speakers was Ann Taylor, the University of Virginia hospital researcher with the role of presenting the case for the accreditation of acupuncture to Congress.[1] Acupuncture, as a major nonmedical field of medicine, had gained the attention of the National Institutes of Health (NIH) in Bethesda, Maryland. The institutes, with congressional funding, were in the process of making a scientific study of it, and they eventually determined that forms of acupuncture really worked. The NIH does not claim to know *why* they work. Those who understand acupuncture know it as an eminently practical, well-nigh technological way to connect with energy—as befits the culture of the Chinese, the people of its origin, who also invented printing, gunpowder, kite flying, and the civil service. Acupuncture works with the help of the fingers' sense of the energy points on the body, as developed by millennia of skilled practice, later in time to be followed by diagrams of the meridians—channels or pathways of chi—and by agreements on the location of the points. At the time of our healers' meetings, I had never come across a close-up personal story told by a subject of successful acupuncture. What did people feel? Did meridians, those pathways of energy in the body that acupuncturists describe, actually exist? Stories were hard to get since acupuncture is so technical; indeed, the diagrams look almost as technical as Grey's *Anatomy*. It is a method of treatment, a known procedure, nothing to do with psychology, not (as far as I knew) fraught with human troubles, nor concerned with human sympathy. At last an anthropology undergraduate, a quiet young woman with long hair, realizing that I really did want stories in my class on healing, gave me what I had been looking for, a close-up account of her own experience of acupuncture.

The sufferer, Julia Megan Webb, was cured by her mother, an American acupuncture healer. Megan described how her mother was first introduced to chi, the life energy of a human body that flows in pathways called meridians. Her mother came to chi through Tai Chi, the widely recognized exercise for gathering chi. Megan described her mother's steps from Tai Chi to acupuncture: "The slow, meditative movement of hand-turned-wing through the air, the deliberate steps placed with careful assurance, and the keen focus on breathing air as clear, clean light in and out of the lungs, led my mother to become aware of an energy gathering in her hands. The hands feel warm, holding energy. After playing Tai Chi myself, I can feel a slight hum when I bring the palms of my hands to-gether in front of my face in a fluid gesture of prayer. Ultimately what Tai Chi teaches is focus and control over this energy. With this control, it can be used to guide one's life or be used for more specific purposes like healing."

Megan gave the link between acupuncture and energy. Acupuncture can work because the universe is rinsed through with energy, just as the body is with blood or our atmosphere is with oxygen. All things tap into this energy. It manifests in different forms like ordinary electricity, or stormy weather, or the strength we feel in the body when we wake up in the morning "full of energy." There is also something we do not have words for. The Chinese, who are quite practical about these matters, reckon that inside the body the energy flows in meridians, twelve of them, and each is connected or associated with a specific organ. They do not think of body organs as static objects—liver, kidneys, and so on—but as active pulsating workers in the body. When a blockage or stagna-tion occurs in the flow of chi, pain may arise. However, the origin of the pain is often in a location far from where the pain is felt, and this loca-tion—for instance, in the hollow of the sole of the foot—is known to the acupuncturist. Thus the blockage in the meridian can be freed. The meridians come to the surface of the skin at different points and can be accessed by applying needles. In the following account, Megan describes her acupuncture experience.

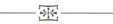

A Personal Experience of Acupuncture and the Meridians: Megan Describes Her Healing

I have been suffering from a precise, intensely radiant pain in my jaw. Now I am to receive acupuncture treatment from my mother. I see her eyes become a little moist and hear her voice waver just a bit. I am aware that she thinks I need to be unburied from something. I agree—how I want to be unburdened from the pain and feel as if I am held back by something I can't quite put a name to.

In the acupuncture room is a wood stove for warmth, a treatment table, and a statue of a man with black points and lines drawn up and down his body connecting the dots. My mother asks me to lie on the table with my feet, hands, and belly bare. Soft music is playing. I close my eyes and I can feel my mother standing behind my head, breathing deeply in and out. This is very relaxing to me, and I begin to breathe deeply too. My mother places a finger at the center of my belly and seems to be measuring distances from something as she slides her finger from various points to a central point, as if honing in on a certain spot. When she is finished, she marks the points with a pen. She repeats this process for every point she marks, sliding her fingers in ever-increasingly small radii to the center point, and then marking it. When she has done, I have marks on my belly, my hands, and my feet.

She then places tiny packets of moss, called moxa, about the size of a fingertip, on the points on my body to stimulate the points. She lights one and tells me to tell her when it gets hot. I do not feel it at first, but then the heat comes fast and sharp at the point and I say, "When." She quickly grabs the smoldering cone and places it on a dish. The smoke from the moss is heavy and feels good to breathe. We repeat the process for each point. Then she asks if I am ready for the needles. I say yes.

She wipes her fingers with an alcohol cloth and pulls a needle out of its plastic wrapping. Then she quickly wipes a point with an alcohol cloth and positions the needle just above it. She says, "Breathe in," and as she takes a deep breath, so do I. "Breathe out," and in goes the first needle in the center of my abdomen. I catch my breath a little when it goes in, but immediately I can breathe easily and hardly feel it. She puts in eight needles in the same way, into my belly and hands and feet. The needles go in and I hardly feel them; in fact, they feel kind of nice.

"Okay, how are you doing?" she asks. I breathe that I am fine, and I close my eyes. "We are just going to let those cook for a while. I'll be back in a little while." She leaves the room and I am alone with the needles.

I close my eyes, breathe deeply, and start to feel very relaxed. I think about the needles and it seems like they to start to whirr a little. Then from the points in my feet, one just below the ball of my foot on the arch and the other in the inside side of the hollow made by my Achilles tendon, I feel a slight building of something rising to the surface from within both of my feet, but especially my left foot. Then I notice that it feels as if another three, maybe four, needles have been placed in my shins. But no one has entered the room. A line of what feels like Christmas tinsel has shot up to the inside of my knee, and it feels as if two more needles have been placed on my knee.

I do not actually wonder at this, but I continue to breathe deeply, with my eyes closed. Then I begin to feel a little excited, then sad, very, very sad. The sadness swells and deepens, and I begin to see some kind of light behind my eyes and I want to cry. I feel my face contort into a crying face, and then I breathe in and out and in and out with shuddering breaths. I am suddenly thinking about things that I have not thought about in years. I open my eyes because it feels that it is too much, and I am surprised to find myself lying on the table. I focus again on the needle points and now, I am not sure if I am imagining it, but there is a kind of string made of light shooting across the needle points, connecting them all across my body from my hands to my belly to my feet. I keep breathing; part of my mind wonders how long I have been here, and I have no idea.

After some time the sadness seems to pass and the flashing light does too. I feel calmer, but somehow sad. Over all of it, there seems to be a kind of lifting taking place. Something is lifting up and up out of my body and I begin to feel very light, although my mind is somewhat shaken by the experience. My mother returns at the door and I am surprised to find that I am in fact surprised to see her, and then I remember that this, what I have been experiencing, is something called an acupuncture treatment.

"How are you doing?" she asks.

"Fine. Good," I say.

"Let's take these out now," she says. She quickly plucks each needle out of my skin. I ask her if she forgot the third point on my hands.

"You only had two points on your hands," she says. I tell her about feeling the other points on my legs. She keeps a blank face but gets out a book to show me how I had felt the next three or four points on the meridian, points that I had known nothing about.

For the next day or so, I felt the memory of the sadness I felt during the treatment, but a week later, I did not feel it at all. What I did feel was *ready*. There are few other words to describe it. I could deal with my problems, my pain was lessened, and my sorrow went away. I no longer felt nervous in difficult social situations. I felt natural and friendly. I felt light. I felt ready and present. This treatment was a turning point in my life after which everything felt different. It is hard to put into words, but a lot of things changed in my life. My mother had applied the art of acupuncture, recognizing the whole person, spirit, mind, and body as one. She had embodied the art so that the energy could come through her and work for the good of another.[2]

What I realized from the way Megan told the story was how she felt chi in her body in energy's own organs, the meridians, and she felt its flow in detail. The points at which the meridians break surface have been provided by our biology, it appears, much as the coconut bears three depressions where you can tap the milk, or the orange politely separates into quarters when you peel it. This is the way nature is; and with us, energy lines whirr beneath the surface all the time and in certain places are quite palpable. The Western doctors say the lines have nothing to do with nerves and do not appear on X-ray photographs or in any other scanner. Yet I can see that it is energy that makes the hands of a healer tingle, or that Singleton felt buzzing in the cupping horn in the African Ihamba.

Megan's experience shows that the sense of energy is a matter of the deepest soul. She went through something rather like a near death experience: first the agony of the blocked soul, then the power in the needles doing their work, then the feeling of lightness and readiness for life.

The next account, after this gentle, intimate, and fully realized story, is on the same theme, energy, and the same manifestation of it, acupuncture—but now I cite a medical student from Harvard, out to get material for his dissertation. David Eisenberg's topic was Chinese traditional medicine. From 1977 to 1985, first as a student and then as a researcher, he worked in China with acupuncturists on the mysteries of chi energy, which he transcribed as "Qi." However, when I give his story I retain the word *chi* because it is better known to readers. Eisenberg chose as the center of his research the Beijing Institute of Traditional Chinese Medicine, and he studied there under experts on chi and participated in their experiments with it. His story, *Encounters with Qi*, written in 1985, has a different tone from Megan's, instructing us from his knowledge of acupuncture. The photographs in his book show various learned Asian professionals, usually laughing cheerfully, and the one American, a very serious bearded student, undertaking experiments with this mysterious force.[3]

David Eisenberg's Story of Chi in China

I asked my teacher, Dr. Fang, "What is *chi*, really?"

"*Chi* means what differentiates life from death, animate from inanimate," said Dr. Fang. "To live is to have *chi* in every part of your body. To die is to be without *chi*." . . . [4]

I was learning to use the needles with a Dr. Zhang. Before sticking others, I wished to be needled myself. I wanted to understand the sensations involved, so Dr. Zhang inserted a needle through a point between my right thumb and forefinger. It is called the *He Gu* point. Zhang started to twist the needle to stimulate the point. After this I begin to feel a sensation of fullness, as if my hand were swelling from inside. Then a feeling of distension went up my right arm into my upper back. I asked Dr. Zhang whether patients always have some sort of sensation when they are needled. He told me that they should feel no pain associated with the piercing of the skin but that thereafter, when the point is stimulated, they will experience pain, soreness, heaviness, numbness, pins and needles, or the feeling of electric shock. . . . [5]

The ancients had a specific name for the phenomena associated with these sensations. They called it *de chi*, which literally means, "obtaining the *chi*." Needle insertion influences the flow of *chi* (vital energy), which manifests itself in these altered sensations. Acupuncturists of the old school insist they can "feel" the *chi* through the needle in their fingers when they have entered the appropriate point or channel. A Chinese maxim holds, "When the *chi* is obtained, it is like a fish that has taken the bait." Some acupuncturists contend that they can not only *sense chi* but also *transmit* it through the acupuncture needle to the appropriate point in the patient's body. . . . [6]

Chinese therapeutic massage (shiatsu in Japan) works on the same principles. Zhu my masseur was totally blind. I lay face down, and Zhu, after being silent for five or ten minutes, positioned himself on his knees alongside me. Then his palms and fingertips scanned my body from head to toe, barely touching me. His hands were like electronic sensors. He was scanning my body by running his fingers along the tracks of the major acupuncture meridians.

Zhu selected a point on the left side of my neck and one on the left side of my lower back. I heard him take in a deep breath, and as he exhaled he began to apply pressure to these two points, using nothing but his fingertips. Then came a bizarre sensation of pressure and fullness and heat throughout my body. By the time Zhu withdrew his fingertips and began to use his palms to knead these points, I was already deeply relaxed. To be relaxed and at the same time aware of every nerve and muscle in your body is an unusual experience.

This was acupuncture without the needles. . . . [7]

Chi Gong, the martial art first associated with *chi*, starts with learning to breathe well. *Chi* means "breath" as well as "vital energy." Then the student is taught to "focus" his or her *chi* at a point in the center of the body. This point is located roughly two inches below the navel and deep within the pelvis. It is from this vital center that *chi* emanates to other parts of the body. With practice, students should sense the presence of *chi* at this point in the form of localized warmth or heat. With further practice, they should learn to direct *chi* to distant portions of the body. . . . [8]

A Chi Gong master said he could feel the *chi* flowing in his body, but he did not pretend to understand its power: "It's inside of me. It's part of me, like an arm or a breath. Can you explain what it's like to exhale? Emitting *chi* is like exhaling for me. Can anyone understand a breath?" . . . [9]

We asked for a demonstration of external *chi* (projecting one's internal *chi* toward another body). Sitting in a chair ten feet in front of me was Dr. Zhao Jun-Xiang, the teacher of teachers of Chi Gong. A bear of a man, Zhao had a big frame and brawny arms and neck. I sat in the chair with my hands in my lap, closed my eyes, and attempted to relax. "Are you ready, Dr. Ai?"

"I'm ready," I replied. Then I felt pins and needles from my shoulders down to my fingernails. The sensations intensified, the pins and needles changed to electrical impulses. It was as if my hands had been plugged into a low-voltage socket. My fingers, wrist, arms, and shoulders tingled and grew numb. In seconds the sensation of electrical impulses in my upper limbs grew in intensity. It was as though the voltage in the socket had been turned up to high. I called to my friend, "I felt this incredible sense of electrical energy shooting through my arms." Seconds later the master stopped, and the abnormal sensations ended abruptly. I was exhilarated but had no idea what to make of this demonstration. . . . [10]

"[In a later statement Eisenberg said]: studying Chinese medicine in China is like going to medical school within the confines of a theological seminary. In the West, we separate religion and medicine. In Chinese medicine, the medical masters, the people who understood material things, were also the spiritual leaders. They never split the two. Imagine if Harvard Medical School were placed inside a large theological seminary, and classes taught jointly. That's in large part what Chinese medicine is about."[11]

Here in David Eisenberg's account are few of the deep matters of the soul that Megan provides, but it gives similar descriptions of the physical aspects of acupuncture and acupressure, this time told by a male experiencer. The features that are particularly interesting are the searching fingers of the healer, aware of the energy in the tracks beneath the skin; Eisenberg's information about the sheer force of this humanly generated power; and how the chi giver takes a little time beforehand to make his connection with the source of energy. The testimonies of both Megan and David Eisenberg witness to the curer's deep attention to the physicality of the patient, the *reading* of his or her body.

Many people can feel the same buzz of energy in their hands that Megan's mother felt during Tai Chi. It is discernible as a tingling in the fingertips of the hand. You hold out your hands with the palms facing, parallel to each other and about three inches apart. You draw them together until they are about one inch apart, letting your fingertips "feel" the presence of the opposite fingertips. Then you draw your hands apart about ten inches, then slowly near to each other again. What you imagined you felt the first time now becomes a positive tingle. This is a sense

Thérèse O'Mahony, Celtic healer.

that people have in their fingertips, and your fingers are feeling energy. The energy the body gives out can also be spotted about three inches above another person's head, again like a tingle. Most healers are quite familiar with the energy field of a human being. The sense can be developed by keeping on the lookout for it.

The sense of the power of a person extending beyond the body is echoed by Jacob Levy Moreno, the introducer of psychodrama, who said that in a true "psychosocial" picture of a person.[12] [The psyche appears as outside the body, the body is surrounded by the psyche and the psyche is surrounded by and interwoven into the social and cultural atoms.] The individual psyche is always intimately and naturally connected with

Thérèse O'Mahony's home and herb garden.

the psyches of others—that is, the "social and cultural atoms." The terms *psyche* and *human energy field* overlap here.

Throughout the world there exists a curious range of metaphors for this phenomenon named energy, not defined by science. In western Ireland a healer in the Celtic tradition, named Thérèse O'Mahony calls her gift of healing power her "electricity," and gives a shiver in recognition of it. O'Mahony's patients feel this electricity too. Before she works on the patient, she needs to become quiet for a time. Once she begins, she uses her thumbs like antennae on the patient's body until she feels the source of the trouble. As soon as she finds it she gets overwhelmed with the desire to heal, and it works: the electricity comes into her hands and arms. The patient feels the jolt of it and the pain is gone. In Malaysia, the healing force is called the Inner Wind of passion inhabiting a person. Far from Malaysia, the Kung of the Kalahari Desert of Botswana and Namibia have their own term for energy, *num*, and they dance to accumulate the energy to heal. *Num* means "boiling energy," the plentifully given energy of healing, real and palpable. *Vimbuza*, "energy-spirit," a spirit especially in charge of energy, is the central element in the healing ritual of the Tumbuka of Malawi, Africa, and they compare this en-

ergy, which they sense is necessary to power the connection with ancestor spirits, to radios and their batteries.

Human beings in different places call this thing, then, *electricity, wind,
boiling energy,* and *radio batteries,* but it is not any of these mechanical
things but something else. In the following sections, I give the stories behind some of these terms.

NUM, BOILING ENERGY: HEALING AMONG THE KALAHARI KUNG

Around that time I encountered a book entitled *Boiling Energy: Community Healing among the Kalahari Kung.*[13] What do you make of a book
called *Boiling Energy?* I thought at first it was an over-intense title. But it
turns out that the phrase "boiling energy" is precisely the Kung's own
term for the energy the people achieve in their healing ceremonies—
"boiling energy." The energy, called *num* by the Kalahari bushmen, is indeed intense, and it does the main work of healing. For the Kung, their
all-night weekly healing dance is central to their lives, this one thing
pervading their culture as an integrating force. Being a hunting people
and used to sharing their food, they also share healing—they give it to
one another.

The dance provides hot energy, *num,* which at its "boiling point"
thrusts the consciousness of participants up to another level of consciousness, a state they call *kia,* which is said to boil fiercely within a
person. Then they can see, sometimes right into the bodies of sufferers, and in the midst of the dance they are able to lay their hands on
the sickness, "pull it out," and heal the sufferer. The San rock paintings of the Drakensberg Mountains in Natal, South Africa, show de-
pictions of a healing dance much like that of the present-day Kung,
which indicate that the Kung ceremony must be at least several hundred years old.

The story begins in the cool of the nights as the band gathers around
a fire on the desert sand. The people are slender, with neat small alert
faces and high cheek bones. They are almost naked, their bodies gleaming, perfectly black, long-legged, and active. The healers bind rattles to
their legs and start to sing, and all, healers and sufferers alike, join in a
large dance circle around the fire. They are intent on what they are doing:
they move close behind each other as one body, some actually touching
the person in front, an arm on his or her shoulder or waist.

---------------------------- ✳ ----------------------------

The Kung Healing Dance Described by Richard Katz

The dancers are calling to the singers, individually or together. . . . "We need your voices!" "Pick up the singing. Louder!"

The dancers call to each other, "This is a night for strong *num*." "Father, help me tonight!". . . .

And the singers laugh to each other. . . . "This is a night for our singing to climb into the skies!". . . .

Kinachau's movements are spare, sharp, and effortless; his body seems almost weightless. Sometimes he does not travel around the dance circle but moves in place, with light, strong, rhythmic steps. Hovering over the ground, hands up in the air, elbows bent 90 degrees, accenting the beat, he is like a giant water bird readying for a landing on a shimmering lake surface.

The atmosphere becomes more exciting, electric. . . . Kinachau is sweating; his face is beginning to take on a pained appearance. He starts to tremble, his legs quivering. His movement around the circle is becoming unsteady. He calls out, "Am I in *kia* so soon?". . . . He does not complete one full circle. He swoons and falls softly into the sand. . . . He has entered into *kia*, sharply and quickly.

Kinachau sits up . . . his look is glazed, and his body trembles spasmodically. He returns to dancing, and after three full turns around the circle, goes to one of the peripheral "talking" fires and begins to heal. As he pulls the sickness from each person, Kinachau's whole body shakes roughly and his legs tremble violently, the tendons sticking out.[14] When the healer starts to pull the sickness out, his jerking hands quiver rapidly over the person's chest, one hand in front, the other in back. He wails painfully, "Errrrr!" and shivers because he has taken the sickness out into his hands. He shakes his hands to throw it away beyond the circle, where the spirits are, and shrieks out the characteristic deep howling sound which expresses the pain involved in pulling out pain—"Xai—i! Kow-ha-di-di-di-di!" Suddenly he stops, and the singing stops.[15]

Then another song begins. Singing and rattling starts the *num* moving again as all the voices form a full, connected sound. The voices life the dancers into serious dancing. . . . Half an hour ago, Bau danced a few turns around the fire, apparently inspired by one of those special moments in the dance when singing and dancing peak to unimagined levels of intensity. Now, still singing strongly, she starts to sway. She falls over, completely limp and moaning, into the arms of the singer. . . . She moans softly and begins to gasp for breath. Bau has entered *kia*.[16]

[Kinachau explains why he danced some rounds before healing.] "Since it's the elders who gave *num* to us . . . you breathe hard and fast, your heart is pounding. You run around because the *num* is shaking and agitating you violently. So you run around with it til it cools down, until you feel that you can lay your hands steadily on those you are going to pull."[17] "You have to be absolutely steady to see sickness, steady-eyed, no shivering and shaking. You need a steady gaze. Your thoughts don't whirl, the fire doesn't float above you, when you are seeing properly."[18]

"During the dance," says Kinachau, "when you look out beyond the fire, you see things. It's light, not dark, even though it is nighttime. You see camps, you see at a distance in the night. You see actual things and people. When the healer talks at the dance and says, 'Go away,' he is talking to bad things that are hurting those he is pulling. . . . You see little things, like twigs . . . sent by god that are troubling people. You see and you pull."[19] Kaha said, "I pull little pieces of metal out of my wife's legs and hips, like little pieces of wire. These bits of metal are tying her leg ligaments up. I pulled her dead father's testicles out of her heart, then I told her father not to pursue her anymore.[20] "You can see when the insides of well people are fine. You can predict the sex of a baby in the womb. You can see the insides of someone the spirits are trying to kill, and you go there. Then you see the spirits and drive them away."[21]

During the death of full *kia*, the soul leaves the healer's body through the head. The soul goes to encounter god and the spirits of the dead ancestors. It pleads for protection for the Kung back at the dance. The Kung say that healers are in great danger at this time. Their soul might wander away or be taken by the spirits.[22] [Returning healers will describe the god's home and their own soul's struggle for the sick person's soul.][23] "When I pick up *num*, it explodes and throws me up in the air, and I enter heaven and then fall down." During *kia* others feel that they are opening up or bursting open, like a ripe pod. This is a kind of death in itself, the final *num*.[24]

Kashay talks about when he was "given up for dead": "There was the time I was very sick, so sick I was given up for dead. This disease absolutely ruined my feet; they were as limp and pale as dead flesh. I was deathly thin. They were dancing for me. They brought me from the camp to the dance. Toma Zho danced over me until the sun rose. I was so sick I couldn't sleep. My eyes were closed but they were full of visions of ancestors. Toma Zho pulled me and pulled me and pulled me until the sun rose. Then I was taken back to my camp, and I said, 'Is today the day I'm finally going to see some sleep?' I lay down,

and to my great surprise I fell into a sound, good sleep. And I woke up saying, 'I'm saved.'"[25]

Num, then, is imparted from spirit beings to humans, or from humans
to humans. Healers in a healing embrace can simultaneously heal each
other. This is because *num* expands when it boils; it can flow easily across
individual boundaries, creating a healing unit more powerful than the
strength of the component individuals. The whole community activates
num, so that the community does the healing through *num* and is healed
through *num*. The healer is using *num* to bring the protective powers of
the universe to bear on the patient and relieve her symptoms.

In my quest for healing accounts, I was moved by this intimate account of doing healing. A professional video recording of the ceremony[26]
brought it closer still. As I watched, I seemed to be flying through the
weird dance myself, crying the great call of release along with the men's
spare forms, the gleaming black bodies in the most meager clothes, running and running like cave-painting stick-men with agile strides, responding to the rising *num*. Their faces began to come clear to me, intent
over wide cheekbones, contorted by the jerk of the spirit, filled from
somewhere with a very satisfying controlled explosion.

Connectedness reigns naturally throughout the performance. People
are aware of each other and are ready to catch a person if she falls. Jokes
fly from one person to another in the circle. It is that very togetherness—
always with music that is able to speak the language of togetherness or
communitas so well—that opens the way for energy and allows the ancestors to bestow it, energy that even enables the healers to venture to
the home of the gods and thus to confirm the unity of humanity and the
spirit world.

The Kung healers venture to the very gates of death for their patients.
They fear the pain of boiling *num* and yet the gift of *num* is their central preoccupation, a gift that makes them Kung, makes a person an "I."
Their sense of the soul is sharp and clear; their courage in flying onward
to the soul's verge is one with that of saints and visionaries. As for me,
for decades as a young woman I could not stand the sentimental holy
books on the saints and great divines of religion, but when I read *Boiling
Energy* I learned from the hunter-gatherers something of what many holy
people must feel. Yet the Kung were a people practicing a way of life reckoned to be the simplest and most archaic in the world.

RADIO IN THE EAST AFRICAN SENSE: *DIVINATION IS LIKE RADIO; YOU OPEN UP THE WAVELENGTH AND YOU GET THROUGH TO THE SPIRITS* (MODERN AFRICAN RIDDLE)

Wind—electricity—boiling: we have encountered three metaphors for energy. Far-scattered peoples have been struggling to find words for what they all experience. There is yet another term used as a metaphor for how healers sense the working of their craft: it is *radio*, an electronic device. The anthropologist Steven Friedson encountered this interesting use of the word *radio* among a hoe-cultivating group of the savannas of Malawi, East Africa, a people known as the Tumbuka. Healers said that when an energy-spirit was inside them they needed drum music to help them to see spiritually and divine the cause of illness. They said that the energy-spirit was the battery for the ancestor spirit's radio. This mystery was revealed in the course of their ritual.

As Friedson knew, the people were familiar with radios, for there were 1,000,000 of them in Malawi, and everybody knew they needed D-cell batteries. Obviously the battery would have to have some energy in it for a person to hear the radio. Energy-spirit? Battery? Ancestor spirit? Radio? What was energy-spirit to begin with? Friedson learned that all people have latent energy-spirits in them, called *vimbuza*, usually benign and friendly. They can exist as a substance in the bloodstream, and thus they are intimately connected with the person. When a person is sick, the people call for healers and drummers. The healers' task is to develop the energy-spirits inside the patient to their full capacity. Everyone is keen to see this happen. The drummers, with an intense heady beat, succeed in heating up the energy to such a pitch that the *vimbuzas* "come out" and become a power in the patient.[27] Now we see how the energy-spirits are the battery, warmed into life by the drummers.

Then, at a certain point, the patient becomes a healer. In order to understand the final connection between the four components of the riddle—energy-spirit/battery/ancestor-spirit/radio—Friedson had to undergo the ritual himself. Being in the ritual taught him how the riddle was completed. He himself broke through the opening into the "seeing" world.

TUMBUKA HEALING

Here I tell the story of a *Vimbuza* healing and initiation in my own words. The patient is a young woman with a serious, round face, deeply willing for this to happen. For the ceremony they dress her in a belt with rattles hanging all around her waist, and they bring her into the gathering, seating her before the main drum with her head almost touching its wooden side. The drummers try for a rhythm. They are searching for the special drum beat that resonates with the particular energy-spirit inside her, and when they hit on this rhythm and play it—a mode with a heady yet skillful tangle between a two beat and three beat rhythm—then the song, the dancing, and the clapping go into a crescendo to heat up the energy-spirit past its critical threshold so that it will burst out into the world of the living. They play. The drumming becomes irresistible. The woman with her ear to the drum suddenly jerks. It is her favorite drum rhythm. She starts to tremble, and she rises. Ah, now she has become the manifestation of a spirit, and she dances before the crowd in the energy-spirit's own dance, the rattles at her waist clashing in a multiple uproar. She is in trance.

What is it like to be in trance? For such a one, the body space feels strangely elastic, with the front part of one's body-spirit stretching outward and upward. The energy of the vimbuza causes one's self to expand, creating a space within one, an opening, a clearing. Along with the expansion of one's body, one feels a tremendous exhilaration.

As the energy-spirit dances in the woman during that first burst, her face is almost naive in its simplicity. The ritual master passes a dove over her head and she seems already to be in heaven. The time is ripe. The heat is at its height, ready for a blood ritual. They give her the dove. In her energy state she bites into its throat and begins to suck the blood. The dove does not struggle at all, and as its eyes begin to lose their light, a bliss overtakes the scene. In her newly-empowered state the woman dances from top to toe, vigorously shaking her belt of rattles until, at last, all her vimbuza spirits come rushing out one after another to dance with her. Now she can dance as much as she likes, finally letting the heat calm down and her mind to grow cool and focused.

The blood of the dove has been given her so that in later life, when she treats patients herself, she will have already been fed on blood and will not want to spiritually drink the patients' blood.

From this point on in the dance, the vimbuza energy-spirits and the drums are at liberty to do a new work. Together they encourage the re-

lease of the woman's own personal ancestor spirits and they push them
to the fore. These ancestors, the spirits of her biological parents and other
dead kin, are the generators of the actual gifts of the healer. The heat,
like radio batteries, is able to open up the channels, and now it is the
ancestors who are getting through to her on their "radio" and connecting with her. They now have primacy and, with their ancient power of
clairvoyance, they cause her vision to clear so that she can "see." She is
now a diviner and can see inside the bodies of patients to the roots of
their illness. In future she belongs to the community, and she must be of
service to her people for the rest of her life or she will be ill again.[28]

☀

"The energy-spirit is the battery for the ancestor spirit's radio": the
riddle is clear. The "battery" is the power of the *vimbuza* spirit when it
comes out. Once that power surge has broken its way through into reality by means of the drummers hitting on the right rhythm, the ancestor
spirit's "radio" can be heard. The person is connected, "is on wavelength,"
"is tuned." It is this "radio" that will send messages to the new healer
when she takes up the task of divining. It releases the ancestral clairvoyance. The mundane radio that one buys in the store is in its own way
manufactured to transcend time and space and tell of things unknown to
the listeners. All the more does the gift of divination tell of unknown
things, learned from the ancestors who have existed among the Tumbuka
from time immemorial. The energy the healer is given ultimately radi-
ates its beneficence back upon the community, reinvesting the power in
them, as it were. It affects the inner selves of all the people it touches.
    The Tumbuka people show in this ritual how vital is the discovery of
the right signature tune or rhythm for the sick woman. In a sense the
group heals by finding the inner love of the sufferer. Treatment by "signature tune" recognizes the necessity of finding the exact tune, beat, or
chant to wake the spirit within the sufferer. It has been seen how the
sick woman sits near the drum in the *vimbuza* cure. When they hit on
her own rhythm she rises, in trance at last, and can take on her power.
Also in Malaysia, the sick man is seated in the midst of the gamelan or-
chestra and the singer tries out various melodies, groping toward the patient's own tune. The tune makes contact, and he rises in great gestures
taken from the martial arts and shows fight at last, the winds running
free. These acts of seeking what really fits a person are especially strong
producers of communitas—just as storytelling is. Hitting on the tune
slides all the community's love, the completest sense of "being-one-with-

you," into the person, so that the person somehow *is* the beloved community, just as one might say, "I *am* home." The result of a body of musicians searching for a person's individual signature tune can be overwhelming—even singing "Happy Birthday" has its effect. The "signature" spirit also resolves some of the dilemma about collective spirituality versus the uniqueness of the personality. Free acceptance of individuality is the supreme style here, taking on the patient's view, while at the same time the group is at one in its enterprise.

Furthermore, Friedson gives details of exactly how the drummers weave the spirit-net of sound that brings the spirit into manifestation. The work cannot be completed without the hands-on material skill that plucks the spirit into being. Friedson's passage on the music of the Malawi drummers and its importance for achieving the "opening" to the spirit realm shows the best understanding of spiritual music that I have ever come across. He tells us exactly and precisely what is happening. He has managed to explain to me how, when Tumbuka healers dance in Malawi, they have reached beyond the place where they are one thing and the drums are another. They are at one with the drums and the people, "equal before the foundation of the world," that is, they have achieved the sense of equiprimordiality, as Friedson put it in one long word.[29] And in a flash the spirits arrive. Dancers, drums, and spirit are all one, transfigured. At this point music is not just a pleasant part of performance It pushes healing into existence. People get better. Musical performance of this kind is not just a mood enhancer, or there for the beauty of the sound, or for pleasure. It is also an act of positive reality.

Friedson notes how the very pattern of Malawi drum rhythm is shaped to seize the mind. The *vimbuza* music itself, the rhythm, consists of a two-beat rhythm combined with a three-beat rhythm, and it varies from time to time as the drummer's intuitions take him, using well-recognized surprises—that is, syncopations that do *not* sound when expected, in such a way that the very arrangement of the discontinuities, gaps, and stutters in the music is subtle and disturbing. Moreover, in its unfolding, this music is hearkening both backward (to what one *has* heard, giving one future expectations) and forward (to what one expects to hear and sometimes does not—which is the syncopation). Thus one does not hear the music in a straight line from the first to the last bar but also, simultaneously, backwards in memory to the first bar. It is not just the first sounds that are marked on one's memory. Each bit of the first passage affects the whole. In Malawi drumming, one is aware of all these things simultaneously—two-beats, three-beats, syncopation, and past and future—and furthermore the people know these features as cunningly woven separate threads.[30] Harmony itself is of this kind, as shown by all of our own Western harmony. This is what made Mozart far more than just a musician; he was a music shaman, in the category of oneness-maker.

In his understanding of what music does, Friedson taught us to revel in this curious now-you-see-it-now-you-don't effect, and he compares it to the sense one has before those three-dimensional random-dot stereogram pictures that stand up inches high out of their print if you squint your eyes for a second.[31] Then you see the lamb, or raindrop, or whatever it is, without squinting anymore, and you see it quite easily, high, and hovering above the paper. You *know*. And it goes away. Similarly, as Friedson says, once a person can hear the music of *vimbuza* whole in its rhythmic depth, then the musical experience is transformed into a kind of multidimensional hearing that transcends acoustical phenomena. The whole is an entirely different, stand-out apparition, showing the spirit presence itself, giving a sudden sense of expansion that bears a terrific charge of energy, heat, and glory—real, not otherworldly but this worldly, belonging to the natural history of the world one is in. One does not have to believe it; the spirits are simply there. The music has slid people out from one level into another, by means of a this-world pattern that uses many things at once with great subtlety. Something in people *can* accomplish this; people are made that way. When they are in that moment, it is pure joy, and it will never end. The shift has taken place. This is far beyond hypnotism or illusion, but simply a matter of being led into the land of joy, which is there all the time, with all one's friends in it. All dance. Hypnotic subjects do not do this.

The *vimbuza* drummers' task is to search and search for this point. They use the interweaving language of theirs—two-beat, three-beat, and syncopation—which is often unexpected and irregular; and somehow this irregularity speaks a language that thumps and knocks and finally shatters the old and rigid walls, and the soul wriggles through to a strange new world. And the people know it.

Friedson describes his own experience like this: he says that when he was in the *vimbuza* dance, "after a while I began to notice that there were moments when I was getting lost in the shifting patterns of the drumming. Threes were becoming twos and vice versa, and I found myself becoming fascinated by this shifting phenomenon. The drums on this night seemed to have a special presence to them, as if the sound were very close to my ears. This sensation of closeness, in which the physical and psychical distance between myself and the sound of the drums seemed to collapse or be enfolded, became more pronounced. I could no longer tell whether the drumming was coming from outside or inside my head."[32]

He comments, "There seems to be an inherent aesthetic interest in this shifting that, for those who are aware of it, captivates consciousness, inviting it to radically narrow its focus."[33] When one gazes at the pattern—if it is a subtle one—it plucks one out of oneself. The flow of attention, if true and focused, joins a person with that thing—and through it to all things. The gift of such a moment heals, stabilizes, produces clairvoyance, and matures one for a lifetime of sureness in the work of reaching the spirit to heal.

I could see that a similar connection of music and spirit is strong in many cultures. Long ago in 1953, Maya Deren discovered that music in Voudoun could take her into another world. She knew the different world into which she was transported. With her, it was the drumming that achieved it:

> The drummer can "break" to relieve the tension of the monotonous beat and bodily motion, thus interrupting concentration. By withholding this break he can bring the Loa [gods] into the heads of the participants or stop them from coming. He can also use the break in another way by letting the tension build to a point where the break does not release tension, but climaxes it in a galvanizing shock. This enormous blow empties the dancer's head, leaving him without a center around which to stabilize. He is buffeted by the strokes as the drummer "beats the Loa into his head." He cringes at the large beats, clutches for support, recapturing his balance just to be hurtled forward by another great beat of the drum. The drummer persists until the violence suddenly ceases, and the person lifts his head, seeming to gaze into another world. The Loa has arrived.[34]

In many rituals in Africa, in Umbanda in Brazil, among Iñupiat dancers, and in a Western choir, at such a point something like an electrical circuit may come alive throughout the group—suddenly there, in everybody—and the participants are like one person acting. Then, music is not merely the vehicle of the spirit, a means. At certain moments, music *is* the spirit; it incorporates all, including spirit, and one hears the spirit playing in the music like the fountain in Rilke's "Sonnet to Love" and like the sound of the sacred loom of Pohjolla's daughter in Sibelius's *Finlandia*. One can ask helplessly, "*How* does music do this?" Another skill is connected with the act of searching across the chords or resonances, not only for the signature tune of an individual, but also for the resonances of all in the community that together make the great collective signature tune. Music helps the group to come together, and its communitas gathers strength. In ritual, active communitas begins to strike off from everybody like flint sparks, like electricity connecting—just as when, in an instant, power touches everybody at once and healing happens. Communitas can actually *happen*, a "running-through-everybody." It is—simply—oneness. And afterward comes the cooling process as among the Kung, and even in Megan's experience of acupuncture after her tears. The power recedes, leaving a wonderful clarity, a being-in-touch with the spirits, a blessed state. The thoughtfulness emerging at this time follows an important spiritual process, one of the discoveries in the natural history of the soul.

Generally, the odd things about music are well known to those who are familiar with it. The piece of music and the audience somehow become bonded in such a way that they are merged into one another and form a single whole for a moment. The players, for their part, know they have to let go and take risks and let it happen. They know, but they do not know in the fashion of book learning. One has to give oneself totally, without reservations. One has to become like a child.

This happened to me in Ihamba, as I related in chapter 1: "I had just found out how to clap. You simply clap along with the beat of the drum, *and clap hard.* All the rest falls into place. Your own body becomes deeply involved in the rhythm, and everyone reaches a unity. Clap clap clap—Mulandu was leaning forward all the others were on our feet—this was it. Suddenly Meru raised her arm, stretched it in liberation, and I saw . . . a large gray sphere about six inches across" come out of her back.

The effect can be very simple. Even spontaneous group harmonizing can bring up the same bliss: we look into each other's faces while creaming out a delicious chord, and we smile. We sing a round. We have given ourselves to a tune, totally, for the time. It is the same sort of thing as the well-known moments of "flow" during sport and sometimes work, when ability becomes second nature, and one's very actions are blissful, locked in a kind of inevitability of perfection—the sense of great soccer players when they are in the zone. Great moments in music are as common as flow.

Communitas makes healing happen and it is very sacred, especially when the group gives of itself to find the hidden signature tune that opens up connections in the sufferer. Getting under the other person's skin is the style, rather than attack and coercion. When exploring spiritual music, one finds that it can appear to play itself, that the music is able to join a music-shaman to the Great Spirit and, through many complex means, including rounds, power songs, and especially the highly layered and unexpected moments of drumming, it gives birth to breakthrough, to the experience of release. Then flow rolls us along, the sense of time is lost, and heaven and the ancestors are here again.

Thus many cultures have a very good idea of what spiritual energy is, its potential, and the connection of energy with the deepest religious experience. Clearly, the different cultures are using somewhat similar metaphors like batteries and electricity to express it. Many people in the different cultures see its similarity to mundane energy and also the differences between the two. The *vimbuza* is yet another way to understand healing energy, linking it with a particular set of spirits personal to oneself. Now we return to our own culture, and see what our own people are doing.

"YOU CAN FEEL IT IN YOUR HANDS" IN SUBURBAN AMERICA: PULLING ENERGY FROM A CLOUD

In the mundane circles of suburban America, nonmedical healing is practiced with its own corresponding understanding of energy.[35] In 1988 the sociologist Meredith McGuire,[36] working in suburbia, was listening to what American women healers said about their craft. They described in some detail exactly how energy was being experienced, and I give some of McGuire's findings here. McGuire reckoned that the background for much of this healing was derived from Eastern religions, especially the practice of meditation and the understanding of psychic power. Now, in 2005, our healers have developed a commonly used practice, mostly without ethnic characteristics, which constitutes a recognizable practice acceptable to large numbers of Americans—American spiritual healing itself. The variations may be many, but the common features are clear to all.

An American psychic healer told McGuire:

> It's like taking a piece of cloud. There's something there. You can feel it in your hands. And you can mould it. For instance in the Bible, it says about being made from clay. That's it. It's like a clay out there in the universe that you can just kind of pick out of the air. It's like cotton; you can just pick a piece off and mold it and put it in where you think the person needs it.
>
> It's not physical. But also remember you're not working even with your physical hands and your physical body. So it's a very fine vibration. It's not

coarse, it's not dense. It's very fine. But still when you're working with a very fine vibration, it's just a little less fine than you are, so it feels like something in your hands. This energy is all over. I've never had a problem finding it. When I need it, I just take it. It's there.[37]

My interest in McGuire's inquiries draws me to emphasize the other parallels to the psychic's sense of a very fine vibration that appear in the accounts already given above, for instance, in Megan's story of acupuncture and its delicate spreading power, and Thérèse O'Mahony's description of her "electricity" and its messages traveling through her fingers to her brain.

McGuire asked a woman patient, "How does it feel when you are healed?"

It feels like a total surrender, a total letting go, a total opening, a heightened degree of awareness of every cell of your body, and a connectedness between your body and your mind and your spirituality, an incredible, incredible connectedness there. Just wonderful! You know a healing has occurred because there's a freeing in your body and your mind. There's more space. There's more energy. And your mind has let go of whatever it was you were tenaciously clinging to. That's the only way I can describe it. I mean, I just know.[38]

Another healer told McGuire, "The source of healing power is probably the whole universe. I'm just thinking in terms of spirituality. There's an energy level that's not to be measured in machines. I think the source is to be in touch with or in harmony with a much bigger force—what some people call God."[39]

Another said,

Healing power is coming from somewhere outside of yourself. There's a very strong spiritual-like atmosphere that's there, and if you plug into that or if you let that sort of roll over you, that's when all these good things can happen. That's the only way I can locate it. Everywhere.

The healing power is released by direct communication, where you put your hand on someone—like E.T. touched a finger, okay?—the contact helps people directly. It's like conducting electricity. Energy is all around. It goes wherever people are receptive, and wherever the weaknesses are, it just seems to flow in. Like a sandcastle when the tide comes in, it just goes in all the little holes.[40]

McGuire's healer friends maintained that universal energy is simultaneously there, everywhere, and yet *within*; we are it.

In addition to McGuire's findings, I have found that the country is full of similar reports of suburban energy healing, mostly lacking even these few words for a close-up description—because when healers tax their brains about it, they often complain, "It's hard to put into words." True enough. The same goes for the vast field of healing in the world elsewhere, which is in progress everywhere. Many of the descriptions are hesitant, a matter of feeling the way, and the speakers know their words are incomplete.

Westerners have been relearning the craft from seers of their own and from different cultures, and are using it to assist healing in unexpected and powerful ways. Strange to say, the exercise of healing gives one joy and peace of mind, for it is good to know that there are indeed spiritual forces waiting to enliven and assist one, working in a close symbiotic relationship. The cures are biological in their effects, that is, connected to our living and bodily existence. This ties in with our growing understanding of the body, and a sense that human beings often have inherent gifts for physico-spiritual healing and for other acts that are beyond psychological analysis—genetically endowed gifts, needing stimulus for their development, and paralleling the predisposition for speech possessed by infants. The brain operates from synapse openings by means of very subtle electronic impulses. There may be readiness cells in the brain, prepared in advance to take on the functions of healing for which a biological predisposition has already made a place. I suggest that the brain is a vital organ which is able to incorporate what we call energy from outside and perform the strange nonlogical acts that researchers have presented here. In addition to the brain, the hands have a great ability to feel and transmit energy. Furthermore, we may find that the internal organs also have some sort of consciousness, as understood by the Hindu chakra system of energy centers. The Chinese are familiar with a maze of communications through the body from designated acupuncture points, to disease points. Our biology is richer that we suppose. People realize we have been starved of this knowledge and help.

HOW TO EXPERIENCE ENERGY: FINDING OUT THROUGH THERAPEUTIC TOUCH

Here are some ways we can actually put into practice what we are starting to understand. Energy is most easily accessed by coming into alignment with its physicality. For instance, we have already seen how energy is discernible as a tingle in the fingertips of the hand.

Karen Johnson is an registered nurse who has worked with Dolores Krieger on therapeutic energy awareness. The following is Karen Johnson's method of assessing the human energy field—a space that extends in a kind of orbit several inches outside the body. In this domain, there is a spread of energy.

> You first become quiet and feel the earth with your feet. Then you move your hands over the body of the other person about three inches away, slowly, pausing for sensations of change in the energy you feel in your hands. You listen all the time to that area extending outside the person until your hands get the sense of where it is alive and how far out it begins to fade away—its outer boundary. [This larger "person" is what Moreno calls the psyche, which interweaves with and melds with the social and emotional vitality of other people—which is why one person's psyche can feel the other person's psyche through the hands.]
>
> Your hands are your guides. You need to look for loose congestion, heat, thickness, heaviness, or pressure. You can locate local imbalances, such as pins and needles, static, a break in rhythm, or confused vibrations. Sweep them away from the troubled area, gathering them up in your hands and throwing them away. Tight congestion or obstruction shows in coldness, blankness, no movement, emptiness, or just leadenness from a long-term deficiency. These parts will need extra energy. So raise your hands and let energy come to you from above and enter your hands. Pluck it out from above you, pick it out of the air. Be aware of what your hands have in them. Treasure it. Keep it alive and convey it toward a weak spot on the person's body. Place your hands firmly on the body. The healing power is released by the direct communication you have with the person. When you put your hands on the person's body, the contact helps directly and will penetrate deep blockages. It's like conducting electricity. You pull the energy from the universe and focus it—you are an instrument.[41]

Now the patient begins to pull gratefully on this good energy. It is not the healer's own doing, but comes from its good source. The two, healer and patient, both have the sense that energy is improved, and both give a sigh of relief. One can recognize the faculty of energy-perception alive in this, like the faculty of eyesight or hearing. Many hands-on healers have the sense.

CONCLUDING OBSERVATIONS: ENERGY HEALING

Then, one may accept that energy healing does indeed occur. Still, what this kind of energy actually *is* refuses to be pinned down. I myself felt the shock of energy at the Hilton—the vivid cold chill, like Thérèse's shiver and like the Inner Wind patient's hair rising, which is a typical reaction that the body makes to the impact of a powerful jolt of energy. My healer at the Hilton in his letter was concerned that the power needed kindred souls, people who have the power, or who could be good conduits, that is, at least two people would have to be involved, people who were alive to the possibility of healing. This agrees with most of the energy accounts—that the energy arrives when people gather in a generous spirit to access it, pull it into the mundane world, and release it here to do its work. Thus the people need to be at one for healing, that is, to have communitas; and the subtle combination of the latent energy with communitas, deep friendship, and prayer, often powered by music, enables the energy to arrive.

Making the step to acupuncture becomes easy in view of the whole spectrum of energy. Our very fingertips feel the same thing in each story, although each is so different. As Eisenberg said, acupuncture is a healing that works inside a system of theology peculiarly Chinese—the Gospel of Chi. If one is willing to get at that chi and experience it, then one can see it on a par with *num*, *vimbuza*, the Inner Wind, O'Mahony's electricity, and the American healer's "cloud." The spiritual knowledge of acupuncture appears to be more precise and exact than the others. Even so, acupuncture is concerned with emotion too. Emotion shows in the reaction of Megan and her mother to the craft in which they are involved. Megan had a conversion, a change of heart. This is echoed in the bite of *num* when it boils inside the Kung healer, the cry of pain, and the fear and hopes rising in the patient with her ear close to the drum in the *vimbuza* initiation. The "catching" or release of sudden energy is overwhelming. Then, the divining gift—almost second nature for the acupuncturist when he feels the chi through the needle—is an endowment that is hard won in the case of the Kung and Tumbuka peoples. For these, it is like the sudden acquisition of X-ray eyesight, having to be carefully calibrated, requiring a steady eye and coolness. I myself sometimes touch very near that sense when setting out so much actual experience in this book, and more and more I feel the need for close attention as I proceed.

Healers, even in different parts of the world, have a sense of their own gift, and the patients know well what they feel. Thérèse, the Irish healer, wields the electricity in her hands with her peculiarly archaic skill. Rene felt the heat when Thérèse healed her and also felt the zap of electricity. I felt the heat in Thérèse's hands; there have been times when I myself have done healing in a minor way and the patient said my hands

were hot—but I never felt them as hot. Something not of my consciousness was going on, in paths extending between healer and patient
that are not even felt by the healer.

During his sojourn with the Kung, Richard Katz uncovered an awareness that has been causing our psychologists and therapists to think
deeply about energy ever since Katz's book came out in 1982. In the
Kung's direct gift for transferring *num*, their straightforward knowledge
that music is the obvious way to rouse it, and their self-confessed *love* of
this dance that causes them so much pain—in all the ways of healing
that are the most profound, they are the masters. The movie of the ritual, */Num Tchai*, is the most difficult ethnographic film to watch, filled
with unearthly howlings, bodies passing and repassing in front of the
camera, faces in agony, and people trembling and falling, clutching each
other in disturbing intimacy. A great doubt assails the viewer: it is an un-
reachable ritual, and one will never be able to understand it. But nevertheless, if the viewer persists, the light breaks; and at last one sees the
event in glory—rather like the listener who is patient with Beethoven's
last quartets—and sees the mysteries of the Kung movie in action, hears
with delight that marvelous howl of discovery when *num* breaks right
through: "Xai—i! Kow-ha-di-di-di-di!" One begins to trust the healers'
skilled readiness to go all the way, well practiced, resulting in the benefits of healing from touching and receiving the full *num*. Whereas in contrast the *vimbuza* process among the Tumbuka looks like a kind of cooking
process—when to turn up the heat, when to take the pot off the ring,
what to add to it when it is no longer scorching hot—that kind of technology. But these are rituals too, not mechanical processes, and they too
can change one's life and the life of the community. Communitas is
needed for the process, and communitas is created by the process.

The curious convergence of energy and spirit—this "energy-spirit"
sense among the Tumbuka—runs through the *vimbuza* process. *Vimbuza*
is the means to acquire the extrahuman faculties, and it is reached
through illness or misfortune. The same identification of energy and religion threads through all the different energy-healing stories of this
chapter, with varying understandings of communitas as the enabling factor, sometimes along with music as a great uncoverer of communitas.

People who know energy do not *believe* in it; they *know* it is part of
their natural environment and that it has its place in everything they do.
Energy of one kind or another, or lack of it, shows up in working together, in music, in illness, in anything to do with interconnection—and
interconnectedness is everywhere. The spiritual fulfillment of energy in

a manifestation as spirit is enormously desired, even at the cost of pain. The bridging of the gap between lack of energy and energy's full manifestation is where the healer intervenes, to heal the body and mend the gap. Into this musically created bridging time comes the possibility of a communitas that has the capacity to bring together friends and foes and to release the forces of healing. The ego that was narrow now belongs to all, and all things become transfigured in the eyes of the seer; all things interpenetrate. Vision, which is ecstasy and knowledge of union with the highest, arrives with trembling, or a shiver, or a shout of joy and pain. The self expands, clearing the way to a communitas filled with joy.

CHAPTER 3

—— ❈ ——

The Experience of Power

I am chary about discussing power at all. Although in practical life the word *power* is likely to mean electric light, its more abstract meaning, as in *power structure*, tends to make us shiver and put up a resistance. We have a feeling that any power structure is likely to be immoral. We know its capacity for corrupting people and we know about its cruelty. *Power* has become a nightmarish word because it can be a terrible danger to humanity and literally make huge holes in cities. In its extreme form, it is military power in the hands of a tyrant—the use of naked force, the way Genghis Khan used it, or the English barons in the Middle Ages. Right now, superior military power is wielded by one power group largely against the will of a great portion of the earth. Again, power shows itself in manipulations with money, which means power over the livelihoods of others. Another subtle kind of power is used by social groups with a class ascendancy over others, and it is very hard to oppose. An upper class may appear to be working for the moral benefit of society, seeming to deserve respect—but the result may turn out to be comfort for the powerful and the degradation of the poor. A similar kind of power is wielded by religious people who have forgotten love and believe it their duty to use "redemptive violence" against those who disobey—in other words, punishment. Yet another form is the scary power that results from spiritual power that has been transmuted by selfish use into sorcery.

Lord Acton's verdict against power in 1887 is instructive: "Power tends to corrupt, and absolute power corrupts absolutely." Power is *bad*.

However, the form of power that dwells in the simple physical forces found in nature, now harnessed by technology and measured in watts or ergs, is relatively innocent—mere natural energy. Somehow, energy seems less corruptible than power. It is just energy. This shades into a much deeper meaning. "Energy is eternal delight," said William Blake, and here he means the energy of a creative human being, including biological energy. Energy healers rejoice in the mysterious availability of the source of energy they use while knowing that it is rather different from the tingly stuff measured in watts. Through the words of healers, one eventually wakes to the realization that there exists a *good* power, not measurable, and that this power has a highly important function in the healing of the world and in religion.

Stories of such healings are found in the book *Black Elk Speaks*,[1] in the books on religions, and now quite often in anthropological literature. They show power of this other kind. By means of the stories, readers may come to understand what healing power is and how it differs from energy. The marvels of spiritual power are particularly seen in the great *wakan* power of the Lakota Oglala Sioux. Another form is encountered far away on the other half of the globe, in the good *shakti* power of India. These powers are blessed, to be used for all people: generous, nonpartisan, founts of life for everyone.

Spiritual power is different from corrupting power. It is sacred; it has an immense range, encompassing the universe; and yet it is discernible, for instance, as the "powers of the weak," felt in the mute status of the most insignificant old starved woman in Africa, a power that, like communitas, represents the ultimate wholeness of the total community along with the sacredness of the humblest person, and may often mean *antistructure* where the structures of society are occupied by the rich and powerful. Its range defeats the grasp of politicians and heads of corporations. There is an irony here, because it is perfectly well understood among spiritual healers. The stuff, power, appears to be impalpable and one cannot touch it, but its healing efficacy is used on the quiet by nurses in hospitals, in massage, and in many different types of therapy around the world.

Spiritual power is more general in character than energy. Energy is well known and enjoyed, but it is a subset of power. We clearly need to discriminate the good and bad "powers," because the beneficial type bears us into religion. It is more of a gift than a phenomenon. One feels that it emerges *from* somewhere, and many people get a sense of where it comes from. Healers give it a listening attention; they have a strong sense that it passes through them to the sufferer. It may be hard for people to distinguish power from energy, but nevertheless different societies have their special words for it, words that have been traditionally translated as *power*. Its name, for Hindus, is *shakti*; for Christians, charism, grace, or the anointing; in the Middle East, *baraka*, arising from holiness; for the Lakota, *wakan*, also the term for the Great Spirit; for Pomo Indians, *weya*; for the Chipewyan of northern Canada, *nkoze*, the hunter's spiritual connectedness with animals; for the Waiwai of Guyana, *ekatu*, spiritual vitality; for the Inuit, *tunraq*; for the Maori, *mana*; for African pygmies, *ekimi*; for Western athletes, performers, and creative people, *flow*, *being in the zone*, or sometimes *time warp*. Spiritual power, where it is recognized, is of central concern to the lives of the people. It is often linked to a spirit being, and the power is given by that being. But it is still recognizable for what it is. It is not exactly energy, nor is it the vision of a god or spirit. It is most often *felt*, bringing awe—flowing, spreading widely, connecting people, the cause of transformations in the material world. Energy more often comes to an individual and is individually felt, whereas the energy of people when they are united is felt as power. Spiritual power is available to everybody, and is sensed by all within its radius of awakening—sensed as the divine milieu, as French philosopher Pierre Teilhard de Chardin put it;[2] or one can describe it as a great cloud of force and glory, invisible to the eyes but sparkling, spreading everywhere, and bringing much happiness. Many would say, "We recognize this as the presence of God."

꧁꧂

The most articulate account of power comes from Suchitra Samanta, a South Asian anthropologist. When I first heard Suchitra's presentations on her fieldwork in Calcutta about the love the people bore for their goddess Kali, I talked to her and begged her for a copy of her paper. This brilliant, active young woman had hit on the real events of people's inner lives to which no other South Asian scholar had got close. The key to this was that Suchitra was of the same mind as the people she studied in Calcutta. Kali of Kalicut did exist and gave wonderful help to the human children she cared for, although her image has been thoroughly demonized by the British because, during the budding Indian independence movement of the nineteenth and the first half of the twentieth centuries, it was her figure that seemed to be behind independence. Eventually I heard Suchitra's full story of the people who loved Kali and her miracles, and it is a rare account. The discussion and stories in this section are paraphrased from her work.[3] Although South Asian scholars are masters of the mysteries of the divine, not many of them give modern living stories of spiritual power in action.

SHAKTI, POWER, AND GODDESS: HINDU SPIRITUAL HEALING

Suchitra Samanta came back from her fieldwork with many stories of healing achieved though the power called shakti that flows from the Shakti goddess Kali. *Shakti*, with a capital "S," is a goddess who manifests herself as a light or as strong energy—also called *shakti*, in lower case. During Suchitra's first fieldwork, undertaken in the hot and dirty alleys of Calcutta, she was given these stories unsolicited as soon as her neighbors found she was willing to listen. Suchitra, being herself a Hindu, did not remain detached, nor did she secretly scoff at them, but she intuited much of what the people could not easily express, empathizing with the subtle nuances of their connection with the power.

The Bengalis of Calcutta often feel the hand of the mother goddess, Kali, bestowing shakti power among them. The power usually comes through a guru, one who teaches the love of Kali. The gurus, generally male in Suchitra's account, are the conduits for Kali's power. For instance, when a guru spiritually heals a dying disciple at a distance, he is giving his will to the shakti power to do the work. He also heals by absorbing the karma or future destiny of the patients into himself, even transferring their destinies between different persons in order to prevent immediate danger and effect a cure.

Suchitra started her fieldwork by engaging the people in general conversation about their religions. When she did this, somebody would often interrupt to tell a story about shakti, how miracles happened through its power, and how amazed they were. With heaving breast, they would give the details of how they actually felt the power of divine love. It was obvious that this is what mattered in their lives. This love, these experiences, were central. The events were beyond logic. Their odd and unexpected quality told the people something about the unaccountability of divine power. Suchitra realized that where was no possibility of rationalizing the experience, it was best expressed in a personal story rather than by objective analysis, for analysis is not a method that is appropriate for living religion and therefore using it results in further obscurity.

Suchitra's conclusion ran as follows: shakti, the powerful current in the relationship of guru to disciple, is central in all devotion. This power or current is recognized as a fluid invisibly permeating the material world, less focused among the morally unawakened but radiant and concentrated in awakened people such as gurus. This power may be communicated by means of food. The disciple makes an offering of food to the guru, who then returns it to the disciple. The disciple eats it as the guru's "grace." The food has become imbued with the blessing of the guru's shakti power. At other times it is the guru's touch in blessing that conveys the shakti power to the disciple, or the meeting of the eyes in an act of being "co-present"—another sacred event. The two, guru and disciple, are drawn together in these acts: the acts are reciprocal, like one act—the devotion of the disciple and the compassion of the guru being one act, bestowing grace. This reciprocal act brings into being a relationship of great power. The guru's gift of shakti to the disciple is transforming and is recognized as a miracle.

The Sanskrit term for miracle is *anubhuti*, whose meaning includes shakti's special, intuitive, spiritual perception that can predict a crisis and give its possible resolution. The indigenous concept of soul, *man* (*manas* in Sanskrit), is an imagining, feeling, thinking, working, reflecting, and recollecting faculty, an active ability like logic or sense, but fierily religious. This active mind-soul is capable of rebirth. Soul (what we might call *psyche*) is the conduit that connects person with person, gods with humans, and gurus with disciples. The power of "seeing" is the gift given by the guru through shakti. Thus, "seeing" is given, healing is given, and the sharing of soul or spirit is given, all through the guru's compassion and the disciple's willingness. This closely resembles communitas. The process of transformation itself, both in the disciple's life circumstance and at the moment when the disciple receives the gift of "seeing," is a spiritual event, a turning point in the disciple's life in which the person discovers his or her own soul.

The guru's experience of the god takes precedence over his knowledge of sacred texts, although texts in India are innumerable. There are so many that one loses sight of what ordinary people experience. For a guru, his own awakening often occurs before he serves as a teacher. After the awakening, the power in him allows him to discern the spirituality in a disciple. Then he is enabled by his shakti power to open his disciples' eyes so that the disciple "sees" as he does. Only the disciple knows how much shakti the guru gives him out of his compassion. The guru is an embodiment of the goddess Kali reborn, and is extraordinarily powerful.

Thus a spiritual connection exists between those who love Kali and their gurus, even though the experience of it may be more than the disciple can understand. Since the guru embodies the eternal shakti power in human form, the power is not lost at the guru's death, but continues to connect him with his disciple after he has given up the body.

One worshiper remembered a certain act of shakti power. He remembered in his childhood once going with his family guru to a Siva temple. In that holy place the guru became especially empowered with shakti and was seen floating on water in the lotus position. Others described having seen a guru lighting incense sticks and setting them to float on a river. They floated and never went out. The guru of another had insight into his disciple's previous incarnations and knew the details. Some of the disciples had dreams in which gurus appeared in waves of light to summon a skeptic to worship at certain named temples, and so on. The guru showed his ability to transcend natural laws to prove to his disciples his intense love for them.

The guru perceives within his disciple's soul his or her spiritual potential, which is described as a "frequency" or "seed-sound" that is peculiar to the god most appropriate for the disciple. This "seed" is as yet unuttered, and is tuned to the seed-sound of the god. When uttered, this seed-sound combines with other sounds to form the "seed-mantra." Once the guru has intuited which god and seed-incantation a disciple is yearning for, he initiates the disciple by whispering the incantation three times into his or her ear. Once initiated, disciples sense that their souls are somehow different, more spiritual. They say that it is like sowing a seed in the proper environment, where it will take root and flower.

One lover of Kali commented, "The power of the guru and the power of Mother Kali are the same. This power is both inside and outside our bodies. The guru's power is really the eternal power of the eternal guru. The guru standing there *is* the eternal guru. The guru is a medium—we need his shakti power to awaken us. He is director and executive. He puts kohl on our eyes, making us see clearly. He shows us the way, he gives us a push in the right direction."[4]

Although the seed-incantations for different gods are openly known, once the mantra is imparted by the guru to the disciple, it is not to be revealed to anyone. It will become the special and individual mantra that can tune in the disciple to the god's frequencies; it is his or her connection with the eternal shakti power. The mantra calls on the god. The ritual repetition of the mantra destroys the self-love of disciples and accumulates shakti power in them.

Initiation first occurs when the disciple realizes that there is a special spiritual potential in him or her. After initiation, many disciples experience extranormal events that they feel come from the guru's power and are his gift to them.

The initiation of Bani, a middle-aged Brahman woman, had been sudden. It occurred in secret in a holy city far from her home in Calcutta.

"My guru seemed to know what god I loved in my soul although I never told him," she confessed to Suchitra. "He whispered the god's seed-incantation in my ear. I was worried I might forget it, but he assured me that he'd always be there in the spirit to remind me of it. After I received my initiation my guru seemed to know about my son's illness in Calcutta—he told me that my child would get better, which in fact he did."[5]

Prafulla, a 60-year-old disciple, described how he had a special experience after initiation. "I've had many miracles happen to me," he said. "They seem to have solved the problems in my life and brought me peace of mind. My experiences have drawn me close to Mother Kali. For instance, I had a long-term experience after my initiation. I found that whenever I looked at my guru's photograph I saw the face of our Mother Kali merging with the photograph. It wasn't a dream or an optical illusion. I saw it with this third eye in here, in the center of my consciousness." He touched the center of his forehead. "I used to see the vision for about four months. Then I told my guru about my experience and after that I never saw it again. Maybe he took it away from me."[6]

Another lover of Kali was Sachin, a draftsman in a tea firm, now retired. He was over 60 years old and ailing. Suchitra's first acquaintance with him was through meeting his wife, Sumona, at the Kalighat Temple, where Sumona was busy washing the steps of the sanctum as an act of merit on behalf of her husband's health. She invited Suchitra to their home. In 1986 Sachin lived with his wife and son in a house jointly owned by him and his brothers. However, his share of the house was a small dark room on the ground floor, with access to a common kitchen and bathroom at the rear of the house. At that time he was frail, struggling to make what living he could. The dark and musty little room, containing a bed, clothes piled high on a wooden rack, a meat safe, and a small altar set with framed prints of Kali and a stone *sivalingam*, was witness to the hardship and penury in which this family lived.

Between tea and hospitality, the couple discovered that Suchitra Samanta herself had been struck by an experience of the goddess Kali. Sachin and Sumona immediately poured out their own experiences in a flood of stories about the miracles that happened in their lives. These ranged from accounts of inexplicable moving lights that urged Sachin on to the discovery of a sacred stone representing another form of Kali, to dreams directing him unerringly toward an uprooted tree branch that was shaped like the elephant god, Ganesh. They kept these objects, the sacred stone and Ganesh tree branch, in their room and they showed them to Suchitra. Sumona also had many experiences to tell, such as the intervention of the Goddess Kali who aided their sick grandchild, and a vision of the goddess who appeared in the likeness of Sumona herself and served food to Sachin and the family.

Sachin discovered many things through his dreams. He had always been drawn to the spiritual life. He next told Suchitra the story of how his shakti first came to him, speaking quietly and simply, saying he did not tell it to just anybody.

———————— ❊ ————————

Sachin's Experience of *Shakti* Power

I especially like Kali. We've always worshiped her in this household. Everyone told me that one day I'd find my dear Mother close by me.

It began when I found my guru. In 1966 I took a flight to North Bengal on business and met a sadhu, a holy man, on the plane. He seemed to be an important person, and the air hostess asked me to move to another seat so that the sadhu could have both seats to lie down on. Of course I moved. After a while we flew into a bad storm. I looked at the sadhu and was amazed to see a bright orange glow around him. I asked the passenger next to me if he could also see the glow around the sadhu.

The passenger said, "It's probably a reflection from the red saris of the women on the plane."

That simply wasn't so. The glow was so wonderful I can't describe it in words . . . so . . . powerful—it was a light, the color of an orange. Then the sadhu called me to him.

I went over and greeted him by touching his feet. He gave me his blessing by touching my head. I might have received my initiation there and then, on the plane, but somehow I felt this wasn't my guru, so I let the matter be.

After this experience I was somehow disturbed; my soul felt as if something was pulling at it.

Then, shortly after I came back to Calcutta, I was on a crowded bus going to work. There were only two empty seats in the bus. A holy man who looked very much like the sadhu I'd seen on the plane came and sat by me. He was wonderful to look at, with matted hair, just like Siva. I wanted to touch his feet, but felt too shy.

When he asked where I was going I said I was going to central Calcutta. He bought two tickets—I have them to this day.

"Have you had initiation?" he said.

"I haven't. Would you recommend a guru?"

"Would you take initiation from me?" he asked. "You'll only need a sacred myrobalam fruit and a sacred thread. Come to the ashram tomorrow at nine in the morning after you've bathed."

I was very excited, and so full of energy that my wife and I arrived at the ashram two hours early, at seven.

I was so happy after my initiation—the gift of my seed-incantation. I was lying in bed that night still awake, repeating the words. It was *my mantra*. My wife and son were asleep in the same room. Suddenly I saw a light through the window—it was around four in the morning. The light was brighter than the sun and it lit up the whole room. At the same moment, the light came in and struck me on the right shoulder and I screamed. Everybody woke up, asking, "What's happening?" My soul was very disturbed by this experience and, as soon as it was daylight I bathed and ran to my guru's place.

The guru's wife was there. She said, "You've received it so soon? It's not so easy. So your guru gave you shakti power!"

My guru said, "It's She, Shakti herself, who gave you the strange light. She manifests herself as light. Such experiences do happen on the path of spiritual discipline."

That guru is my father, and he's also all the gods at once, Brahma, Vishnu, and Siva. My guru is especially close to me and loves me dearly—he's stayed for more than a month in my house.

I used to be afraid to do the rituals for Kali at home even though my guru gave me instructions and tried to reassure me. This goddess can be dangerous and demanding. My guru said to me, "Sit on your prayer mat and remember me in your soul before starting your worship, and I'll protect you." Since then, whatever I've wanted in my soul I've received. Two years after that I received my guru's shakti again. My guru came in a dream and gave me the mantra for the fire sacrifice. Also at that time I didn't know how to worship Krishna and Radha. I dreamed my guru was standing in the middle of three streets giving me the ritual instructions. I awoke and wrote down the instructions immediately.

The next day I went to see Baba, my guru, and he said, "You've received the primal mantra, '*Om.*' You'll receive plenty more; go cautiously, don't waste anything."

My guru used to study forensic medicine at a medical school in Calcutta. But he gave it all up to be a Tantric and perform esoteric rites to Kali at the cremation grounds.

He's an attractive person. While he was studying medicine, a certain event inspired him to ask the meaning of life. One day, coming out of medical college, he saw a man dressed in saffron picking food out of a heap of bloodied garbage. "That fellow must be mad," thought my guru, and then saw that the man was actually a friend of his.

"Don't do that," said my guru. "You'll fall sick." His friend asked for a cigarette. As their hands touched, my guru felt an electric current pass through to him.

The friend said, "Will you drop me off home in North Calcutta? I'm your friend, I'm going to give you something. While I'm alive you won't realize the significance of what it is. Only when I'm gone." What he gave my guru was the god Vishnu in the form of a black oval stone in a bag. The friend told my guru that as a new guru he was destined to renounce worldly life.

When my guru's friend died there was a tremendous storm. You couldn't see three feet ahead. And his prediction about my guru came true.[7]

Sumona, Sachin's wife, described her own initiation, which was also full of spirituality. She received it along with her husband, and recounted an experience she soon afterward.

It was the annual festival of Kali, who's a dark goddess—and this is important. We decided to make a special cooked offering to the goddess at our home altar. While I was cooking, two small dark children came up to me and asked me for some of the food. I told them to wait in another room till after I finished my prayers. I laid out the food in front of the deities and performed my worship. I pleaded very hard with Kali to accept my offering, to give me some proof she'd done it. I cried as I prayed. I then left the room and came back later to find to my amazement that the image of Kali had food on her mouth and hands as if she'd just eaten. I forgot all about the children. They came again the following day, and I crossly asked them why they hadn't waited for their food the day before. "Why," they exclaimed, "We weren't here yesterday. We didn't even know you were celebrating Mother Kali's festival!"[8]

Shakti power is central to any understanding of Suchitra's accounts. An invisible and divine power, shakti is felt as the fluid force that merges the faces of gurus and of gods on a picture, erasing the natural boundaries between them, so that the goddess herself becomes visible through the third or divine eye (at the center of consciousness) as in Prafulla's waking vision. Shakti is manifested as the light surrounding a holy man, or as a bright and moving light without an apparent source. The dark Shakti goddess, Kali, coalesces with a human manifestation in Sumona's story, in the form of the dark children who came to eat the food offering and who then vanished.

The soul is the conduit between god, guru, and disciple. If initial experiences "pull" at the soul of the disciple, the guru is able to read that soul by the power that is in him. The guru can also read the disciple's secret predilection for a particular god, and the guru initiates the disciple with the mantra concerned. When disciples know that the guru has recognized their potential, this draws the disciple along the new road to faith. Faith is a journey that is made in the soul that gradually becomes aware of the possibility of equilibrium as the aware self becomes more and more tuned to the eternal Shakti herself.

Again, the very random nature of these experiences, the fact that they come when they will and are not a matter of a neat proof like the end of a geometry theorem, is central to their meaning. Shakti and its mysterious manifestations are not easily explained. What the shakti manifestations are about is, in one way or the other, the love the guru feels for his disciples. Love is the special faculty that shakti bestows as a gift. The experiences arrive, bearing intuitive knowledge of what is happening to the soul. The experiences are miracles, bringing about what was not there before. By means of one single event, they can transform the physical circumstances of life, change the nature of life's crises, and bring to the fore the spiritual and moral consciousness of a person.

The guru, as soon he forms a relationship with the disciple through tuning in to a devotion that works for the two of them, sustains the disciple by constantly dwelling in his soul with love, becoming familiar with the disciple's inner wants, fears, and feelings. The miracles are achieved through the guru's shakti power working through his touch, glance, or verbal assurance, and also through certain rituals, such as sacrifice or "self-offering" where blood from the guru's own chest or right arm is offered to the goddess to give healing power.

Dinu, the husband of Bani, the Brahman woman, recounts stories of his guru. The guru was an old man, vividly alive, with little goggling bright eyes and a huge gray beard radiating from above his ears and around his entire lower face. He was dressed in white.

On one occasion, when the guru was staying with Dinu's family, Dinu heard him suddenly shout something in the middle of the night when everyone was asleep.

Dinu, irritated, called out, "What's the matter?"

"The son of my disciple Gaur is very ill! Go and open the altar room door."

Dinu complied, and the guru went in to the altar room. He seemed to know beforehand where all the items of worship were kept. He lit three sticks of incense and began to pray.

After a while he said, "The boy's better now. Go and make us some tea."

By now it was 4:45 A.M. They drank tea and prepared to leave. Asking Bani for some food to take with them, Dinu and the guru took a taxi to Gaur's house in North Calcutta. Gaur was fast asleep, exhausted, having been up all night with his sick child. His parents were there too, weeping because this was their eldest grandchild. The guru advised a change of doctors, which was done. Within five days the boy recovered.

When the boy was well the guru asked Gaur to offer worship at the ashram on the night of the new moon (auspicious to Kali), and to take the requisite cloth, fruit, and clarified butter. The guru gave Gaur consecrated flowers, telling him, "Put these in an amulet, and put the amulet on your son. It'll protect him." The child was now in good shape and remained so.[9]

On this healing occasion, the guru did self-offering for Gaur's son. Kali is an unpredictable goddess: if her rituals are not performed properly, there may be consequences to the worshiper. But the guru has the ability to absorb into himself any such consequences on behalf of his disciple, even though he himself might lose years off his life by doing so. It was by absorbing the illness of another that this guru met an early death. When one of his disciples became sick with an incurable brain tumor, the guru offered sacrifice and "took on the weight" of the tumor. Not long afterward he marked the calendar at a certain day and time, and he passed away on that day.

The healings were done by his shakti—which manifests itself in his ability not only to precognitively "know" that a disciple is unwell but also to effect a cure. The guru could transfer and change fate itself, including his own—resulting in the loss of life span for himself.

Through the Hindu perspective, it becomes clear that people often relate to each other more through shared religious experiences than through definable relationships such as kinship, friendship, or business. A religious relationship is really a matter of shared miracle. People experience one another through this mysterious linking power in a simultaneously emotional, intellectual, and intuitive knowing.

Such experiences, well received, may result in the disciple acquiring various powers such as the ability to resolve marital conflict, to heal and protect, and to predict the outcome of events. When the disciple finally dies, he or she may continue to intervene in the lives of loved ones, as indeed a dead guru may. Dinu realized that because of his relationship with his guru he came to be more aware of his own true self: "I have seen my soul, I have touched my soul."[10]

The miraculous event initially moves the person to wonder, and then further events occur that sustain and strengthen the soul, accumulating shakti power in it. The steady transformation increasingly brings the soul to purity, to peace, and to stillness. It is this focusing of shakti in the soul over many reincarnated lifetimes that finally brings the cleansed and purified person to blissful union with God. People rarely speak of this ultimate closure. They do, however, speak of experiences of transformation along the way.

⌘

Spiritual power has rarely been better expressed—the power of healing and love, not the power of the police and money. Shakti power penetrates everything and sometimes even takes primacy over the gods themselves. All the careful tuning is through power. Dylan Thomas, a Celt, said it: "The force that through the green fuse drives the flower drives my green age."[11] The peculiarities of each person are set into vibration by this power. Spiritual power is intimately related to the individual soul, for it is on the soul's wavelength that help can get through. In Malaysia, also, the Inner Wind is one's true temperament with which the rhythm of the music in the healing ceremony strives to resonate, finally releasing the pent-up power. The same thing is sought in Africa at the Tumbuka *Vimbuza* ceremony, when the drummers search for the special mode that resonates with the patient's own energy-spirit. Here, clearly seen, is the recognition of the individual's own particular soul. Even when I do something as simple as look for a word, I know I am looking for a particular vibration precisely necessary to hook myself onto the power grid. Each word is a kind of personal pass code to a human-spiritual power, giving extraordinary pleasure. Suchitra saw that pleasure in the eyes of Sachin and Sumona in their humble room when they discovered that the intellectual American-trained anthropologist also felt the shakti.

The power of a god is felt too in certain Christian circles in America, in churches and halls where the power of the deity, here also called God, heals the sick, and while doing so sometimes gives them a brief sleep called *resting in the spirit*. This blissful phenomenon was studied by Thomas Csordas, an anthropologist and psychologist who uses the theories of phenomenology to explain it. A deeply caring man, he could see the good mindset that lay in the people who had so "rested." These were the Catholic Charismatics. It is curious that when I first read an essay on this research, I made up my mind to have nothing to do with such a narrow-minded group as the Charismatics. They went too far, I thought, and anyway the whole performance of resting in the spirit appeared to be a matter of suborning the will of an individual to that of another and was distasteful. But then I discovered later publications that included the transcripts of the healers' stories: I found I was wrong again, as I had been with my condemnation of "energy." The good old magic still dwelt in the Charismatics too—they knew what they were doing. Thomas Csordas's material and the telling transcripts fit neatly into the examples of spiritual power, revealing fascinating and startling stories that spoke for themselves.

The Charismatics and the Power of God: Stories Recorded by Thomas Csordas

In the prayer hall, which is a school gymnasium, the priest-healer prays with the congregation and sprinkles them with holy water. He explains what it is that Charismatic congregations have been experiencing: it is healing power.

"When God decides how he wants to deal with someone his power comes out of the blue. The power of God brings a person under control so it can do something for her. The person falls over, 'resting in the spirit,' in the darkening of the ordinary consciousness, while God takes over. The power is then free to speed up the healing process and achieve in minutes what otherwise might take a long time. The power is a force bigger than a person, a force you feel yet you can't explain, and it works miracles and gives people unlimited joy."[12]

Many of the people in the hall are already in the mood and sing Charismatic songs. Then the healer asks for healing stories. One man tells what happened to him:

"I was in an accident at work years ago and badly hurt my shoulder and the sciatic nerve in my left leg. The pain was so bad I couldn't drive more than four miles without getting out and resting on the hood of the car. I even cried from the pain. The doctor said they'd have to cut the nerve, but instead my wife said she'd take me to a healing service. Okay. Although I wasn't a Catholic I believed in miracles, and at one time I used to go to Catholic shrines. I'd get a feeling there. Then I came here. Nothing happened at the healing services for a bit; then one day I went forward with the others to be healed. They all prayed on me, and it was like a heat coming from above that went right through my body, that I've never felt anything like that before. I never felt it after. Then somehow I was down on the ground. I let go of all weariness and felt the divine power sweeping over me—heat flowing through my body. I was light as a feather, not wanting to go anywhere but to stay in the presence of God. I gathered afterward that someone caught me when I fell, but I had no fear. They called it 'resting in the spirit,' and it was.

"I was there for a while and then went to my seat, energized. A woman came and said, 'Would you come in front with me?'

" 'Yeah, okay.'

"So I went in front, and she sat me on a chair. She said, 'Did you know you have one leg shorter than the other one?'

" 'Yeah, it's almost an inch shorter. The doctor says it's getting atrophied.'

"She put both my heels in her hand and they were stretched, and she was praying, and I saw my leg stretch right out in front of my own eyes to the same length as the other one.

"I came home and said, 'I can't believe it, but it has to be so.' I put my feet on the chair in front of me and looked. That day and the next day I had pain you wouldn't believe, and then it subsided, subsided, and it went away. My wife had to sew my pants so that they were the same length. Now I can do anything."[13]

The witnessing was over. Now Csordas describes how those who wanted healing gathered outside the door of a room kept aside for healing, where one by one they were invited in for the laying on of hands. Three or four healers were waiting, each with a special group of healing ministers called a "team," ready to support their efforts. One sick woman was called in to the priest himself and his team, and other sick people to the other healers and their teams. Some of the sick were in tension or sorrow; some had physical troubles. The woman who was called to the priest came and stood before him. The team of four gathered around. The priest listened to the trouble of the sufferer, who then suddenly "prophesied," that is, she spontaneously came out with what she knew in a flash what was wrong.

The team members put their hands on the sufferer, one woman on her left with one hand on her left arm and the other arm on her right shoulder. Two of the men were behind her with their hands on her shoulders and her upper back. The other man stood at her right and laid both his hands on her shoulder.

Now the group around the sufferer prayed aloud in tongues, rapidly, while the sufferer also prayed. The priest looked intently into the woman's eyes, speaking in a deep, unswaying, yet gentle tone—a voice filled with authority. To the sufferer there came a sense of absolute presence, a sense of total encompassing. This was the moment. The priest touched the sufferer's brow with holy oil and, placing his hand firmly on her head, prayed, "By the power of God, be healed!"—and the woman left consciousness, overcome by the power of the divine presence. Her body drifted backwards and the team laid her gently on the ground. She lay there in peace, one with God.

Those who experienced it told Csordas that in falling, they are moved by a force, and once down, all gives way to passivity. Then the power is like electricity flowing through the body, like waves of peace flowing up and down the arms, a sense of ministering angels rushing through one, or something that unexpectedly comes upon a person—warmth. One is unaware of pressure from the floor on which one is lying, forgetting self and earthly feelings, being in another world. It is through this power that healing comes, a sense of the sacredness in all things, and often miraculous foreknowledge.[14]

The power is called *the anointing* by Charismatics: people may have certain spontaneous bodily experiences in a meeting that show they are receiving power or are able to give healing. These are trembling, lightness, heaviness, heat, the coming of an inspiration out of the blue in answer to a problem, other signals such as a burning sensation in a healer's ear because one of the congregation is being healed of an ear problem, or the heart beating fast for the healing of coronary disease. The Charismatic healer Francis MacNutt[15] says that a sense of heat is the most common of all physical phenomena connected with healing, centered upon the affected organ and sometimes remaining as an indication that the body is being healed long after the prayer is over. Also the hands of the healer may shake as a kind of current of power moves through them, lasting as long as the prayer continues—like an electric current or a feeling of power. If healers feel this sensation during a prayer meeting, they know through experience that someone in the group needs healing and can receive it. The sensations frequently come without being sought.

A priest said, "You pray for the anointing, the sense of God's power. You have to get from the natural to the supernatural because of your human condition. I guess it's through hit and miss, you have to work yourself into it. You have to begin to walk on water, the way Peter walked on water. It's something that can't be learned or taught. It's something you have to kind of go through. With me it's a feeling of a heaviness sometimes on me, or a heaviness sort of stuns me—comes on me; and if you are very sharp and discerning, sometimes your sixth sense, your spirit, it's very, very sensitive and when you get revelation knowledge, it's intuitive. It's not so much up here"—he pointed to his head—"it's through the heart. And you kind of flow with that, you kind of flow with that. Your heart on the deepest level, the real you, is where God lives with you. And He works in you on that level. He's Spirit. Spirit gives witness to Spirit. So you're working on this deep, deep level."[16]

A Charismatic psychologist and healer told Csordas the story of his first experience of resting in the Spirit.

"Well, the first time it happened, it was really scary. I was in a pew with my friend that took me. And I was watching these people go up to get prayed over and I was watching them fall over. I'd never seen that, either.

"And my friend was kind of egging me on, saying, 'Go ahead. You're chicken.' So I got in line and I went up, and when it was my turn I went to a priest and a woman. I told him I needed some prayer and I forget what it was about. I looked at him and I said, 'You know, I'm really scared. I don't really know what's going to happen.'

"He took my hands, and said, 'Hold onto my hands, and don't worry about it. Just close your eyes.' And he started to pray. And I could feel myself going. I just grabbed ahold of him, grabbed on like, 'I don't want to go over.' And finally I did, and it was really peaceful. Unbelievable. That's how I learned to trust."[17]

A healer told Csordas a similar story, this time about a priest who thought people were faking the falling. This man became a healer himself.

A Healer Explains How a Doubting Priest Rested in the Spirit

"There was a priest I know well, Father X. He came with a couple of friends to Father C's service, and we met as I was coming in. We all came into the church together, and Father X sat in the same pew with us. He was invited up to concelebrate Mass, and after Mass, before he came back to his seat, Father C asked him, 'Do you have the gift of healing?'

"And Father X says, 'No.'

" 'Would you like to?'

" 'Oh, yes.'

" 'Then I'll pray for you that you'll receive the gift of healing.'

"So he dipped his hand into the blessed oil, and anointed Father X's forehead, and Father X went crash and the catcher knew it would likely happen and was right there and caught him.

"Well, so much for that: Father X didn't believe prior to that time in being slain in the Spirit. He was very outspoken, even in prayer groups; a holy man, but mistaken on this matter. He didn't believe in it and publicly said so lots of times. So he went down like a ton of bricks, and when he got up he lined up with four other priests, and people formed lines to come to them for a blessing. He would just raise his hands, and about half of them would collapse. Among these were two people who were also nonbelievers in resting in the Spirit, and *they* went down. They'd been slain in the Spirit by a priest who'd been an unbeliever ten minutes before.

"Now there's an end to this story. Between the Mass and the evening healing service the whole bunch of us who had come in two cars and met accidentally set out together to a little place for lunch. And Father X says, 'That was a marvelous thing, wasn't it? Some of you know that I haven't been a believer in this. I thought people were faking or putting it on, or it was wishful thinking, or something like that, maybe psychosomatic or something? Being a nonbeliever and going down like that, I was totally out. I believe it was because I'd seen Father C do it beforehand and I expected it, but I didn't feel it or see it because the next thing a couple of seconds later I'm on my back looking at the ceiling.'

"I said, 'Father, did you say a few seconds? Group, how long was it?'

"We agreed it was somewhere between five and ten minutes. He could hardly believe it. He was so totally out."[18]

❊

It can be seen in other episodes in this book how the "passing out" phenomenon, which launches a full living human being into the realm of bliss, is one of spirituality's greatest gifts. I have felt it myself among nonsectarian healers. When seeking relief from aches from a group of hands-on healers near Charlottesville, I was invited first into a quiet circle of meditation, then taken to an upstairs room among the healers and laid on their treatment table. Two people were in the room to work on me. I shut my eyes. The healer's hands came over my head using therapeutic hand sensitivity—I could tell the hands were there. The hands seem to have generated between them and me a big dark power, and then, everything—all my thoughts—went into darkness, quite gone. I was interested, but still "out." Another pair of hands took my knees in a warm grasp, then yet a third pair took my ankles. It was utterly good, with the happiness of love in the warm darkness. After a little the activity passed and my pains felt better. I could have just stayed there, it was so good, but it was over. The lights went on, and there were only two people in the room. I asked Jim, "Wasn't there someone else healing me?"

"Just Mary and me, and of course we invite angels and spirits we know, to help—"

"Aha," I said, "Sure enough."

This was like the darkness the Charismatics were able to enter. They well understood it. They had enabled it to happen many times, yet each event was spontaneous, a matter of "letting it happen," releasing the power—a skill and also a gift. It often happened in the middle of their church services, and it was by no means uncommon in Christianity. One may compare their trance with that of other sacred trancers. I have seen the apostles of John Maranke of Zimbabwe—a Christian syncretistic movement—go into a trance of bliss, but standing, not falling. In the first chapter of this book the doctor Singleton worked in full consciousness, on his two legs, invested with his tutelary spirit, and it was the patient who fell, at which the fearful ones among the singers blamed witchcraft, while the doctors saw in her the approaching release—and sure enough, out came the trouble.

In our country, in the same era and on an equal footing, here, one can recognize among the Charismatics their gift of peace and nearness to the divine, just as Sachin in Calcutta found the gift of shakti as the light touched him. This matter of "being-out-of-this-world" is different from being deprived of the senses as in anesthesia, which does—mercifully—take away one's senses for surgery. How is it different? The purpose of "slaying in the spirit" is not to take away one's senses but to make way for a better, extraordinary experience, the sweeping power, the beauty coming from out there like a great hand bestowing total rest for which one has starved for so long. Those who experience it know they have come through to something else. The heat is upon them, the weightlessness. Their battery is recharged and overflowing. And *then* the healing can take place. The sufferer comes through death into new life, and is helped up by the servants of the new life, the Charismatic ministers of healing, the chanters of heavenly words in the mystic speaking with tongues, glossolalia, beyond understanding. The hands are placed on. The great prayer and great command are uttered, and the disease is freed and leaves, simply leaking away.

The healers call it the power of God. Various phenomenologists and psychologists classify it, pin it down, and turn it from side to side, noting what it does to the personality. They say it is the self curing the self, the work of the individual body.[19] One may question who decides what actually happens. The sick person? The psychologist? The matter is under discussion.

So the power comes, and healing is possible. The body knows this first before the mental consciousness knows it. With some people, the mental consciousness actually fights it.

However, in this same America exists another healing process that has been practiced for generations and needs no religious conversion in order to access it. It belongs to the Plains Indians, and they have a custom of healing by means of the power of the Yuwipi ritual, an old and well-worn ceremony.

WAKAN: THE POWER OF THE OGLALA SIOUX

The account here is based on the words of the Sioux medicine man, Lame Deer, who taught his readers the power they call *wakan* and described the Yuwipi healing ceremony of the Oglala Sioux, on the Rosebud Reservation in South Dakota.[20] Lame Deer's photograph is instructive. Here is a very old man. A life of strong understanding and conviction is written in the terrible wrinkles of his face. His lower lip is hunched forward in critical judgment. His eyes, semislitted, are quite steady. He himself knows; he has done the ceremony.

The story of the Yuwipi ceremony is supplemented here with details from the account of the anthropologist William Powers, who witnessed Yuwipi many times in the adjoining Pine Ridge Reservation, South Dakota.[21] Bill, at the time I came to know him, was a young and extraordinarily enthusiastic anthropologist who could dance, and he knew communitas. He and my son, Rory, a drummer, could raise a group of neuroscientists and theologians to a kind of visionary height, there in the 1984 Star Island, New Hampshire, conference of the Institute of Religion in an Age of Science (IRAS). For decades Bill and his wife, Marcia, have worked in the reservation villages in South Dakota. These areas are hardly more than a scatter of tar-paper shacks, rusty house trailers, disintegrating log cabins, and toppling privies. Some people even live in abandoned auto bodies. The far countryside, on the other hand, consists of beautiful prairie meadows and bluffs that support horses and white-faced cattle. Richard Erdoes, who collaborated with Lame Deer on the book, tells of his first experience of South Dakota:

> Before me stretched an endless ocean of hills, covered with sage and prairie grass in shades of silver, subtle browns and ochres, pale yellows and oranges. Above all this stretched the most enormous sky I had ever seen. Nothing in my previous life had prepared me for this scene of utter emptiness which had come upon me without warning. I stopped the car and got out. There was emptiness of sound, too. The calls of a few unseen birds only accentuated it. I found myself overwhelmed by a tremendous, surg-

ing sensation of freedom, of liberation from space. I experienced a moment of complete happiness.[22]

Bill Powers describes a similar sense of wonder at the quietness of the landscape, alive with the spirits the Oglala know. Despite their poverty the Oglala have a sense of a "Great Spirit," *Wakantanka.* The Great Spirit is with them always; his power is seen in the thunder, in the eagle, and in the mountains. Erdoes records how when Lame Deer was young, he asked a medicine man, "Tell me about the Great Spirit."

"He is not like a human being, like the white god," said the medicine man. "He is a power. That power could be in a cup of coffee. The Great Spirit is no old man with a beard."[23] This answer made the young Lame Deer happy. Lame Deer gradually learned how to sense *wakan*, the power, as his people did, and was later called to heal with it in the Yuwipi ceremony. He tells the story of Yuwipi as he experienced it.

The Yuwipi Healing Ceremony (Based on Lame Deer's Material Supplemented by that of Bill Powers)

A large room was used for the ceremony. We all helped to empty every bit of furniture out of the room, including any shiny and metal objects. Anyone who had eyeglasses or wrist watches left them behind—anything that would reflect light. The spirits who were coming were distant ancestor spirits and they didn't like modern metal and glass things. People sensed the spirits as tiny, about three feet high, extraordinarily active.

Much sagebrush was brought in for the floor. We each wore a little sage behind our right ear, and we tucked a sprig into any electric wiring that was around the room, to bless it. All windows and doors were completely darkened with blankets, used as curtains and screens. We sat around the walls, leaving a space open in the middle for the sick person, who was a man suffering from long-term back trouble. With him in the middle was "the Yuwipi man," the shaman, along with his outspread objects that he'd taken from a suitcase, useful in lieu of a medicine bundle. The girls had been making strings of small tobacco bundles made of cloth of the four sacred colors. The Yuwipi man took the strings and made them into a wide rectangle on the floor, which became the sacred space. Each corner, in each of the four directions, bore a flag of the right color, with a feathered stick between two of them. That feather was an eagle's feather and it held that power from above, the wakan. Behind the cen-

ter staff was an altar, a heap of pure, fine, mole-hill earth which the Yuwipi
now smoothed with delicate waves of his hand, using an eagle's feather, and
then he marked the earth with the sign for healing, Wakantanka, the Great
Spirit. The Yuwipi got ready a pair of rattles that each contained tiny ants' stones
and a scrap of flesh cut off the arm of a well-wisher of the sick person. These
rattles made the sound of thunder and were full of cleansing power. They
talked, and could be understood if one used a certain herb in the ear. In the
ceremony, when a spirit entered the room he would pick up the rattle and make
a noise with it, and he might hit the body of a sick person to make a cure.
That rattle travels so fast nobody could ever catch it. This had to do with a
certain "power that moves." The rattles were put crosswise on the altar area,
and we laid the Oglala sacred pipe before the rattles on a bed of sage. Now
the altar was finished and we went to the doors and nailed them shut, altogether shutting ourselves in.[24]

We lit sweet grass and spread the smoke on everything, and finally the
Yuwipi raised the sacred pipe and filled it, praying to the Great Spirit that he
may gain knowledge to heal the sick man—chanting the words in repetition,
first in a high, intense, vibrating voice and lowering it at the end of the phrase—
"I pray to Wakantanka so that we may gain knowledge." Now we singers
cleared our throats, beat our drums, and sang in a vivid tremolo. Our high
falsetto pierced the air above the tiny clamor of the drums. We used the words
of the Yuwipi's own spirit, telling him again and again that he could work the
healing.[25]

"With this pipe I send a voice to Wakantanka."[26]

And now the Yuwipi man stood before the altar, took off his shoes, and
faced west. He put his hands behind him, for he was to be tied up. He was a
shaman; and tied, blanketed, and bound, he would heal the pain of the sufferer. We used bowstring rawhide for this, starting with his fingers, tying each
finger to the other. The spirit would strike as with a bow with its bowstring,
quickly. We took a large blanket and placed one corner right down over the
Yuwipi's face, hooding it. Two other corners lapped across his chest, the left
one from left to right under his right arm, and the right corner across his chest
and over his left arm and chest. He was now shrouded. We tied a thong tightly
around his blanketed neck, then around and around his body in slip knots seven
times, all down his back. Then we bound his ankles together. At each knot we
tucked in a sprig of sage.

The man was thus feeling how we people felt. We were being tied together,
ending the isolation between one human being and another; this tying was
making a line from humanity to Wakantanka—a harnessing of power. The spirit
could now come and use him. It would pull the people together and teach us.

The Yuwipi man had to be tied up to make the spirits appear. Untie him, and they would go away. Sometimes they didn't come at all. Sometimes we just felt a furry hand, soft as a kitten, on our shoulders and neck.

Two men lifted the Yuwipi and gently placed him face downward on a bed of sage, facing west, with his head near the altar. While he lay on the floor in his blanket, his spirit could be hundreds of miles away in the far hills, conversing with the ancient ones. He ceased to be. It was up to us to bring him back and help him through his spirit work. The singers began, joined by women with extremely high-pitched voices that strongly penetrating the space, all of us praying within ourselves. The one lamp was extinguished. The total darkness now helped us to concentrate. All of us had to use our powers the right way or the Yuwipi could be killed, helpless as he was. Lightning could strike him dead. In the darkness we were seeing with our hearts instead of with our eyes. We couldn't see, but our eyes were opened. We were isolated, but we knew that we were part of the Great Spirit, united with all living things.[27]

We were ready with the drums, the songs, and the prayers. We sang:

> From above coming down to the earth
> I have been promised a power to use among the people.
> Here come the dancing spirits.
> They are praising the mystery power with songs and rattles.
> They are dancing and they are happy.

Now the spirits were reaching us. They might touch us, but we couldn't touch them. Amidst the roaring of the drums, the sound of prayers, the high-pitched songs, our ears caught the voices of the spirits—tiny voices, ghost-like, whispering to us from unseen lips. We heard the clatter of rattles striking the floor and walls of the darkened room. First here, then there, next to us, then above our heads; now against the floor, now against the ceiling, against the walls, the rattles bounded about with abandon. Soon, in the blackness of the room, tiny sparks began to appear wherever the rattles struck the floor, like faded streaks of luminescence scampering playfully about in the darkness. The lights flitted through the room, almost touching us, little flashes of lightning coming at us from the darkness. Rattles were flying through the air, knocking against our heads and shoulders. We felt the wings of birds brushing our faces, felt the light touch of a feather on our skins. They came from above and beneath, making the walls and the floor shake and tremble. And always we heard the throbbing drums filling the darkness with their beating, filling the empty spaces inside ourselves, making us forget the things that cluttered up our minds, making our bodies sway to their rhythm.

And across the black nothingness we felt the presence of the man lying face down in the center of the room, his fingers laced together with rawhide, his body tied and wrapped in a blanket, a living mummy, through whom the spirits were talking to us.[28]

The sick man grabbed the corner flag that was nearest to him, then turned and faced the wall. He could hear a whispering in his ear in a high-pitched voice, asking him "Are you well?" "No," he said.

To his surprise, he heard, "I'm really thirsty. Does anyone have a beer?" Everyone laughed. We liked it when the spirits were entertaining.

The rattles sounded for the healing. They danced near the sick man's feet, then over his head, until eventually he experienced a touch. Something not quite discernible made contact with his hair, then pressed against his head. It touched his head very gently in a number of places, then moved to the back of his neck, across his shoulders, down his spine. There was an odor of sweet grass; it passed before his face and into his nostrils. He felt wind pressing against his head, a fanning motion across his face. Then another touch. Once the contact had been made, the spirits returned to their violent dancing, emitting sparks along their paths. Quickly they danced along the rectangular line of tobacco offerings, accepting the gifts from us as we made to leave the meeting and return to our homes. Finally the singing ended, the luminescence disappeared, and all was quiet.

The lights went on. We saw the Yuwipi sitting unwrapped and untied, existing once more among us. The blanket that had constrained him was folded neatly by his side, and on top of it was the thong that had bound his hands and the longer one that had bound his body in the blanket. Next to the blanket lay the long string of tobacco offerings, neatly rolled into a perfect sphere. He finally looked up at the people and said with a grin, "It's really stuffy in here." We laughed and began to talk.[29] Each of us in turn had something to say, something good, how we felt and what we experienced. We asked him questions about our health, about family problems, about somebody or something which has been lost, and the Yuwipi answered us. The spirits had already told him the answers to our problems while he was lying inside the blanket. At last the Yuwipi lit the sacred pipe again and we all had one more smoke. Then we began to clear up the room. The Yuwipi went to the man with the bad back and asked him how he was.

"The pain's gone and I feel better," he said. "I'm glad to be back with the old ways, and I'm going to offer up another meeting next year."[30]

These people *know* they can enter the circle of spiritual power for healing. There are ways to do it, and these are of ultimate concern. It is useful to remember that Quakers, with almost nothing by way of ritual, do it in their quietness, if not in the darkness, and much more simply. But certain humans have been given the Yuwipi ceremony, and others have the African Ihamba, and the Bushman have *num*, and the Hindu have *shakti*, and the Malays have wind, each using curious means to sharpen the senses and to open to the power. In the case of Yuwipi, it is a matter of binding a person—veritably putting him into suspended animation—done publicly, sacrificially, for the sake of a sufferer's backache, the shaman submitting in order to be one with the people, as Lame Deer put it. What the Yuwipi man himself experienced while bound in the blanket is never told. First he is bound, then comes a long darkness, then he is seen unbound. Among the Iñupiat of northern Alaska, a shaman used to be bound inside the underground house; yet, said my friend Molly Oktollik, he rose through the skylight with one leg cocked under him and traveled 300 miles to the village of Shishmareff, and was seen walking about there. It is from this kind of tomb of trance that the body rises in its sense of death, and with the power it achieves it can work healing at the spirits' bidding and give help to those who have problems. The Kung bushmen call the change they experience *the death that kills us all*. The Ndembu of Zambia assign a state of "death" to their puberty-age girls, who lie in a "death place" under a blanket, prone and quiet for an entire day of their initiation, and thus are able to rise later in their dance of transformation. The Charismatics used to call the experience of falling as being "slain" in the spirit. These "dead" are with God. At the back of one's being, there always remains a scene that is the inverse of death: a scene of life, where one senses the power, knows the unity with other beings, and feels one's ancestors as active forces.

What is beautiful about Yuwipi are those little trails of light, sparks flitting, flashing, playing, one's hair lifting in wonder, the spirit passing over the scalp, the dance of the tiny ancestors. In darkness the rattle sound is everywhere, its susurration like a rasp creating energy until one's fingers tingle. These are the bodily responses to the accumulating power. The women's giddy screaming chant takes over everything—and that can bring anything to birth. Then those tiny whispers right in the ear—is this what our saints hear? What Elijah heard after the earthquake, the still small voice?[31]

In Yuwipi they turn off the lights. In the *angin* ritual in Malaysia, they gather with the fiddle, drums, and gongs, creating a scene of visible beauty, while a trancer sings of magical times. The words from the spirits through the medium's mouth spread their power over the gathering until the sick man is taken up into the empyrean, into the hurricane of energy—a special gift for the individual. *He* it is who now acts, rises, and dances the martial gestures. Among Charismatics, the seeker is thrown down and lies with Christ. During the Ihamba of the Ndembu the sick woman falls, while simultaneously the whole community undergoes the birth of the consciousness of oneness for her. In Yuwipi, the darkness cuts off ordinary vision for all, and almost immediately the spirits come, with the rattling of strange unseen inhabitants everywhere. Then pass the whispers, even amid the noise, messages where there is no light; and the touching, so gentle, like the touch that we sometimes feel, given by a dear one who has left us. The kitten-shivers. Sparks. Now it so happened that once, when the great symbolic anthropologist Roy Wagner was meeting with other spiritual experiencers along with me, he suddenly grasped a point in the conversation and spoke. I saw with my own eyes a line of sparks come from his outstretched hand. This was just minor, but spiritual matters are strange, with strange effects, especially with light.

CONCLUDING OBSERVATIONS: THE EXPERIENCE OF HEALING POWER

At last we can treat with respect the stories people tell about their experiences of religious healing—Sachin, so excited with his encounter with the light in Calcutta that he woke all the household; the Charismatic man with the short leg, seeing it creaking itself out longer to obey the miracle, and then the sewing to lengthen the pants leg; not to speak of the jovial unbelieving priest-psychologist with his catastrophic downfall like a felled tree. We can practically see Tom Csordas, the anthropologist of religion, grinning faintly in the background—like us. And there indeed was Bill Powers, alive with cold chills in the darkness of the old yet new Yuwipi, aware that he was carrying on the teachings of the great Lame Deer. In that room Bill had been one with a praying body of very serious First Americans, and both Lame Deer and he have contrived to hand on the privilege to us, the readers.

Tom nearly fell to rest in the spirit, but not quite. I was on a bed when I blanked out among the Charlottesville healers, which needs no faith at all. And the gentle Suchitra, the native anthropologist, showed the flag better than any of us.

CHAPTER 4

———— ✠ ————

Scenes of the Imparting of Power

In my fieldwork in northern Alaska, I worked with a number of people who were eager to tell me about being healed by some particular person. It was the person, they said, who had the touch and could transmit the healing. So and so had "good hands," or had "the blessing." The first story in this chapter is my own tale about Claire of the Arctic, a well-known personality noted for the healing in her hands. I studied under her while she worked intimately on people's suffering bodies, transmitting changes in the body directly through the hands.

I also found that this power in the hands existed elsewhere. Good stories came from New Zealand and Mexico, and I give them here. In yet another way, transmission occurs through healers who by their very presence enable the healing to happen, as in the celebrated story of Black Elk's first healing, and in another account of an inspired personality, a Jewish rabbi in Morocco who had the gift.

POWER IMPARTED BY TOUCH: THE HEALING HANDS OF AN IÑUPIAT WOMAN IN NORTHERN ALASKA

Among the Iñupiat, hands-on healers attribute the power to a helping spirit. The "spirit" in modern times is Jesus. The account that follows is more fully told in my book, *The Hands Feel It.*[1] I give a close-up view of the work of Claire (a pseudonym), a mother of a family and a healer well versed in the ailments of her fellow villagers. When I first met Claire in 1987, I could see she was a busy woman. Her face was interesting— and of course she was looking at me, interested in me too; she had oval strong features, somewhat like the dark-haired sibyl in Michelangelo's Sistine frescoes, only with a serene expression. In her eyes, different from the sibyl's, one could see the more delicate epicanthic structure of the Native American. This woman possessed the gift of healing.

Claire was employed in communications and the organization of tele-conferences in the city hall of this isolated place, a village with a popu-lation of 680 living from the products of sea, ice, and tundra hunting. Claire kept her CB radio always by her, and when someone was sick would go at once to the house. While I was working on language with Claire one day, the CB radio spoke, "Claire. Claire. Come in please. There's been an injury. It's little Lee, he's hurt." Lee was 3 years old. Claire went, seizing her jacket and putting it on as she strode out to her ATV Honda three-wheeler—then waited an instant for her 7-year-old daughter, Jeanie, and me to get on behind—and we whirled off. She en-tered Lee's house, all gentle, already knowing the trouble through her gift of clairvoyance.

Inside, the child was screaming. He had taken a jump off the high-up empty stereo shelf and gone crash on both knees. Now he could not stand or walk and was on his mother's lap crying. Claire brought up a chair and sat opposite Lee, with young Jeanie kneeling close by to watch. Jeanie was fascinated, like me. Claire took the injured foot gently and turned up the pants leg. The knee was puffy and swollen like a balloon. Lee's crying got worse. Claire turned her hand over the throbbing knee, almost not touching it.

"I can't hurt you, *I can't hurt you,*" she told him as an obvious truth, in her most musical voice. "Look, I'm making it better." At this stage she was *seeing* inside. It was like an X-ray picture, she would say, all inside was as clear as daylight: she could see the mushiness of leaking serum in the damaged tissues, and, most important of all, her hands could read the message of misery. The mother held Lee, and Claire felt both his lower legs, just the lower legs. Lee's crying began to give way. She felt down the muscles of each leg, drawing down the legs neatly and placing them together. She worked each ankle, the flat of the foot, the toes, bending them gently until they were flexible, showing Lee how good they were. Her hands went back to the knees. The right one bore the bruise and the big swelling that came from around the kneecap. She placed both kneecaps centrally and pressed them gently into position as if they were jigsaw pieces, completing the action by pressing carefully with her palm. Now she worked the good dimpled surface of the left knee, while swiveling the leg back and forth. Then she returned to the swelling on the right knee. I noted that she left the trickiest bit until last. She pressed the swelling slightly here and there, and I saw it diminish a little. She left that work alone for a time and turned down Lee's pants legs. He slid off his mother's lap and tried a few steps, using his legs like little sticks.

Claire chatted to his mother about this and that. She turned to Lee, "Auntie Claire's going to sew some mukluk boots for you. How about that, eh?" Little Lee had been making eyes at Jeanie. He looked up.

"Come on," Claire told him, "Auntie's going to feel your knee a bit more." She worked on the swelling again, showing me how it was going down.

"See? It's simple." Before my eyes the swelling went away altogether, leaving the normal muscle curves now visible around the kneecap. I was attending carefully. I too had experienced, when I asked for healing in this village, how the pain seemed to leak away and just not be there any more.

Claire drew down Lee's pants legs and let him go. He walked easily. She went to the sink and washed, getting rid of whatever it was. "The pain goes into my own arm," she would tell me. "My hands gets hot. *Hot!*"

Claire and the mother went on talking. The mother was hard up, awaiting a welfare check. The place was not at all luxurious, lacking a carpet, with torn vinyl chair seats and only a garish, paper-rainbow window shade to cheer the place up. Lee was now jumping from the empty stereo shelf onto the sofa.

"That's how he did it in the first place," said Claire. "Jumping and falling on his knees. Stop that." We left before more treatment might become necessary.

Claire kept saying, "See, it's simple," and so it was; it only needed the actual doing. It was healing that was empirical in essence because it was so particular. The hands knew the details of the inner tissues; they were involved in the tissues, not just laid on the outside. I compare it not so much to Christian laying on of hands, nor to the treatment of the therapeutic touch healers who pass their hands around the body a couple of inches away from it, nor the work of Umbanda healers with their embrace-like clutches, but to that of Singleton, the African healer in Zambia, with his mongoose skin bag and horn, stroking and feeling and coaxing the damaging Ihamba tooth out of the back of the sick person into the cupping horn, and aware of the right place on the body to do it, as described in chapter 1. In both Claire's kind of healing and Singleton's, what was at work was a kind of practical consciousness, a consciousness of which the practitioners were aware, and they used it knowingly.

This is how Claire put it: "I can't really say I learned it. I *feel* it. I get the symptoms from those people. I—they get sick. That's the most important part, the feelings, and I know it, I always felt it. I could *sense* it. The old people would hardly ever let anybody watch them work on a person. I had the authority to do it, authority to watch, I was *given* the authority by the old people. I could heal, my grandfather did, my grandmother did, my great-grandmother did. It went down from generation to generation. I'm one of the very few people that could work on myself. It's very rare.

"I have to pray about it a lot of times though. I don't do the healing myself, I know the good Lord gave it to me so I'm not going to take all the credit for it. I just never *doubt* it too. I *don't doubt* and I *refuse* to doubt. It's one of the main things.

"Like the other day I was getting bad symptoms in my side, in my stomach. I lay down but I *couldn't* get the pain away. And the next day a woman came to me with all the symptoms that I'd had the night before. I couldn't eat and didn't want to eat, I wasn't really nauseated but I was uncomfortable. And here she was, thinking about me all the time. Every time I work on her I get her symptoms beforehand. It's more powerful when they think about me. I was affected really easily by that, badly affected. Sometimes I just feel for them to come, and I know they will. You talk about somebody and they'll walk right in. It's happened like that so many times; I always know it. But I could block it off. Another good thing about it. It goes on until they come and then it'll go away. So any time they come in, after I work on them it goes away. If they don't give me anything in return I just constantly have it, and I don't like that. Most of the time I ask to work at their house so that I can get a bite to eat or something to drink. They're giving me something."

Claire was living within the ambience of mystical participation. She felt the communications taking place in that world; she was interested, attributing her healing to the good Lord; and she was grateful for it.

Claire taught me a little healing herself. One day she told me, "I'm tired. I'm having that pain on my rib all the time. It happened when I had a Honda accident. The machine got my rib here." She put her hand to her back on the right. "It's been bothering me for four months."

I was checking the oven and turned around. "Shall I rub it for you?"

She didn't say yes but went to sit down at the table. Her hand went back to the rib. "It's not badly hurt, but—" I put my hand there and followed where her finger showed the spot. Had she broken a rib? I remembered how in 1941 a horse had crunched my body between his cart and a gate, and how the pain had gone on for months. Maybe that had been a broken rib. Yes, there on Claire's rib was a clenched thing, about 1¼ inches across.

"That's it," she said.

"Yes," and I showed her the size with my finger and thumb. "It's clenched up."

I merely caressed it, as Claire would have done. Around, and on top. The thing seemed to dwell greedily on that rib, scaring the body into believing it was sick. A lump all right. It was body stuff acting up hard in the wrong place. I sighed. My hands *knew* this thing was sore. Now, astonishingly, Claire was letting the thing go into my hands. She let it go and let it go. The clenched part was mainly softish now, but I could feel within it a little long section still hard, say half an inch long, and I handled it a bit in the place where it was hard, inside. You get a little picture of it inside there. Now there was only the shadow left.

"That's better," said Claire, so I went to wash my hands. She told me later that the pain had not recurred.

I was not the one who was doing it. It happened from—doing the right action? Not exactly. It was more as if there were some X intervening when the two elements were there, that is, the person in pain, and a person evidently able to transmit it away.

The perception of the trouble was not "extrasensory perception," outside the senses, but an actual fine sense—existing contrary to expectations—in the fingers, somehow resulting in the transfer of the ailment. This sense perception of the fingers seemed to be actually real; and there grew a knowledge, a certain awareness in the human consciousness, of a link between oneself and the sufferer, empowered by a kind of rushing of one's own consciousness into that of the other. This, whatever it is, is the concrete meaning of *sym-pathy*, "feeling-with"; and it followed a palpable path, through the fingers' understanding. In this experience, it was something to do with the cast of feelings. When the feelings are open— they cannot be forced—the channels to the other person are open. Somehow nothing happens if the person is not sick; it is the hand's sympathy with the person's sick tissues that opens the way. The "sympathy" that passes is not undifferentiated energy and heat; it is too personal for that.

Whatever it is, it is the cause of the "opening" that takes place at the hands' contact with the sickness. That joining of one's consciousness with that of the other person—that sigh, I think—is exactly the spirit in Iñupiat parlance, called *the good Lord*. It is not one's own doing; it is one's own allowing. It cannot be forced but is prayed for; "prayer" is of that nature and is rather mysterious. A nonegotistical intention is necessary, but intention is not the whole matter. It is the *allowing* of an opening.

The practical part of Iñupiat healing is to create a conversation between the two bodies by means of the hands' work. The hands say, "Hello, are you hurting?"

The body says, "Yes, just you feel *this*, it's *sore*"—and the hands do, they feel the misery of the tissues as an uneasy "twinkling," a kind of bad-tempered resistance to the hands, a kind of "dinner-plate" effect over the site of the pain, a "chewed string" effect along a sinew, or even a frozen response, not the easy feel of healthy tissue. But the body seems to wake up and say, "Ah, thank goodness you're here. Take it, for heavens sake"—and over the misery goes, into the hands.

The hands thus intimately work at the pain, repositioning organs and attracting the pain into the hands, which are "Jesus' hands." The healers sometimes say, "They are God's hands, not mine." The trouble will enter as far as the elbows, where the healer blocks it off. Then she washes out the bad things she has drawn into them.

Some people learn the healing easily. The reader can try from the few words of description that I have given, and will be able to tell when it works. The moment when the fingers *know* that the tissues feel sore—that is, when the healer sighs and the sufferer sighs—that is the moment when the pain is simply not there any more.

Here we see Claire's touch of release bestowing cleansing power, liberating the body from some cruel pressure. Touch healings depend on the presence of what Keats called "negative capability"—which means just the opposite of "an inability to manage," for which it has been mistaken; it means the melting of one's resistance to power and letting it come in. It is how creative strength can come through the willing artist or healer, through the daring act of "allowing" it. This example shows something of the deep value and sacredness of bodily touch, the power that is transmitted by the potential of love in a person. Interestingly, it is very similar to the Maori gift of *aroha*, an account given by Joan Metge,[2] an anthropologist in Auckland, New Zealand. She describes what happens to a Maori who experiences a sudden lack of *mana* power, causing a state of body and soul called *whakamaa*. The stories illustrate the act of restoration of the power, an act of curing called *aroha*, unconditional love—a word related to the Polynesian *aloha*.

Power Imparted by Touch: Whakama and Aroha among the Maoris and the Healing of the Shattered Spirit (as Described by Joan Metge)

The healing of the condition of whakamaa is most often effected or at least begun by one simple act. If, for any reason, an individual feels that their personal mana (spiritual standing) has been diminished, whether it be a child openly criticized in a white school, or a person who has committed some misdemeanor in the community and been reprimanded, the person will suffer from a collapsed spirit for several days and literally cannot raise his or her head. One person so afflicted is described as standing: "stock still, head bowed, arms hanging limp, looking at the ground. She did not move a muscle; she did not raise her eyes; she made no reply. I was reminded of a house that has been shut up: windows closed, blinds drawn, showing no signs of life. . . ."[3]

The cure with whakamaa begins when someone goes and stands alongside or behind the afflicted one and puts an arm around her. A touch given in aroha (caring love) goes a long way to healing whakamaa. . . .[4]

In school situations or in a culture group, when a person does an action wrong or says a line that is not meant to be said and they all start laughing, that causes whakamaa. Or if a ball is thrown at a window and the window breaks and the person knows they have done something wrong, that is whakamaa. Or if a child is put down by a teacher, or put down by a friend, especially when he is with friends and it is not like him to be put down, that causes whakamaa. People described the appearance of whakamaa in these words: "Someone who is whakamaa looks like a wooden post. They stand there petrified. . . . It is almost as if they have lost all power of movement except for their eyes moving. . . . He stands there not seeing, not hearing, not answering. . . . He is at a loss for words. They are only there in the body."[5]

This is the dominant pattern of whakamaa behavior: given certain conditions, whakamaa also manifest itself in other ways.[6]

The inward feelings of whakamaa cover a range far wider that its manifestations in behavior: they include feeling shy, embarrassed, uncertain, inadequate, incapable, afraid, hurt, depressed, and ashamed. Often several of these feeling are intertwined.[7] Whakamaa varies from mild to severe and in duration from minutes to years. Those more seriously affected report feeling "deeply wounded, hurt inside, a crumpling inside. . . . It really hits you right in the core.[8]

The cure is deeply social, just as most of the causes are. The Maori have always recognized mana, which has the primary and basic meaning of "spiritual power and authority." Deriving from the spiritual realm of God or the gods, mana becomes manifest in the world of human experience, indwelling in individuals and groups. The knitting together of the mana of each individual with that of others is the very stuff of what Victor Turner called communitas. Whakamaa occurs when a person has to withdraw from this precious social unity or for whatever cause. Maori recognize whakamaa as no mere psychological state but as a diminishment of their mana, their store of spiritual power. If a young person has a tendency to flaunt their mana and the importance of their ancestors, their elders remind them that they carry their mana of their ancestors when they visit other communities and should take care not to trample on anyone.[9]

In very mild cases persons afflicted with whakamaa may come out of it on their own, but in most cases they need the help of others. "Try as you may, if you are whakamaa, there is nothing you can do about it, unless someone else does it for you."[10]

When the minister of a Maori Christian church found that members of her congregation drew back when asked to read from the Bible during services, she dealt with the situation by "getting behind a person and saying, "Come on, you can do it, quite well, too." Getting behind and putting her arms round, enveloping him with love, so he feels, "She feels I can do it, well, I'll try."[11]

When a person is perceived to be whakamaa, somebody else make the first move at a certain point, when her withdrawal has lasted long enough and she shows signs of readiness, such as a relaxation of body tension or minor movements of hands, feet, or eye. Recalling how her grandfather dealt with her whakamaa when she was a child, a woman said:

> My grandfather, he would be extra, extra tender. Or he would come and put his arm round me or something, and not say anything, just take me away from the conflict I was in. Even as young as four I remember him looking at me and not saying anything, or touching my hair or something, when I was feeling particularly down about comments made by other people.[12]

⁂

Aroha has been called a truly divine love because it knows no bounds, and is infinite. The *aroha* touch is a striking form of the power of the loving touch, to cure a trouble linked with the very awe that Maori people feel for the spirit of a person, their *mana*. This is no ordinary stage fright, loss of face, the committing of a faux pas or solecism, or paranoia. Because of the very high consciousness of the presence of *mana*, the consciousness of its lack in oneself is like death, as when Vincent van Gogh shot himself, or when William Blake suffered seven long years of the dark night of the soul. One might look at it this way: in a society that had once been living spiritually with the *mana* of the gods from eons past, any member who experienced being cut off from it would feel the deprivation as a kind of hell.

THE SENSE OF TOUCH IN HEALING AMPLIFIED BY THE USE OF STONES

Some healers gain certainty in their diagnosis by using a very stable object like a stone or crystal, bringing it near the body and sensing through it what it says about the inside of the body. Janice Reid describes a Yolngu healer in Australia diagnosing a woman's injuries. The healer, *marrnggitj*, takes two magical stones and places one between the patient's breasts. The other is placed against her side. He leans down, peering intently and looking through her body in the line of the two stones. Then he use another stone to treat her internal organs.[13] This diagnosis, made as if through glass, is part of an extra faculty of which the healers are aware, the faculty of discernment. The sense is concentrated and enhanced by the healer's two stones. His fingers have some affinity with the special stones: these, outwardly, are mere things, but they are numinous additions to perception.

Crystals have the same effect of enhancing healing. An Otomi shaman in Mexico named Don Antonio told the anthropologist James Dow what it was like to use a crystal to amplify his fingers' sensitiveness while trying to locate a harmful intrusion in a patient's body. James Dow, a member of the Society for the Anthropology of Religion, started his studies early in his life with a great interest in mathematics. Subsequently he found himself caught up in an interest in Otomi shamanism, and documented it thoroughly.

————————————— ⊠ —————————————

The Healing Crystal, in the Words of Don Antonio

One crystal is for yourself alone, because if you have something in your own body, a pain here or there that can't be alleviated with medicine, if you can't get well, you need this crystal. First sprinkle it with a little white rum and start to pull out the illness. The crystal will pull it up. You can use it over here if you have a problem in the middle of your back. You can feel the illness moving inside as you pull on it with the crystal. Another crystal is used to cure your patients when the illness is so deep in the body that you can't use your mouth to suck it out. In that case you use the other crystal. The crystal will bring it up to right below the surface of the skin. Then you can get it yourself. You place the crystal on the body. So, the crystal begins to dance by itself and begins to pull the illness up toward the surface. When it's close to the surface, stop using the crystal, put a bit of cigarette in your mouth, and get down to suck it the rest of the way. So then you've got it.

Each time you're going to suck out these bad things, the patient will say, "It hurts me here. It hurts me there, or over there on this side." Right at that spot where it hurts are the bad things in the body. These are always induced by sorcery. To cure this, chew on these cheap cigarettes. Since the tobacco is strong, five or six cigarettes will be enough to cure a person. When one is finished, take another. The tobacco neutralizes the power of the things you suck out. They can't withstand the shock of encountering the strong tobacco. The stuff that's pulled out is like vermin. The tobacco stuns it. These evil things behave like animals.

When I suck objects I spit them out into a paper cone, because the stuff is so rotten. Sorcerers implant cow meat, pig meat, sardine meat, chicken meat, or whatever meat there is. They implant it, and so these bits of meat are cooked inside the body of their victims by the heat of the blood. So when you're about to suck out this stuff, you won't be able to stand its foulness. So this is why you use cigarettes. At the moment the illness is about to surface in the body, put a piece of cigarette in your mouth. If a piece of flesh is coming up, you won't be able to resist its rottenness. Spit it out.

Pull it up with a crystal. This you'll have. But the thing will not pop out on the surface of the skin. It's inside the flesh. It's below the surface, and then it comes up into your mouth.[14]

✳

Why it doesn't it pop out on the surface of the skin, instead of remaining below the surface and then coming into the mouth? This was the same kind of dilemma that faced me in Africa about the sighting and extraction described in chapter 1, except that I was able to *see* the bad shade come out. In Africa the patient's skin showed no huge tear, only the small razor mark. But the large spherical blob was just suddenly there. No one was going out of their way to hypnotize me; I simply joined in a collective seeing. As Singleton said afterwards, "The thing we saw [i.e., the Ihamba], we five." Don Antonio's account in Mexico contains no hint of hypnotism or autosuggestion—it is very pragmatic. His story brings to mind a picture of a skilled man listening carefully to something in the body of a sufferer, something that is physical yet with a spirit component. It is the spiritual component of the healing that brings about the transfer out of the body. What also seems odd to Westerners is that an apparently inanimate object, a crystal, was clearly helping Don Antonio, just as the Yolngu healer was guided by stones. Crystals are tense with their tightly ordered molecular structure; for instance, crystal goblets ring when tapped. The way a crystal grows is a mystery, and the order they achieve—unfolded in a steady, mathematical, yet mysterious way—makes them good electronic transistors.

Even rough stones are interesting too. They have great density; they are ancient, often rubbed smooth by time; and their old forms bespeak a kind of consciousness. Power has accreted to them—more slowly than it accretes to sacred relics or to an aged seer, yet people are sometimes aware of the presence of power in stones. Pilgrims in many sacred shrines touch the stones where the holy person has been.

Don Antonio's case is not an example of a mere oddball doing magic in the outback of Mexico. His direct shamanic perception at an enhanced level is a hard-won faculty that has value because it represents an endangered gift, not only because it aids him to heal the sick.

Then what about the nature of *persons* who heal with power? Particularly strong spiritual healing power can be found pouring through certain visionaries or people of sanctity. For instance, buried in the famous book *Black Elk Speaks* appears the story of the first healing done by Black Elk, holy man and seer of the Oglala Sioux, an event that probably occurred in the mid-nineteenth century. The words show his humble genius.

——————————— ⌖ ———————————

The Imparting of Power through a Person: Black Elk's First Healing, in His Own Words

One day in June when everything was blooming I invited One Side to come over and eat with me. I had been thinking about the four-rayed herb that I had seen in the great vision when I was nine years old. I knew that I must have this herb for curing and I thought I could recognize the place where I had seen it growing that night when I had lamented.

One Side was willing to help, so we rode over to the top of a high hill above the creek, and there we got off our horses and sat down, for I felt we were close to where I saw the herb growing in my vision.

Then I began to sing alone a song I had heard in my great vision:

In a sacred manner they are sending voices.

After I had sung this song, I looked down towards the west, and yonder at a certain spot beside the creek were crows and magpies, chicken hawks and spotted eagles circling around and around.

Then I knew, and I said, "Friend, right there is where the herb is growing." We got on our horses and rode down the creek until we came to a dry gulch. As we neared the spot the birds all flew away, and it was a place where five dry gulches came together. There right on the side of the bank the herb was growing, and I knew it, although I had never seen one like it before, except in my vision.

It had a root about as long as to my elbow, and this was a little thicker than my thumb. It was flowering in four colors, blue, white, red, and yellow.

I made a prayer to the herb, and said to it, "Now we shall go forth to the two-leggeds, but only to the weaker ones, and there shall be happy days among the weak."

It was easy to dig the herb, because it was growing in the edge of the clay gulch. Then we started back. When we came to the creek again, we wrapped it in some good sage that was growing there.

Something must have told me to find the herb just then, for the next evening I needed it and could have done nothing without it.

I was eating supper when a man by the name of Cuts-to-Pieces came in, and he was saying, "Hey, hey, hey!" for he was in trouble. I asked him what was the matter, and he said, "I have a boy of mine, and he is very sick, and I am afraid he will die soon. He has been sick a long time. They say you have great power from the horse dance and the *heyoka* ceremony, so maybe you can save him for me. I think so much of him."

I was afraid, because I had never cured anybody yet with my power, and I was very sorry for Cuts-to-Pieces. I first offered the pipe to the Six Powers, and we all smoked. After that I began to make a rumbling thunder on the drum. The voice of the drum is an offering to the Spirit of the World. Its sound arouses the mind and makes men feel the mystery and power of things.

We went into the tepee. The sick little boy was on the northeast side, and he looked as though he were only skin and bones. I had the pipe, the drum, and the four-rayed herb all ready. They placed a cup of water before me; and then I had to think awhile, because I had never done this before and I was in doubt.

I understood a little more now, so I gave the pipe to the pretty young daughter of Cuts-to-Pieces, telling her to hold it, just as I had seen the virgin of the east holding it in my great vision.

Everything was ready now, so I made low thunder on the drum, keeping time as I sent forth a voice. Four times I cried "Hey-a-a-hey," drumming as I cried to the Spirit of the World, and while I was doing this I could feel the power coming through me from my feet up, and I knew that I could help the sick boy.

I kept on sending a voice, while I made low thunder on the drum, saying, "My Grandfather, Great Spirit. The water in the cup that you have given me, by its power shall the dying live. The herb that you have shown me, through its power shall the feeble walk upright. You have said this to me. To you and to all your powers and to Mother Earth, I send a voice for help."

You see, I had never done this before. I was so eager to help the sick little boy that I called on every power there is.

Standing there I sang thus:

> In a sacred manner I have made them walk.
> A sacred nation lies low.
> In a sacred manner I have made them walk.
> A sacred two-legged, he lies low.
> In a sacred manner, he shall walk.

While I was singing this I could feel something queer all through my body, something that made me want to cry for all unhappy things, and there were tears on my face.

Now I walked to the quarter of the west, where I lit the pipe, offered it to the powers, and, after I had taken a whiff of smoke, I passed it around.

When I looked at the sick little boy again, he smiled at me, and I could feel the power was getting stronger.

I next took the cup of water, drank a little of it, and went around to where the sick little boy was. Standing before him, I stamped the earth four times. Then, putting my mouth to the pit of his stomach, I drew through him the cleansing wind of the north. I next chewed some of the herb and put it in the water, afterward blowing some of it on the boy and to the four quarters. The cup with the rest of the water I gave to the virgin, who gave it to the sick little boy to drink. Then I told the virgin to help the boy stand up and to walk around the circle with him, beginning with the south, the source of life. He was very poor and weak, but with the virgin's help he did this.

Then I went away.

Next day Cuts-to-Pieces came and told me that his little boy was feeling better and was sitting up and could eat something again. In four days he could walk around. He got well.

This was in the summer of my nineteenth year.[15]

This is almost beyond words. As Black Elk knew, his story and the way he walked were sacred, and it is shown excellently in the account written down by John Neihardt. I could see a similar consciousness of sacredness in Singleton and Fideli, Megan with the acupuncture, Thérèse O'Mahony, the suburban healers, the Charismatic practitioners, Claire, and Don Antonio. They are enveloped in power.

Another figure who healed by his sanctity was an extraordinary Jewish rabbi who helped and healed many people in his Jewish enclave in Morocco, and was much loved.

THE IMPARTING OF POWER THROUGH A PERSON: RABBI YA'AQOV WAZANA, JEWISH HEALER OF MOROCCO

The account is given by Yoram Bilu, an Israeli anthropologist.[16] On a hillside near Meron in Israel, Yoram Bilu, the Israeli anthropologist Henry Abramovitch, Vic, and I had many conversations about holy *zadiks*, saintly rabbis of Israel and Morocco. Our two Israeli friends showed us an ancient low cave where Jews hid from the Romans in the mass killings of the first and second centuries. Standing on the pebbled cave floor, Yorum bent under his great height and enthralled us with his stories. He told us of the healer Rabbi Wazana and the Jewish community in the first half of the twentieth century, living in a remote mountainous region of Morocco among Berbers. Their homes were clay houses without electricity. Many children were born but many died in these out-of-the-way regions, even though the land was fertile.

Rabbi Wazana was a tall man with a natural authority. Like other helpers of the sick, he made alliances with earth spirits, called demons by the people. Healers were able to contact the earth-spirit world, seeking to control its inhabitants in order to alleviate the misery and suffering they caused; and healers could also exploit the earth-spirits' constructive powers for curing and divination. It was said in Morocco that the goodness of Wazana was strong enough to survive his using such "impure" power.

The following healing, narrated by the patient Masouda, shows Wazana in action.

A Woman Ready for the Grave: The Story in Her Own Words

I was staying in the house of Rabbi Wazana, my husband's uncle, and I was sick. I fell victim to sorcery—a woman relative must have thrown poison into my food. The rabbi was away in Casablanca at the time. While I was so ill I had two children and I lay on the floor, helpless, for three years. Nobody would take me in, and my parents lived very far away. I don't remember a thing about that time. Other people took my children. There were no medicines, no doctors.

Then he of blessed memory came back to the village. My husband went to him at night and begged him, "My wife is very sick—she's going to die."

Then Wazana did what he did. He held my hand, and read many verses to me. I was seven months pregnant with twins. He gave me medicine from the French in Casablanca, but people said, "Maybe she'll die because of the medicine."

He said, "No, she won't die, she has much time left. But she'll be sick and she may even seem to die in the next twenty-four hours." He warned them strictly, *"Don't take her to the cemetery."* One woman relative was near me, very jealous.

The rabbi knew what was wrong with me. He told the people, "Whatever was in her belly died three days ago, that is why she's nearly dead." He gave me medicine—may he rest in peace—and what was in me miscarried and came out. Afterwards the poison came out. My mother told me it was like a big yellow flower. I don't remember anything.

Then the Jews said the Shema funeral words. I really was going into another world. People went and dug a grave ready for me. I can just remember them getting a bucket and soap and ritually washing my body. They even sewed my shroud.

Then two Jews said to the holy man, "Give us the woman so we can take her to the cemetery."

"No."

"We'll fetch the police. You must."

"No."

A policeman came and said to Wazana, "Give the undertakers the Jewish woman who died yesterday so the people can go home."

But Wazana wouldn't be pushed. He answered, "I won't let them take her. They may not have her. She's my nephew's wife. Tell the people to go home. Tomorrow she may be dead, then I'll take her to the cemetery myself." He didn't let them take my body away.

One of the Jews accused Wazana of wrong-doing. He said, "Put that body down so her soul can depart." What did Wazana do? He put on his cloak— it was wintertime. Then suddenly all the dirt that was inside *me* came up in- side *him* as well—it reached him up to here [pointing to her throat], and he didn't eat or drink for twenty-four hours. He just prayed. That is a saint. [She sobbed.]

Then Wazana told somebody, "Go and get a small chicken, a chick." I don't remember that, my mother told me. They gave him everything he asked for. They cooked the food, and he gave me three drops of chicken soup in my mouth. At four in the afternoon I opened my eye, only one, not the other.

I was still sick after that, maybe for a month, but I got better. Now every- one is happy, and the man who said the saint did wrong didn't go out for a month, and then he died. He was walking along and met what he met, and fell down.

That is why every year I make his feast.[17]

The saint himself died at a relatively young age because the local Moslem sheikh had appealed desperately to Wazana to save his sick daughter. She was under deadly attack by demons in revenge for her habit of killing their allies, the snakes. The demons reminded Wazana of his usual arrangement with them, and warned him that he must on no ac- count save the girl this time because that would frustrate their own per- sonal vengeance for the snakes' death. Yet Wazana persisted. He said that even if God himself forbade him to save the girl, he would. The very next day she was completely cured. But the demons did what they threat- ened and took Wazana's vitality, and in three days he was dead, in his prime. The people were in awe at such self-sacrifice. After his death he was often seen in this world, appearing at times of prayer and going about to heal the sick. The people became passionately devoted to him.

⌗

Yoram Bilu, recording the story, found himself taking the rabbi's gift seriously, amazed by the supergenerosity of the man who would heal, never mind what. The power that came through Wazana was real power; he never discriminated about its religious correctness. Wazana eliminated the boundaries between the human and demonic worlds. Whatever healed, whatever worked for the good of the people, he would do. He also disregarded the boundaries between Judaism and Islam. Furthermore, Wazana had no material wealth, no home that he stayed in; he befriended women, children, and layabouts; he did not go in for prestige; and he seemed unmarked by age. He was never one of those venerable old scholars. He miraculously brought back a lost wife to her husband; he enabled young girls to find spouses, while never marrying himself; he helped the barren, though he had no earthly children; and he restored sexual potency to other men, while his own sex life was meager or nonexistent. He did not marry "on earth," but he was different and married "below earth." It was said that he was married to a spirit woman, a "demon woman" as the people supposed, and he had two spirit sons. This family miraculously appeared to someone in the community.

His spirit was gifted with a tremendous store of energy unhampered by the unreal social boundaries between the religions and spirit hierarchies of the society he was in. He was open, like the shamans of the hunter-gatherers, connected to people and their spirits as the hunters were connected to the animals. He died self-sacrificially, giving his life for the young. In death his body stank and had to be buried quickly. I myself remember how this happened to the body of Father Zossima in *The Brothers Karamazov*—and the circumstance gave unexpected joy and wonder to Alyosha, the monk in *Karamazov* who loved the earth greatly and was not afraid of earthy things. A similar strange story is told by W. B. Yeats in the play *The Countess Cathleen*, in which two servants of Satan in the garb of merchants came to the good countess and offered to buy her immortal soul in exchange for food for the starving people of Ireland. For love of the people, she agreed and had to die. The people were fed, but when the merchants came for her soul to complete the agreement, her soul was unexpectedly taken up by the angels, in spite of the wicked business deal. Similarly, after death Wazana lived on. Curiously, Wazana was as open as the humblest Bushmen and pygmy healers who take these powers for granted as simply "what we do." He was not concerned about Muslim or Jewish or Christian or demon-worshipers' beliefs. Such healers are innocent of the disparagements and exclusionism of civilization.

There is a darkness that fertilizes. Jung was drifting toward this idea with his "Shadow." West Africans and Brazilian Umbandistas well know the double power of Eshu or Exu, the god with two heads, bad and good, the heads of Satan and Jesus. Claire, the Iñupiat healer, had her bad times, and during terrible depressions she saw Satan on her left shoulder. When they were over, Jesus would come to her, and her healing would be better than ever—always after her bad times, as she kept saying. Healing needs this human humus, this dirt, this impurity.

Here one can see true spiritual power, in no way concerned with social pressures and the power of the state. Victor Turner called it "anti-structure" and connected it with what is now recognized as unconditional love. Carl Jung glimpsed it in his notion of the collective unconscious. We have seen it in shakti, in the experience of resting in the spirit, in those tiny strange spirits in Yuwipi, in the Maori power of *aroha*, in Claire the healer, and now in Wazana.

People do heal. Certain people heal by their mere presence. Some find the power to heal suddenly given to them. Moreover, in many of the initiations of healers, the first coming of the gift is involuntary.

CONCLUDING OBSERVATIONS: POWER HEALING

What is spiritual power, this force given to people from "out there"? This rich sense that pervades a group of people and makes them sing with joy, that makes them unbelievably happy? Not everybody "passes out" at its arrival, though one would give one's eyes just to be present at an occasion like that—say, to be at the scene of Pentecost or at Yuwipi. Most people have actually experienced the power, sometimes at their weddings, in the dance of the bride in her wide dress, full of delight; or marching in a huge throng for human rights; or just after one's baby is born, a time of total gladness. Yet—just as with healing and those who "lay on" that power by means of the hands' touch, as the gentle sympathetic Maori friend does—one still asks, what is going on?

Going right back to the highest level, to the problem of how all things are, one sees sometimes how all things are knit together with power like the muscles in an entire huge working body, all parts being able to move as one, everything from time immemorial able to communicate with everything else—but nobody realizes it. Maybe the ancients were aware of it. The anthropologist Lucien Lévy-Bruhl, in describing "how natives think," called it "the law of mystical participation"—a perfect term for this power. Teilhard called it the divine milieu. One senses that the power derives from interconnectedness, and, as the Buddhists see it, is involved with the activity of the universe in its ongoing acts of creation, which the Buddhists term *interdependent co-origination*. The people that heal grant that healing comes from elsewhere, not from themselves. Old positivist scientists would have denied these arguments. But looking at science now, I can see that scientists accept there are mystery gaps opened by chaos theory and quantum theory. They are trying to find suitable tools to fit what is actually happening in the physical world, tools such as more subtle studies of the brain. Is the brain by any chance an organ for the reception of messages from what is "out there"? Is there a power given to the brain or body that alters material conditions outside of itself and can work miracles? As for the healers, they know that something not yet scientifically defined is happening under their hands and that the power is present.

CHAPTER 5

———— ✢ ————

The Presence of Spirits in Healing

Energy, power—the accounts begin to thrill the fingertips. Mine are tingling as I write. Being open to the presence of a power opens a person to that further field of mystery, that of spirits. However, congregations in churches are told the verse from the Bible that goes, "No man has seen God at any time."[1] The people humbly shake their heads. Somehow they are not supposed to have had an actual experience of God; they are just to believe. The fact is, their joy at being there and praying is the gift of that very experience. All have it, more or less.

Do people have real experiences of spiritual beings? I had one. Moreover, experiences of the presence of the dead are quite common. Many people who have been bereaved have told me how the dead, maybe a parent, relative, or mentor, have come back to help or comfort them as they struggled with their grief. A spirit figure—often Jesus or, for instance, Sai Baba—may also come and heal a sick person, or call into existence a new healer. This chapter opens up a wide range of stories about the role of spirits in healing and in the lives of healers. I start from close to home, North Carolina, with a Pentecostal healing, then to Ireland, giving an intimate account of poor peasants in the presence of the Mother of God. After that we go further to a case hidden within another great religion, Islam, showing the visitation of caring spirits that bring healing to the oppressed women of the Sudan, in the Zār cult. In the next four stories the spirits are even more purposeful and finely directed. These stories concern the making of healers, and all show the workings of a spirit in detail. The stories resemble conversion experiences, but the events show more than that: the subjects find themselves with a considerable destiny in front of them. The subjects become healers themselves, the agents of the spiritual world to act for the physical benefit of the human world.

Some of the experiences are almost too serious and humbling to talk about, and it is very hard to tap into these stories unless one is a Suchitra and can get the stories flowing. They are about a deep sense of a divine presence. For instance, when I sing in my church choir, I *know* the Holy Spirit is there. Everyone smiles. (This is a complex matter, because there exists an entire religion behind it.) I am loved. I know that the others have a sense of the spirit too; it is in their singing voices. The Holy Spirit is flying about in the place. When it is over, I cannot wait till next Sunday. But this matter is hard to put into words, and I am only just beginning to talk about it.

So with great respect, I open this section on spirits with a Holiness Pentecostal church miracle in North Carolina. What the story is about, at root, is the continuous sense of the presence of God in this church—felt in the hearing of the Gospel and in singing from the heart. The Gospel that is their life says, "Love, forgive, listen to God, pray." The people know the Gospels, and they know the story of the love that floated unharmed over the great wave of death.

The account of the miracle was written down by Douglas Reinhardt, a graduate researcher in anthropology in North Carolina, working among several others on a project for James Peacock, Ruel Tyson, and Daniel Patterson on the religious experiences of lower-middle-class and poorer churches in the American South. Jim Peacock was recently head of the main American Anthropological Association, a tall benign man with real vision about what it means to be a born-again, a Muslim, or a Buddhist. He is a master of comparative religion. Jim, Ruel, Vic, Dan, and I would meet, discussing the fascinating results of the project. It was showing that upper-middle-class and upper-class churches spoke little of religious experience, nor did they enjoy fervent singing. This confirmed us anthropologists in what we could see, which was that the converse of this is true: humbler societies are nearer to religious experience.

A PENTECOSTAL HEART PATIENT IN RURAL NORTH CAROLINA TELLS HIS STORY

The members of the Holiness Pentecostal Church are white, school-educated, small farmers and God-fearing white-collar workers, people who often experience the baptism of the Holy Spirit as the apostles did at the original Pentecost.[2] The "baptism" is an ecstatic, rapturous event. People will dance, shout, shake, and roll for pure joy on the floor. Some may have the gift of tongues, and others will be given the discernment to understand it. Healing occurs. Explaining their own history, the Pentecostals jocularly say, "The Lord took the Baptist water and the Methodist fire and made that Pentecostal steam."

One of the members had a strange story to tell. This man suffered two heart attacks and was really ill. He gave his story.

Testimony of a North Carolinian

Since those attacks, I'd gone back to work. I was taking medicine for my heart—glycerin—but I began to get depressed about my condition. I had pain in the left side of my chest, I felt bad in general. The doctor told me, "I'll send you to a specialist and he'll give you a stress test and catheterize your heart." I was afraid of that—I was against that.

I went for a year and all at once I decided to go ahead with the catheterization, and the doctor made the appointment. On Tuesday night, over a week before my catheterization appointment, about three o'clock in the morning, I woke up and sat up in bed with this on the tip of my tongue: "Healing, claim healing." I was right by myself there—of course my wife was in the bed asleep—apparently I was saying this over and over. It came to me later on: this is the Lord speaking to me, in my words. There was no audible voice. I rolled over and went back to sleep, and didn't mention it to no one. That's when it was done.

It took time to unite this so far as man is concerned. I went to the doctor that afternoon, Wednesday, and my wife went with me. I went up there to be examined but the doctor said the stress tests and catheterization had to be done. I wanted to go back home, but the doctor insisted that they must be done right away. Well, that scared me.

The examination started the next day and nothing turned out. It didn't make no sense to them. They thought I was up there to take a rest or stay out of

work or something. Well, my healing was being manifested. I knew I didn't
have no pain. The doctor came to see me three times a day, but I had no pain.
But I'd had it previous to that about every day. I knew then that I'd been healed.
I was supposed to go home after they had catheterized me on Monday.

They X-rayed me, they ran cardiograms on me. They said, "Are you sure
about this?" Everything was all right. Monday afternoon they run me over. They
put me on that treadmill and I ran for nine minutes. He didn't have no idea I'd
go for three minutes. And unbeknown to me the heart specialist called my doctor and told him, "I want you to show me some proof that this man has ever
even *had* a heart attack."

I didn't ever have the catheterization, but I knew that He healed me—Jesus
Christ. God is just as alive today as He ever was when He walked the streets
of Palestine.[3]

The man tells us exactly how it happened. It was a true experience,
and it was naturally embedded in the church experience that had a seamless meaning for him, the world of the Pentecostal experience of the baptism of the Holy Spirit. His healing went beyond salvation to a release
from a physical threat.

His church's God told him, "You shall receive power after the Holy
Spirit comes upon you."[4] In the service itself one can sense the rising of
the Holy Spirit. First the congregation sings and sways: the joy swells.
Then the woman preacher tells a vivid story of how Jesus helped a person's problems, and she breaks into tongues when she gives praise, which
is followed by the great amens of those who discern the meaning of her
words. The pastor turns to another sick person and says, "Woman, face
this audience." He talks very firmly and he says, "Audience, God revealed
this woman's face to me while I was praying. God has heard your prayers
and he's going to heal you. It is God that does the healing, not man."
The pastor asks the brethren and sisters to gather around and touch the
afflicted as prayer is being offered. When they have assembled, yet others form an outer perimeter touching those who are touching the sick.
Then the pastor calls out loud in Jesus' name and commands the disease
to come out of her. At the same moment as the healing touch is given,
the minister gives a sudden involuntary shaking of his body, followed by
a huge bodily quiver on the part of the seeker. The seeker sinks backward to the floor, held safely by catcher helpers. She lies motionless for
several minutes. She is "slain in the spirit."

This is how she described it afterwards: "I felt a light, cool touch on
my forehead, and then I was down on the floor. It was a warm secure feel-

ing. I didn't feel afraid in the least, only totally warm and as if I was feather light. I kept praising God inwardly as I remember, and the warm feeling intensified. I didn't wish to move from that spot. My husband guessed I was on the floor five or ten minutes."[5]

This is the same falling in the spirit as among the Catholic Charismatics, though here the accent is more upon the spirit than on the power.

Another church in North Carolina, the Pine Grove Holiness Church of the Lumbee Indians, also in the Protestant tradition, has a sense of the spirits that are about us. The testimony of Sister Annie Mae at a revival meeting gives witness to her visionary moment.

Praise God. I thought about an older person, their hair turned white, praise God. And you know, I seen some, when they are just about to cross over, praise God, and some of 'em say they could see angels, and they could hear the angels sing, and ask one that was standing by, "Could you see the angels?" And they tell 'em, "No." But *they* could see the angels.

You know one time I was in the studio, praise God, and the power of the Holy Ghost fell on me, and it just shook me all over the place, praise God. And you know it seemed like . . . I just felt as if I was in heaven, praise God!

Hallelujah!
I got it!
I got it!
I got it! [Annie Mae spoke in tongues.]
It's real, praise God! [She spoke in tongues.]
It's real!
Oh yes, Jesus!
Thank you, God!
It's real.

Oh praise God!
I'm healed,
I'm healed
I'm healed, praise God.
He's a healer,
He's a healer, praise God
And he will heal you
He'll do for you what he'll do for me. Praise God.
Hallelujah![6]

The message of excitement and joy is clear, and the sense of wonder—"It's real!"—tells of a blazing sense of certainty. Intellectual
Catholics shake their heads about these events and say, "It's all hysteria,
cotton candy—there's no theology." But it is raw experience, *apodicticity*,
as the phenomenologists term it, which means the sense of absolute certainty. It is given to many. One sees it best among peoples without highly
structured social systems or theologies, such as people of the American
South, Sudanese Muslim women, Irish peasants, east African cultivators,
Californian Indians, Alaskan Inuit, Nepalese mountain people, and Zambian medicine men. The faculty survives better among the poor. When
the Holy Spirit gave a Zambian Catholic archbishop[7] the gift of healing,
the Vatican demoted the archbishop. That is the pattern. It does not go
with the authority structure.

What about a case where fifteen people see the same spirit figure? In
1971 and 1972, Victor Turner and I did a fieldwork study of the curious
cult that grew up in the wake of this event, becoming participants in the
pilgrimage. This fieldwork had simply transpired; nobody planned it. In
Manchester, England, where we had earlier joined the Catholic Church,
the city had been full of Irish laity, Irish priests, Irish intellectuals, and
the very poor Irish—but the important factor in our interest was Vic's
love of Celtic culture. Numberless Irish folk confidentially advised us to
"go to Knock," wherever and whatever that might be. We decided to go
where we were directed and do fieldwork in Ireland, a country that had
suffered deeply in the past and was scarred from the colonizers' cruelties.

We found Knock to be a small village in County Mayo with an ordinary Catholic church. Much fame is attached to the place because of its
great event. One rainy evening in 1879, a very bright light arose at the
back of the church with a divine woman at its center. Everybody said it
was Our Blessed Mother. It seems that somehow or other a kind of determined lightning bolt planted itself in that western bog village, a marvel that became a source of healing for many. Within the light and dazzle
were seen sacred human figures.

THE HEALING LADY OF KNOCK, IRELAND

I relate this event in story-telling style, to give the sense of being there
and to avoid the formality of the church accounts.

The story begins in 1879 in the middle of the second great potato
famine, in Knock in County Mayo, Ireland, a country greatly oppressed
by Britain.[8] During the summer, rain had been falling steadily: the whole
countryside was sodden. Earlier in the year in the fine weather, the young

potato shoots had shot up green and firm. Now, in most of the villages, the leaves were turning bronze and starting to loll again with the potato blight. Soon entire fields were lying black and mushy, every plant dead. The new potatoes underground became slimy masses of pulp. I myself have seen this blight in the 1930s and dug up that slime. Many in Ireland went hungry again. The people of Knock were in dread of the future, for hardship and political oppression were their daily lot and no one could forget the suffering of the first great famine of 1845, when the people's one food crop simply disappeared.

It was at 8:00 P.M. in the evening, Thursday, August 21, when the visitation occurred. It came in the middle of the relentless rain that was the ruin of the potato plants. Fifteen people witnessed it as they stood in the muddy lane behind the church. Between the stone wall of the lane and the church grew meadow grass, lush and high, and that August the grass extended right to the back gable of the church. Women were passing along the lane with sacks held over their head above their black shawls, chattering in Gaelic. Their clothes were worn and their feet bare. They were hungry. One of them, Mary Byrne, her sack over her brow against the rain, skidded rapidly past in the mud and then stopped dead. "What's that?"

They looked and saw a vast light radiating out of the gable end of the church, and in it glowed a brilliant array of holy personages. They gaped.

"What would they be doing out there in the rain?" said a woman. They looked at each other, smiling, wondering.

"Did the priest order new statues?" said another. "And why would he put them out at the back?" No one knew.

It was very overcast and gloomy overhead, but despite the curtain of rain a blaze of light was pouring out from the saints at the wall—*radiating* out from them. The light arched over the whole black evening. In the center of the light was the Blessed Mother, tall, with the glimmer of a crown on her head and her hands spread out toward the people—they could feel healing power between those hands. Other saints stood by: St. Joseph was there on the left, bowed toward her in his old age; St. John stood on the right with a book from which he appeared to be teaching. All of them shone in their own glory but did not speak. A rush of feathery radiance flickered around them.

Mary Byrne said in a low voice, " 'Tis the Mother of God Herself. Our Lady has come to us carved out of light." She paused. "Our Blessed Mother."

They gazed. They raised their eyes to the lady in awe. She was tall, in a robe of light, with folds and drapes around her, a veil over her head, and a crown upon it: she was there in majesty. She was utterly holy—and so were the figures around the tall enfolded lady, dazzling them all in the rain.

"There's St. Joseph by her," Mary whispered. "And when you come to think of it, the young fellow with the book—that must be St. John. I know that one. I was after seeing his statue in Lecanvy church."

Three children further down the lane stood transfixed. They pointed and started to climb over the stone wall. "Lift me up," said the smallest boy to Patrick, who was bigger. "I want to see the grand babies."

"Wait a minute now," said old Mrs. Trench. She waved them down. "I'm coming with ye." She lifted up her skirt and clambered over the wall. The grass on the other side was high and soaking wet, but she pushed through, holding her skirt up a bit. The old lady was soon through the grass, up by the gable, and then in the middle of the dazzle—and she had the children all around her. She knew that this was as near to heaven as she would get in this life. She held the little fellow to her side.

Mrs. Trench gazed at the being before her and at the hands outspread. "A hundred thousand thanks," she burst out. "*Ceid mille failte!* Thanks to the good God, and to you, our glorious Lady, for giving us this manifestation."

The saints were afloat—three dazzling beings ablaze with light, hovering two feet above the ground, with their feet scarcely touching the tops of the tall grass. The grass underneath the lady looked dry, so Mrs. Trench felt it with her hands. "'Tis dry." She went forward to embrace the feet of the shining lady, but her hands went quite through. There was nothing you could touch. Young Patrick stood on tiptoe by St. John and tried to see into his book. The words shone so much he could not make out what they said. He whispered to his aunt, "I'm thinking it must be Latin." After watching the vision for a couple of hours, they were soaking wet, so they went home.

The morning after the appearance, the archdeacon of the church made his own track to the gable, following the trail of old Brigit Trench and the boys when they first approached it. The archdeacon had not been present the evening before. He looked at the spot. Those tall grasses at the gable, their delicate tips, had borne the insubstantial weight of the light of the vision. He prayed, shaking his head a little. Next day pilgrims started coming, and healings occurred. Ten days after the vision young Delia Gordon, who had a painful ear disease, drank water mixed with the mortar from the gable wall. She was cured. Very soon people from all around the country wended their way to Knock and knelt at the gable. The area was full of tracks. Two or three cripples experienced cures and left their crutches against the wall as tokens of the miracles. The men brought boards and knocked together a small table with a shelter above it. They placed it as an altar on the spot where the lady and saints had appeared. Everybody crowded to the wall and touched it with the crosses of their rosaries, picking out bits of cement to make miracle water. Others passed over the ground picking up mud and even rainwater. The church was continually packed with an excited throng; one in ten of the sick was receiving a cure. The delight, the happiness, was high. Crowds of people circled around the church in an anti-sunwise (counter-clockwise) direction, the old Celtic direction, saying their rosaries. In the meadows nearby people sat around fires, brewing tea and eating soda bread. Hawkers appeared. The accounts emphasize the spontaneity of the development.

Time went by. Through the end of the nineteenth century and throughout the twentieth, the numbers of pilgrims rose, reaching a figure of 1,500,000 a year at the end of the twentieth century. In 1971 and 1972, when Victor Turner and I were doing fieldwork in Ireland, healings were occurring all the time. We met James Greenan, now a strong limber man, who had suddenly been restored to his feet at Knock after twelve years on his back after a fall. He certainly took his cure with a good deal of sangfroid. If we had said to him, "You recovered suddenly, by chance, this is a thing that can happen among any large group of sick people in hospital, or anywhere else, praying or not praying," he would have seen that we simply had no understanding of the matter at all. Not only did he know all about the power of Our Lady who had worked cures at Lourdes and Fatima; not only did the unceasing prayers of the Irish people go up to Jesus, Mary, and Joseph; not only did James live in a continuous communion with the saints, the land, his kin, and his very history through the power of the blessed St. Patrick, but he also *experienced* it at the shrine at Knock. He *knew* it as an act of healing. Here is this Irishman describing himself before the healing, sick in his house in the town of Boyle, not even enjoying his good strong tea and soda bread, as he told us:

I was so sick, I got so I wouldn't speak to anyone. One day friends came to my house and told me they could take me to Knock. I didn't answer. They said, "Why don't you speak?" At last something inside me said, "Go! Take a chance on it." So I did! I was praying to St. Anthony, asking him to pray to Our Lady. Whatever she wanted for me, that's all right, I said.

I didn't expect anything, mind. When we got to Knock, the blessing of the sick began and I prayed as much as I could, resigning myself. Just when Father Concannon passed me with the Blessed Sacrament I felt myself lifted up—it was a feeling all through my body—a feeling of strength. I said to the nurse, "I want to stand up." The nurse was trying to make me lie down. But I stood. I felt a bit shaky for a moment, and I asked the nurse to be near. Then I felt grand. I walked over to the medical bureau, without sticks or anything. The doctor there, he said, "But can you bend over?" "Why?" said I, "I haven't tried yet." And I bent right over and touched the ground.

Here James demonstrated with perfect ease. "That was quite impossible before," he said. He told us that after the healing he became a steward at the shrine, carrying Our Lady's statue and doing jobs for the shrine. He said to us seriously, "May God be praised and blessed for the great favor, and may Our Lady of Knock be known and loved in every part of the world"—which was like Mrs. Trench's exclamation at the vision itself. In 1972 when we met him, James—a self-effacing man—looked fit and cheerful.

When we ourselves joined the processions at Knock we could see around the procession of the Sacrament a very serious attitude developing, a kind of magnetic field, wherever the Sacrament was carried. People clasped their hands and prayed with all their might. It was a time of their completest being.

※

One might put it like this. The woman spirit flamed into existence in response to the people's love, in the hopelessness of their lot. The people recognized the appearance of the Mother as her personal act of love. Although the appearance of divine figures may be the same in a general way as the awareness of the presence of the dead, the stunning occasion of a vision of light eclipses all our experience of powers and personal healing.

It seems such events most often happen to insignificant groups of people, to children, and to the poor. "Significant" people may well lose that negative capability so necessary for mystical participation. Yet one asks questions, one feels impatient: the history of the event ought to have at least a little logic about it. Did the vision of Knock help Ireland in its predicament? Why don't holy figures act logically? But the real question is "Why do people like James and the Pentecostal man experience a breakthrough?" For the Pentecostal man, the breakthrough was "Claim healing!"—told in his own voice as an undeniable command. And consider James's "I didn't expect anything, mind"—then his experience of being lifted up. Spirit figures exist, and they are pretty sure of themselves. The Blessed Mother is a spirit. She was profoundly sorry for the people of Knock and for all the starving. The Pentecostal man's spirit, the Lord, could not bear the doctors' shilly-shallying over his diagnosis. "Get to it" was the tone. Those of the spirit world actually have fine mature humanistic feelings, better than those of their counterparts on earth. In the case of Our Lady of Knock, it so happens that around the time of her appearance, a large protest campaign was active in the area calling on the British rulers and landlords for justice. The movement was known as "Michael Davitt's monster meeting campaign." Not only this but, as the pilgrimage to Knock developed, the consciousness of the pilgrims became fixed on the crown that the lady wore. She was a queen. The people saw the point: she was not only our mother but also the queen of Ireland, which cut out the claims of British royalty to that title. The history of Irish independence was indeed involved in the appearance at Knock. Irish people to this day take a quiet pride in that odd insignificant village of Knock and the hidden implications of the heavenly vision.

The focus now crosses to another continent and another religion, and settles on a muddy village near the banks of the Nile, in an area where the anthropologist Janice Boddy did fieldwork inside a cruel social milieu hitherto only studied by men. The recent breakthrough in women's studies of oppressive societies has been an eye-opener, making me proud to be a woman researcher myself.

Boddy showed that here, too, in the Sudan, the people have a sense of spiritual beings. This time the sense rises strongly in the private lives of Muslim women, and their stories show that oppressed people are not without personality, color, and even unorthodox spiritual events in their lives.

POSSESSED BY THEIR OWN UNIQUE SPIRITS: HEALING AND GLORY FOR THE OPPRESSED WOMEN OF THE SUDAN

The women of the Nile live their lives dominated by men, who own nearly everything: land, property, and children.[9] Both men and women are busy growing crops, and the women in addition have their families to tend. Both boys and girls in this society undergo circumcision; in the case of the girls, it is done by removing the clitoris and performing infibulation, that is, stitching to make the genital aperture smaller, a practice intended to prevent premarital sex and to assure the men when they marry that their sons are their own. However, even in this repressive society, there is something that outweighs the rigid controls under which the women live—something they love. It is called "Zār," a kind of women's club for acquiring a particular, fussy, affectionate spirit who has a desire to heal a person and give relief to a woman's passions. The women meet together frequently and go into trance, becoming incorporated by these roving spirits, beings who first afflict them and then heal them. The spirits are good to them in a way unique to Zār, for this is a cult full of spontaneity and color, with access to an entire repertoire of spirit figures mostly well known to the people—Holy Men or Women; Ethiopians; North Americans; Hindus; Chinese; Colonial Officials from Egypt, Turkey, or Britain; Desert Nomads; Syrian Tinkers or Gypsies; West Africans; Western and Southern Sudanese; Black Africans; Witches; and Crocodiles—a fascinating collection. During the sessions, in which the women "go down"—as they call it—into trance, neither the participants' bodies nor their costumes belong to them; they belong to their spirits. Zār rituals are always fraught with tension and surprise, for at any moment a woman might be seized by a new spirit whom no one knew existed and she did not know she had.

In *Wombs and Alien Spirits*, Janice Boddy takes the reader to a session held in a courtyard dancing ground, bounded on three sides with palm-fiber mats spread on the ground. It is evening. Here sit several dozen chanting women: they are the spirit-possessed. Their faces peek out from cotton shawls, fine brown faces with tattoos, shapely faces with long noses and shining eyes, keenly attentive. The priestess beats out a syncopated rhythm on a drum, and other women play clanging brass household utensils. The rhythm intensifies. Now a sick woman rises to dance. She is possessed by a Western military officer. A cloth covers her face, yet she flourishes a cane like an actor in a vaudeville burlesque. In her dance, she is an officer of the desert corps conducting drill. Every so often she bends rigidly at the hip and, cane pressed to her forehead, bobs her torso up and down. How she came by the cloth and the cane—also cigarettes, belt, and a radio—was because the spirit requested them.

In the waning eerie light the chant changes, and a woman—now a spirit—performs a strange pantomime with a sword, crouching low, sweeping the flat of the weapon back and forth along the ground. She dashes through these postures with skill and grace. She is a hunter flushing game, a soldier wary of enemies lying hidden in dense vegetation. Another woman struts down the clearing smoking, with a walking stick held perpendicular to the ground at the end of her outstretched arm, pompous and indifferent. She is a Mandarin. A portly gray-haired lady wearing a red head scarf with crenellated designs dances through a series of gestures; at one point she performs a benediction. She is host to the Catholic Priest spirit.

Another chant, and immediately a young woman starts flailing about on the mats, out of control. She is guided to the center of the dancing ground and left to kneel at the feet of the priestess. She is going down into trance. The music stops; she continues to move convulsively. The priestess asks the spirit in her, "What do you want?" The spirit whispers, "A purple cloth"—which they give her—and the woman dances, then falls to the ground.

In another session a woman begins to cry. She gets up and says in a deep voice, "Unless you put on a ceremony for her, she won't recover." It is a man spirit speaking about the woman herself. Then he, the spirit, says, "I want a dress like that one there, and I want henna and incense!" This time he is speaking *as* the woman.

Another woman is possessed by the spirit of an Ethiopian man. When she goes down into trance, she says, "You must make him coffee right now!" This woman is speaking *on behalf of the spirit*. They make "Him"— the spirit—some coffee and she, the woman, drinks it; that is, "they" drink it. She becomes quiet and emerges from her trance.

Another woman says, "I want so and so," and they do it for her, that is, for her African Cannibal spirit. She says, "Bring Him meat, raw meat"— speaking on behalf of the spirit. The woman/African Cannibal eats it.

Boddy says that this ambiguity, this risk of confusion, is essential to the understanding of what possession trance is all about. "She is he; she is not he." It is interesting that what might be dreaded in our society as a case of multiple personality is regarded as beneficial in this ritual situation, where the other personality, if recognized, has a healing role. The woman's awareness is not diminished by this: rather, it is heightened in sympathy with the incoming spirit's identity, for spirit and host exchange experiences. The patient gradually learns to accept that it is her failure to recognize the spirit that is the source of her affliction. The spirit, on its side, is learning to communicate with humans—something it very much wants to do. The spirit heals; the spirit and the human being agree to help each other.

Why the spirits possess is because they want to. They take the initiative. They desire access to the human world and have a job to do there. They love cleanliness and beauty; they desire gold, fine clothing, and delicate perfumes; and they demand similar good taste in their human hosts. When appearing in human form they are always bathed, well dressed, and lovely to behold. They prefer their hosts to eat clean foods—white, enclosed, expensive foods that increase and strengthen the blood. A spirit occasionally signifies its presence in a woman by drinking straight cologne or demanding to smoke perfumed cigarettes.

The spirits are always near, just above their human hosts, influencing their perceptions and what they do. A woman has to learn *not* to resist a spirit's attempts to enter the human world through her body. Because spirits take the initiative and are entities greater than a woman herself, acting of their own will, the startling possibility exists that at any moment a woman might not be who she usually is. The spirits endow her with a sense that something important has happened, that she has seen more than she has observed.

For a woman in Zār, the spirits are present in all the twists and turns in her life: childhood illnesses, betrothal, marital difficulties and pain, anxiety surrounding pregnancy and childbirth, nostalgia for her mother's home, and even, perhaps, a beloved daughter's death. And as a woman lives on through the decades, she develops her relations with the spirits, and the clues come through easier. To those who experience possession, spirit world and human are delicately combined.

My own comment, after Janice Boddy's insight into the phenomenon, is to glory in the strangeness of such events, here shown in one of the most complex spirit rituals known, involving multitudes of spirits. One can begin to understand the autonomy of the beings in the spirit world—a state of things accepted in all spirit religions. The beings are not invented by ourselves. They simply come, as they wish. Northern Sudanese women are a section of the population endowed with extraordinary strength and persistence in the face of a Khartoum-centered political system, in the face of warlords, extreme poverty, the laws of Islam, and patriarchalism in its most primitive form; and yet they come out from under. The women have the power of seeing through the eyes of others. Janice Boddy's Sudanese friend, Asia, said about the trance:

> When it descends into you, you "go the limit" until the drumming stops, and then the person stops. When the drums are beating, beating, you hear nothing, you hear from far away. You have left the dancing ground, the place of the Zār. And you see, you have a vision. You see through the eyes of the European. Or you see through the eyes of the West African, whichever spirit it is. You see then as a European sees—you see other Europeans, radios, Pepsis, televisions, refrigerators, automobiles, a table set

with food. You forget who you are, your village, your family, you know nothing from your life. You see with the eyes of the spirit until the drumming stops.[10]

The individual's soul is dormant, and the body is filled with another spirit. Actual contact is made. In so many ways, the search for healing moves ahead of us into a great mystery.

As for the Zār women, what may be happening is that the participants are following the deep connectedness and oneness between people, that is, between these women in their confined lives and the very different figures who are their spirit mates, separated from them by circumstance of life, class, and—curiously—time and space. The Zār women are experienced in reaching the connections. Their works become acts of genius, works of the spirit, bringing about events that seem beyond understanding.

We will gain more understanding when we go back and look at stories about the first intimations of a healer's vocation, accounts that trace the first budding and flowering of the gift, the beginnings of "the call." This is a matter we have not touched on as yet. In the sharply etched and dramatic stories that now follow, the reader may begin to appreciate what the call is saying to the person, in event after event, stage by stage. What the stories portray is what eventuates when healers are confronted with the crisis that changes their lives.

One healer was British, another an Iñupiat from northern Alaska, another a Nepali, and the last one an African. These people could hardly have been more different in their cultures. However, the common features become clear. For instance, in each case the call to heal came from a spirit.

The Britisher, an anthropologist named Roy Willis, is a tall man, a bit clumsy on one leg because he once had polio. He is the sort of person who achieves a gentle rapport with everyone. He tells how in 1983 he himself had a strange experience and was gifted with healing—he, Willis, an anthropologist and a social scientist.

The Healing Vocation: The Anthropologist in Trance, Given in the Words of Roy Willis

The discovery that I was a natural healer came in my early fifties as a complete and rather disturbing surprise. The idea that I could heal would have been absurd. Nothing in my training as an anthropologist quite prepared me for the experience to come. Then, quite suddenly, I was overtaken by a profound, indeed shattering, mental, physical, and emotional crisis. Everything in my life—work, career, personal relationships—seemed utterly devoid of meaning. None of my outward achievements as a scholar and social scientist seemed to mean anything. It seemed as if my very ego, my sense of personal identity, was dissolving and leaving me the helpless prey of long-suppressed and violently destructive emotions rooted in half-forgotten childhood conflicts. I was weighed down with a sense of waste and guilt about the past.[11]

It was 1983 and I was visiting Egypt. Before going to Egypt I recall having a strong premonition that something significant was going to occur there. On Friday March 18th in Egypt I decided—though I was thoroughly depressed—to go on a sightseeing tour of Alexandria. It was when we arrived at a Roman monument known as Pompey's Column that the strange events began. As I started to ascend a small hill topped by the massive column I stumbled over a stone and fell flat on my face. I got up, unhurt but shaken. An old man then invited me down steps and along a passage until we were standing directly beneath the mighty column itself. Emerging afterwards, I sat on a stool. It was then that the really weird stuff began. I became aware of a voice speaking in English with a fluent delivery from a source at once immensely distant and right inside me. The message was to the effect that my sufferings were the payment of a debt about which I would understand more later—that the debt was now discharged, and I was—this bit was strongly emphasized—guiltless and free. I had come home. I was then told and was given "one commandment," to enjoy life to the full.

I felt I was being immersed in cool, healing water. I could sense the life-giving liquid over my whole body, and instantly the psychic pain I had known for so long "switched off." Then happened the most astounding thing of all. Gazing through this watery element in which I seemed to be immersed, I beheld a strange, multidimensional, oval, floating object, glowing with a soft amber color. I could see it with a startling degree of clarity much superior to ordinary vision.[12]

Then I came to, out of what I assume was a trance state, and returned to my hotel. There in the seclusion of my room I wept without restraint. Afterwards I felt as one reborn. The experience was much sharper and more real than real reality. Its meaning still escapes me. Was the object some kind of angelic messenger?

A few months after the Alexandria experience I became aware that I had healing powers. The discovery came as a shock. It happened during a social science research project I was doing in Scotland on non-orthodox therapies.

As part of that research I had enrolled, as a spy if you like, on a course given by the late Bruce Macmanaway, a renowned natural healer. Listening to Bruce talk of his conversations with spirits I was immediately reminded of my work as an anthropologist with traditional healers in rural Africa and the way they had explained things to me.

To my surprise, Bruce invited me to "treat" one of his patients, a middle-aged woman suffering from upper back pain. I placed my hands on her shoulders just as I had seen Bruce do in his course demonstrations. After a minute the woman startled me by saying she felt "deep heat" in her upper body and then declared that all her pain had gone.

This could just be an illusion, I told myself, merely the result of "suggestion." There was no way known to science that a genuinely pathological condition could be dispelled by such a trivial action as resting one's hands on the sufferer's shoulders.

I made further tests to see if this unexpected result could be replicated, and then I healed a number of troubles, arthritis, sinusitis, eczema, asthma, hypertension, migraine, sciatica, frozen shoulder, pain in the head and back, rheumatoid arthritis, and accidental injuries to joints and soft tissues. The gift was 85 percent successful. I was onto something both important and deeply mysterious.

What causative agency, force, or whatever, is at work here? In almost all successful cases my patients spontaneously reported unusual sensations of bodily heat or warmth during the hands-on phase of treatment. One woman compared it to sunbathing on a tropical beach. Those suffering from severe stress felt pleasant drowsiness during and after treatment. This evidence suggested that some form of beneficial energy was being transmitted through me to the patients.

I do not feel tired after healing, rather the reverse. When I heal it feels as if my mind has been pushed out of gear as in a car and is running in neutral while someone else takes over the steering wheel. It is a restful sensation, akin to meditation. I feel detached from my ordinary everyday self. The dominant sensation is one of *flow*. This flowing sensation seems to include both me and the person I am treating. It is both gentle and powerful and, I often feel, intelligent. It knows where to go and what to do. But wherever this power or energy comes from, it works regardless of my own or the patient's volition. It exists as an objective fact of the natural world.[13]

Back to my own commentary. Just as I myself in the Hilton Hotel felt healing energy and had to change my views, so did Roy Willis, the trained social scientist, have to change his views after this cataclysmic event—

one that was destined to benefit a large number of people in a disturbingly nonanthropological way. When the news of Willis's odd side step away from the discipline first came to the ears of his colleagues in the discipline, they were not so much amazed as puzzled; they wondered, and then forgot about it. I was one of those at the time. I did not know there were features in the story that were fascinatingly similar to the reports of initiation among healers in many different societies. I simply did not know, then, how often those features repeated themselves: there was the element of surprise; the crisis of the psyche—the depression, seen elsewhere as demons; entering the place of the dead; words from an unknown source; trance; fuzzy outlines; a glowing floating object; clarity; the power of "seeing"; a sense of rebirth; further teaching by a guru; and the gift of healing. Now, as the stories proceed in this section, it will be seen that the features in Willis's story will be continually repeated—features that impel one to recognize the phenomenon of the gift of healing as an objective fact, "replicable," as Willis puts it. Here again one may look at the study of healing in the spirit of natural history as if healing were a strange plant. One would have to state: "Such and such is what actually happens; see how this plant or animal actually lives; one may mark its features, draw sketches, give habitat, source of nourishment, reproductive processes, and so on."

After his experience Willis planned to go back to his old study-continent of Africa, but this time his topic would be healing. He wondered if he would be able to enrich his study with this new spirituality—would he be able to share it with those Africans who seek to cure the soul?

OPENING TO THE SPIRIT: THE *NGULU* DANCE OF NORTHERN ZAMBIA

Willis hoped to participate in the people's healing and be open to its power.[14] In 1990 when he first returned, he visited the Lungu of northeastern Zambia, a Bantu-speaking people living a little south of the equator in upland forest. He heard rumors of their *ngulu* healing sessions, and was told that certain medicine people, usually women, beat drums to persuade mysterious spirits called *ngulu* to reveal themselves to their patients, and when they did the patients would be healed. These *ngulu* spirits were also capable of causing sickness and distress—they were alien powers who were not concerned with any particular person's family and history. Nevertheless the Africans knew that when the spirits were well honored, they would serve the interests of life and its increase. A difficulty existed for Willis, however. *Ngulu* had become a secret cult, frowned on by the churches who regarded it as primitive and pagan. To study healing at such a time seemed impracticable.

In 1996 Willis went for a second visit among the Lungu with a stronger determination to reconnect with the spiritual aspects of the healing, this time by dint of lending himself completely to the African way of healing and practicing it—a method now called the anthropology of experience. He had the good fortune to meet with a medicine woman and with a patient who had fevers, cold, and heart palpitations. A ritual was to be held, and it was the first of many that Willis attended. The rituals featured beginning rites to invite the spirit; then tranced healing events that were held in private places "set aside," that is, outside in the forest, beyond the reach and rules of ordinary life; and lastly, ending rites, the dismissal of the spirit. In other words, the ritual was a rite of passage, passing the patient from the ordinary to the nonordinary and back again, healed, into normal life. The spiritual transformation took place in the middle phase, taking the patient out of ordinary existence altogether and reconstituting her as a healthy being. It was a social event, but in a different way from what is usually considered "social"—that is, not intended to enhance the authority and business system but with another agenda. Many people took part, and a number of them went into trance along with the patient.

Willis's understanding of these matters was already rich. This is how he recounted the inner core of the rite, commenting on the sense of *flowing*, a camaraderie between doctors, musicians, anthropologists, and patients, something quite remarkable.

————————— ❖ —————————

The *Ngulu* Dance, in Willis's Words

It began in the village at dusk, at the house of the principal medicine woman along with her friends. We made offerings to the spirit, and at that, the medicine woman sank to the ground, breathing heavily and uttering strange cries: she was in trance. She could do this at will and did not need drumming to achieve it. Suddenly she sat up, smiled, and hugged the two people nearest her, then went out with her people, wending her way down the dark trail to the forest clearing to begin her task, the care of the patient. A crowd of fifty people had already gathered, along with three men drummers, who immediately started to play. The medicine woman went to find a mat that bore white signs. She spread it out in the middle and settled the patient on it. She placed the sick woman sitting upright with her legs straight in front of her, then laid a cloth right over her head and body, covering her.

"What must it feel like under there?" I thought, watching. The patient betrayed no emotion. The medicine woman, all the time in trance, incensed her with smoke, then rested her fly-switch lengthwise on the patient's cloth-covered head as if it were a lightning conductor. Chanting broke out among the crowd, while the drummers built up their insistent di-*DI*didi di-*DI*didi beat, working creatively against each other to magnify the throbbing summons to the powerful ngulu spirits, drawing them to this special cleared space in the night. The patient was alone beneath her cloth in the very center of darkness, under simultaneous assault through several sensory channels. Soon she was going to lose her sense of social selfhood, her name, her wifehood and motherhood, her village and tribal identity.

For some minutes the veiled figure was motionless, the drumming and chanting becoming increasingly urgent; then the first trembling movements under the cloth signaled the onset of spirit action. Everyone's attention was concentrated on what was happening there, on the imminent revelation. The movements became convulsive, the cloth fell away, something was struggling massively in her, urgently seeking to emerge. We saw her round black face raised, her awestruck eyes. Those around her stooped to listen, straining to sift intelligible words from the semi-babble of glossolalia that they heard, in order to learn the name of the spirit entity stirring in this woman.

"Mbita!" someone cried, triumphantly repeating the newly uttered name of the patient's ngulu spirit, along with four other names. A moment later the spirit-filled body of the patient ceased its convulsive quivering, the wordless cries of pain or ecstasy ceased, and, amazingly, the figure rose to its feet, suddenly whole, reborn from suffering and chaos. And now, in its new, changed state and moving with the continuing rhythm of the drums, the spirit danced before us all, visible, revealed.

It was the spirit dancing, in a slow languorous way, a smooth gliding movement, sensual too, with simultaneously gyrating hips as the human-spirit-body turned through a wide arc, then a spiraling movement through the cleared dancing space, going through this sequence of gliding, swooping movements several times. Now the whole group was dancing with "Mbita-who-was-the-patient," the new spirit, in a dance of spontaneous joy at her epiphany. All were filled with divinity.

To end the session the medicine woman went to the patient and twisted the hair on the top of her head to bring her around from her trance. The patient had no recollection of her altered-state experience. She literally had no words to describe it, nor had the medicine woman.

For us all, the drumming and the movement had pleasantly dissolved the boundaries of ordinary selfhood. Now I felt in a spaced-out state. There had been a hard-to-find "gentleness" about the night's performance. I was lifted out of normal consciousness into a state where ordinary perceptions of time and space were drastically altered. I knew that we are all related, different versions of each other, but that there were no fixed boundaries to selfhood; there was a permeability and flexibility between self and other, an infinite flexibility, and again this sense of everything flowing within the all-encompassing rhythm of the drum. I experienced the dissolution of the ordinary sense of time and space, the coordinates of ordinary selfhood, the sense that "I" am a person with a particular inventory of social characteristics, including a "position" in society, living at a particular time—all these defining and localizing criteria temporarily vanished. I was indeed in Victor Turner's state of *communitas*, intensely aware of myself in relation to my fellows. Interestingly, I could "see" myself more clearly than in ordinary reality, when self-perception is typically more fragmentary, tied to one or other fleetingly relevant social role. Then, in the moment of *communitas*, I saw myself whole and objectively. I was "at home" and among, as it seemed, "kinsfolk." I discovered that the state of *communitas* provides access to those transpersonal entities or forces commonly called "spirits."[15]

I myself reflect here on what Victor Turner said about communitas.[16] It is the sense people have when they relate to each other in full direct connectedness. Then they recognize it as a special occasion and talk about it with delight. People feel their own lowliness in it and are aware of the gift that is flowering between them, and are often aware of where it comes from. Communitas, if it is present even in the dullest jobs, is richly charged with emotion and pleasure, and it gives people strength to go on and on as if by magic.

Here, then, was Roy Willis in Africa with the spirit upon him, in that very world of communitas. Where indeed does this visionary state of communitas come from? Here it seems connected with spirit presence, and, moreover, it is becoming clear that spirits are easily called forth in communitas. Compare the first of the spirit stories in this chapter, especially the collective prayer scenes in the Pentecostal church in the American South. What followed the big "togetherness-action" of praying together—which one may now identify as a ritual of pure communitas—were the curing and other extraordinary benefits that resulted. Roy Willis in Africa also spotted the connection of healing and spirits with communitas, which was never developed by Victor Turner. Oddly, owing to recent research by the more humble of my students, I found that one could indeed use the old word *communion*, "sharing" or "oneness," for the high spots of communitas in teenagers' bands and jam sessions. This was communion, which has been stamped with Christianity and colored with only one religion's meaning. The Lungu of northern Zambia and Willis danced in blessed communion with the spirit-filled patient woman. *Communion* was a true term for it.

One sees in these experiences the intimate union of spirit and material things—and somewhere in each story, the message comes through of the spirit's good intentions for humanity.

The next story deals with an initiation by a spirit among the Iñupiat Eskimos—just one decisive episode that changed the life of a village.

THE HEALING VOCATION: A ONE-EYED ANCESTOR SPIRIT GIVES POWER TO UMIGLUK, THE IÑUPIAT SHAMAN

This is a classic personal history of a shamanic experience, told to an archeologist in the 1930s on the icy north slope of Alaska, in the days of underground sod houses and fur parkas. Froelich Rainey, the archeologist, was well liked by the Iñupiat. It is told he would sit on the floor with them and not on chairs as the missionaries would have insisted. Rainey had discovered the remains of something of the nature of a city of 3,000 inhabitants, thriving on the skilled sea hunting. In 1908 the numbers were down to 179, owing to induced alcoholism and infections brought in from outside. Rainey also wrote down their oral history. His story tells how the shaman, Umigluk, taught shamanic powers to his village. In my own time in 1987, the Umigluk family still kept a framed photograph of the shaman in their prefab house on the wall beside the dining table. The photo shows Umigluk, a stocky man, wearing a parka with an enormous fur ruff. You could see the eyes in the somber face penetrating you and going beyond. The grandson of Umigluk was a sensible, practical man with a gift for listening to the animals. He told the story of his grandfather to the archeologist Froelich Rainey, whom he liked. In 1988 Claire, my healer friend, gave me a copy of Rainey's account, which was part of a recent teleconference course she was taking in anthropology. What it described seemed to be the key to the spirit-created shaman initiation.

It was the story of Umigluk's flying boat and his strange vision.

———————— ⋈ ————————

Umigluk Tells the Story of His Own Grandfather, Umigluk

Once when Umigluk was a young man he was making his way home along the Arctic shore after a hunting trip. He heard above him a sound like paddles dipping slowly into water. He looked up and saw a boat high in the air, circling around and around as if it were descending from the moon. Men were evidently in the boat paddling, but when it came nearer and landed on the earth before him, he couldn't see anyone. Soon a man at the steerer's seat stood up in the boat. Umigluk recognized him as Alungok, a shaman who had died some time before. He was known to have been a speedy runner, particularly when he took off his outer boots to run in his small inner boots. Once Alungok crossed a pond without even wetting his boots. This man had died during a vision because, while the vision was in progress, the villagers had been banging about with buckets and talking loudly. Unfortunately, Alungok's spirit was trying to get back from its visionary journey at the same time and could not manage it because of the noise. So Alungok died. At the time of his death the people saw the same sky boat arrive to take his body and spirit.

Now, Alungok had returned. Standing up in the boat he spoke to Umigluk asking after those he'd left behind, his wife and daughter. Umigluk replied that they were fine. Then Alungok disappeared. Another shaman rose in the boat, Anguluk. He wore fine clothes and his mittens were decorated with pieces of copper. He seemed to have one big eye instead of two, with a protruding brow and the eye in the middle of the big brow. When he danced, the copper ornaments on his mittens rattled. At the sound, a white ermine came up from inside the boat onto its edge and went down into it again. A brown ermine followed. Then to Umigluk's delight the brown ermine followed the white ermine in a chase around the gunwale of the boat. Alungok reappeared and told Umigluk that they had come to take him away just as he himself had been taken, but they couldn't because of the smell of beluga whale blood that was on him from the hunting. Here the vision ended. Umigluk looked about him but nobody was there. He took his path home to his tent and on the way the scene vanished from his mind.

Late that night he awoke and started up naked to leave the tent. His wife called, "Umigluk, come back, are you crazy?" She made him put on his clothes. The man was like a crazy person and kept wandering away. He continued crazy for four days, getting worse whenever he ate anything. After four days he began to improve.

Shortly afterward the people came together in the main underground igloo to play their drums. During the drumming Umigluk's spirit left him. All went black. Then the spirit of Anguluk, the one-eyed shaman with the mittens, entered Umigluk's body, beating the drum instead of him and singing instead of him. The shaman within him taught him eight power songs, which now became Umigluk's own personal songs. All this was strange to Umigluk, but the people began to understand it was Anguluk inside him, teaching him. "Teach us," they said, and he agreed. So they used to gather in the underground meeting igloo. Still with his power in him, Umigluk taught the people to sing his eight songs, playing them quietly at first until each person learned theirs. He taught them to carve masks of Anguluk with the protruding brow and single round eye. When it came to the October feast of the whale's tail, the eight Iñupiat sat in a row as in a boat, finely dressed with decorated mittens, and they sang and danced like Anguluk. He taught them how to let their spirits go out from their bodies and come back in, pulling themselves back into their bodies as if they were pulling themselves backward into their underground igloos. The songs gave them power, power to heal the sick, to eliminate mortal wounds, bring animals to the hunter, change the weather, and speak with the dead.[17]

Such is the way a shaman is made. The vision, the four-day crazy period, and the coming of the shaman's powers appear in all the stories of the creation of an Iñupiat shaman. This is in the general pattern of the worldwide shamanic initiation, happening to a person by the action of a spirit and preceded by something like a near-death experience or frightening depression. The framed photograph of Umigluk on the wall of his grandson's home has a telltale look in his eyes of being somewhere else, the same look I have seen in his great-grandson when he danced the caribou and caused the animals to approach the village, a power even seen in his young great-great-grandson who was gifted with clairvoyance. This telltale look, interestingly, is also to be seen in two people unrelated to the Iñupiat, two anthropologists studying West Africa, both of whom were initiated into the craft of the medicine man. Rembrandt in one of his pictures caught the same look in the eyes of St. Paul, who had such a spirit initiation too. All these shamans knew that a shaman must never renege on his craft, he must never refuse to heal, he must cause no harm by the power, and he must not attribute the power to himself. This is the shaman ethic, and it is found everywhere.

Claire herself belonged to this unspoken sisterhood of shamans,[18] for shaman power still exists in northern Alaska, along with its curious "time-out," blanking-out feature. Claire, who was a Christian, experienced at different stages of her life at least four episodes that psychologists in our culture would diagnose as fugue or even psychosis—but these episodes do not derive from psychosis. They were the irruptions of shamanic powers just as the ancient Iñupiat knew them, typically lasting four days. In early times the breaks began with a meeting with something fearful, a spirit of the dead or a dangerous animal, some entity who first afflicted the budding shaman, then changed and became a helper.

The account of Claire's first recorded break was supplied by a friend of hers, a white woman whom I met in Fairbanks. It appears that in 1970 Claire was in Anchorage in an expensive hotel, alone for four days, for reasons unknown.

"There she had some kind of transformation," said Claire's friend, looking disturbed. "She told me on the phone—I was at the airport—she told me she'd had some kind of revelation about me. There were certain things that would happen. A person who didn't know Claire's powers would think she'd gone crazy. She was uttering glossolalia. That was a bad time for Claire."

The friend bent over her coffee, saying. "I can't think what Claire went through in that hotel for four days all by herself."

That was one episode. In 1984 when Claire was not doing much healing she had another visitation, a very disturbing one. Claire would continually see a devil figure in her peripheral vision. In the negative phase of the episode, Claire uttered a torrent of blah-blah-blah nonsense words that nobody could understand. It was glossolalia again. It greatly upset her relatives. Claire told them irritably, "Don't be like that. You don't think I'm anything, do you? I can't help it; it comes to me." But at the end of the four-day period Claire was able to pray again to Jesus, and afterward her healing power was stronger than before as it was after each of these events. Jesus was the obverse of the devil, and if he were her helper spirit, he then would be her guide. Here was something like the same switch from dangerous to helpful that manifested itself in spirits in the precontact days.

Claire went through another encounter with her trouble, whatever it was—maybe the devil again. On Thursday, January 14, 1988, I found her lying on her couch, very depressed, in what psychiatrists would call a state of fugue. She had her eyes shut and would not speak. I was frightened, thinking she was angry. Four days later, she was herself again. What I saw had all the hallmarks of a shaman episode.

During a visit in 1991 yet another repeat of it seems to have occurred. I had newly arrived to attend the annual whaling festival and heard that

Claire had returned from the hospital, where she had been a patient from May 28 to June 2. I went to her house.

"Where's Claire?"

"Washing dishes," said young Ann.

I approached the kitchen. A small dark figure was at the sink, and she did not turn around.

"Claire, Claire. Look at this. I've brought you something." She still did not turn. Her gray hair was scrawny, her figure thin. I immediately thought, "An episode again? Isn't this fieldwork pitiful! My dear friend caught up in . . . something so mysterious. Okay, I have to try to understand it."

Claire peeked into the shopping bag I brought and saw peacock blue velveteen for a new parka, plus insulating lining material and a peacock blue zipper. She turned convulsively and flung herself into my arms. We were crying. I stroked her wild gray hair and haggard face.

"Dear Claire. You've given me everything, my sweet friend." When we recovered, she told me the doctor at the hospital had given her the wrong medicine. She was really mad at him. "I'll get an attorney," she said. Now she was off all medicines and was feeling better by the minute. I wondered what the doctor thought he had prescribed the medicine for.

⚶

In this journey that I was making through the experiences of healers, various understandings were coming into focus, not only about spirits but about the human soul. One was about the phenomenon of the fall to the ground. Among the Pentecostals and Charismatics, a person was slain in the spirit and fell; in the Zār ritual, a woman "went down" into trance and lost her ordinary self; and among the Lungu the *ngulu* spirits struggle with the human being to allow them to appear, and there is blackness at first. Both Umigluk and Claire experienced these cruel breaks in normalcy without realizing there would be a gift at the end of it. The break is a matter of the deepest being, a matter of that "thing" beyond value, the soul. The break comes, and afterwards there follows the entry of a beneficent spirit with overwhelming power, causing shock and blackness at first—as with St. Paul on his horse. It is even more of a transformation of one's total way of life than the one a baby experiences when it emerges into an oxygen-laden world and its blood has to take a path through new arteries to engage the lungs.

The soul exists in reality, sensitive, and can be brought to attention as if it were a bell struck by some insubstantial bell ringer—and it rings out. *Then* one knows one has a soul. Yet again, that thing, the soul, does not hang helplessly inside. The heart hangs there, resonating, yes, when the breakthrough occurs; the lungs suddenly spread wide with a kind of recognition—with a gasp, like the baby. The very pores quiver. One's organs operate quite well to indicate that something is going on. It is one's consciousness that is changed; it is set at large, "with no fixed boundaries." "There was a permeability and flexibility between self and other, an infinite flexibility," as Roy Willis described it. This soul is not in our own hands. It does not operate by the laws of ordinary consciousness.

❇

The next account, full of similarities, is set in Nepal—some 6,000 miles away from northern Alaska, among stone huts straddling the mountain slopes of the Himalayas. Here, villages are perched on the ridges of vast mountains where the people raise livestock and grow maize and potatoes, while some emigrate to town and work in sweatshop factories making clothes for Westerners. The religion is shamanism and animism, with a trace of Buddhism. In 1976 the anthropologist Larry Peters was working in Nepal when he encountered the shaman Bhirendra. Larry is a well-put-together and serious man, and he persisted in his research and practice with Bhirendra until he received in good measure the shamanic trance himself, although he belittled his own success. In his analysis he viewed the phenomenon from a psychological point of view, then left the problem alone for a long time. Later, he linked up with Michael Harner and has done much good by helping the revival of the ancient shamanic skills of the Tuva people of eastern Russia.

Bhirendra told Larry the story of how he became a shaman. The episodes turned out to proceed in almost exactly the same manner as in the other vocation stories in this chapter: affliction, followed by benefits. The story Bhirendra told sounds like magic, but Bhirendra truly experienced these things, as Peters, himself a shaman, confirms in his book. Bhirendra is photographed in a tall crown of peacock feathers, wearing crisscross beads. He is bending fondly to his drum. His mouth is open, his brows raised, the resonant chant pouring out of him. He is intent on the power of the song.

------------------------------ ✖ ------------------------------

The Healing Vocation in Nepal: Bhirendra's Story, "How I Became a Shaman"

When I was 13, something came over me. I started shaking violently without knowing why. I couldn't stay still for a minute even when I wasn't trembling. My grandfather was making me mad through possession, and I ran off into the forest, naked, for three days. During those three days I ate only what was given to me by my grandfather and the other spirits, forest shamans, who wore pointed hats over their white hair and were only three feet tall. Their wives had black hair, long breasts, and were very fat. When one of them came to get me I was scared, but my grandfather's spirit stood in front of me to protect me. One of the forest shamans wanted to teach me. He showed me how to have power. He told me the prayer words to say, and he tried to feed me earthworms.

"Earthworms?" I asked.

"You have to eat them," he said, "or you'll die."

I reached out for the worms, but every time I did so one of the wives whipped my hands. She carried a golden sword and each time she whipped me, she cried, "Let's cut off his head."

"No, no," said my forest shaman. "I want to teach him." He said to me privately, "This is the way to eat. Take the food on the back of your hand." I did so and no one attacked me.

Finally the villagers came looking for me, shouting, "Bhirendra! Bhirendra! Where are you?" But instead of hearing voices, all I heard was the sound of dogs barking and I ran away. Finally the villagers caught up with me. I stopped my shivering and came to myself. They took me home and tried to make me eat, but I wouldn't take anything.

"What's the matter with you?" asked my parents. That night I started shaking again, but this time I looked around for a drum and took one that belonged to my father who was a shaman. I found myself outside. Some kind of path opened before me and I knew where to go—the gods made a path for me. The villagers couldn't follow me because no one could see the path I was taking. They would have walked into trees and thorns and fallen off cliffs. I found myself where three rivers cross, in the cemetery. The cemetery was terrifying. Out came a horde of demons with long crooked fangs, and others with no heads at all and eyes in the middle of their chests. Some of them carried death flags, and still others brought decaying corpses along with them. I ran. They chased me and leapt on me and started eating me. This was the end.

"Help, help!" I cried. "Help me, gods, I'm only a boy!"

I drew out my grandfather's magical dagger to defend myself, but I dropped it. It fell on a rock and there came out a long spark of light. Immediately everything changed. It was daytime and I was alive. The demons were gone.

When I got home I told my parents everything. They said, "That spirit who helped you in the forest, that was your grandfather. It was his dagger that saved your life. You have to know that your grandfather went off to Tibet nine years ago and has never returned."

My father said, "You're going to need a guru. It's best for you to have your mother's brother, he's a very powerful shaman." So my shaman uncle started to teach me: rituals, prayers, everything. My good grandfather's spirit, the one who made me mad in the first place and who protected me, was with me all the time, inside of me, and I had lessons from him in my dreams. That spirit became my very own. I could call on him at any time. He'd correct me if I made mistakes in my prayers and I'd feel him slap my hands in my sleep.

I had no choice in being a shaman. I was chosen. If I'd refused, I'd have gone completely mad and committed suicide. I'd never have been able to stop shaking. I was cured by becoming a shaman.

The learning began. During the first stage, I played the drum and shook. The more I shook the more the gods talked through me and the more visions I had. At the second stage the guru and I, both with drums, drummed together. The guru could bring my grandfather's spirit into me that way, and I knew when the spirit was there because it made me shake violently. Then I was able to bring my spirit easily. I could feel him riding on my shoulders. At the third stage I learnt to make offerings and do healing rituals. I learned the ritual to open the top of my head and let my spirit go out on a journey accompanied by my protecting spirit, in order to seek lost souls separated from their bodies.

The fourth stage was the ritual of the vision in the cemetery, the climb to the highest heavens. For this the people went to the cemetery and erected a temporary shelter on stilts, like a rice granary, and they decorated it with hundreds of white soul flowers. Leading up to the shelter was a nine-rung ladder, each rung named for each level of heaven. I wore a white robe and a peacock feather headdress. I and my guru climbed the nine steps and entered the sanctuary, and there for the first day we played our drums together, praying and singing to call the gods to possess us. For the next six days I played alone, fasting. I had visions of ghosts and spirits. On the seventh day I saw myself walking into a beautiful garden with flowers of many colors. A pond lay there and golden glimmery trees spread their branches. Next to the pond rose a very tall building that reached up into the sky. It had a golden staircase of nine steps leading to the top. I climbed the nine steps and saw at the top Ghesar Gyalpo himself, the supreme god of the shamans, sitting on a white throne covered with soul flowers. He was dressed in white and his face was all white. He had long hair and a white crown. He gave me milk to drink and told me I would attain much power, *shakti*, to be used for the good of my people. This was an unselfish power, granted to relieve the suffering of others, a power that would create a bond between me and my people.

I left the sanctuary and returned to the village. The people and my guru were on the way out to meet me and they carried me back cheering.

It's hard to explain this experience to you. It—it makes me cry. It was the most significant experience of my life, and from then on, my entire life changed.[19]

The story shows precisely the same days of confusion and wild action as with Umigluk, even the story of running off naked. Here in addition is a ladder to heaven, like the tunnel in the near-death experience and, in the story of Jacob's ladder, the radiant path to the light.

Shamans are given the gift of healing through spirits, and their miracle medicine is beneficent power. Their call is to take up a different mode of being in the world, a mode taught them by the spirits, sometimes called the shamanic state of consciousness. In this state the experienced shaman is able to release his soul from his body and "fly out" to the place, perhaps, where the soul of a sick person is wandering, lost. This last is an extraordinary process and is called *soul retrieval*. It is one I myself have used, following Michael Harner's instructions in *The Way of a Shaman*.[20] The active intervention of someone willing to "fly" in this manner and take positive action to look for the soul of a suffering person in whatever form in which that soul may appear somehow does the trick, and people recover. The soul is real.

The next story of the healing vocation is that of an African medicine man, Muchona. It tells of Muchona's first initiation into the work of spirit healing. Muchona was known as "the Hornet" because of the way he would pounce on an important point in an argument. In 1953 Victor Turner took down in handwriting the story of this excited little guy with whom he felt a deep rapport. If Vic himself was not a hornet, he was at least a subtle dribbler in the art of soccer, and could get past any opponent. In the same way, he got past much of the wearisome structuralism of his day and made for the gaps—liminality. Muchona and Vic relished each other's company in the grass hut that was our home.

THE HEALING VOCATION: A BUDDING MEDICINE MAN OF ZAMBIA IS CAUGHT UP IN THE SPIRIT'S PURPOSE

Muchona was a great talker, and also a noted healer, herbalist, and diviner of the Ndembu people. The Ndembu were the same forest people of northwestern Zambia whose ritual is described in chapter 1 in this book. They inherited through the maternal line and lived by hoe cultivation and hunting. Victor Turner first met Muchona in 1952 when he and a friend were walking along a dirt road in the Ndembu area playing "find the herb" among the roadside bushes. The two players were so absorbed in their rivalry that they failed to notice a swart elderly gnome who was padding perkily beside them. He was evidently a keen observer, for he joined in their sport and soon took the lead. It turned out he was a doctor for many healing rituals, especially for diseases of the heart and

A Ndembu medicine man uses his spirit telephone to call for help in healing a baby.

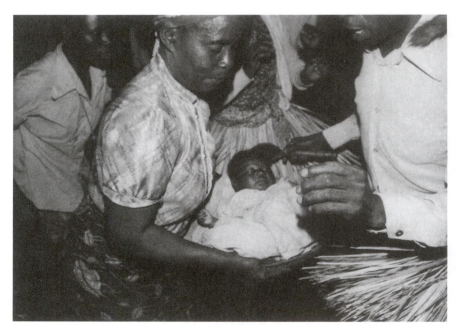

The Ndembu medicine man touches the baby with his switch of power.

lungs and to help a patient gain a teaching spirit. Muchona had been born into a slave family and had worked hard to emancipate himself. He was small in stature with narrow features, but he had a needle-sharp, pin-bright mind, and was known as somewhat of an outsider in his village. At the beginning of his career before his induction as a healer, he had married. His vocation to be a doctor started with an affliction caused by the spirit of his dead mother, who herself had had women's troubles and whose spirit, after her death, wanted Muchona to become a curer. Muchona described the spirit attack and the cure that began his career as a medicine man.

Muchona Tells the Story of His Vocation

I kept getting ill. I was caught by a very heavy sickness in the body and I found it hard to breathe. It was like being pricked by needles in my chest, and sometimes my chest felt as though it was blown up by a bicycle pump. I could only mutter, "*Boyi, boyi.*" My ears felt completely blocked up. I was like a drunken person and kept slipping to the ground in a fit. Then I kept dreaming of two of my mother's brothers and of my father. And I dreamed of my mother. My relatives went to a diviner to see what was wrong. When the diviner tossed the objects in his basket, the seed of the palm tree came up on top of the objects in the basket. It is the tree they use for palm wine.

The diviner said, "That means you're suffering from the sickness of *Kayong'u*. It's the sickness that comes before the call to be a doctor and diviner. Those four spirits in your dreams have come out of the grave to catch you and enter you, because they want you to become a diviner and treat people's illnesses. I can't make out who that fourth spirit is, the image is too weak." That one was the shadow of my mother.

So I realized that four spirits were determined to make me take on this difficult job. And it's a dangerous one! I could tell the divination was true: it was my destiny to take this course, the spirits wanted it. So the drum ritual for making a doctor began. All night long the senior doctors washed me with medicine. I kept shuddering convulsively to the Kayong'u drum rhythm; the spirits were doing whatever they liked with me. Every time I shuddered it was like being drunk or epileptic, as if I was suddenly struck in the liver by lightning or beaten with a hoe handle and stopped up.

Early in the morning while it was still dark the doctors seated me before a new ritual fire of green wood. When it began to be light, the old doctor who was in charge, a hunter-diviner, came up to me holding a red rooster by its legs and at the top of its head. The rooster, who crows in the morning, was there to end my sleep, to wake me up. The Kayong'u spirit also wakes up people it has caught. It makes them breathe hoarsely, like a rooster or a goat. The same thing happens when an initiated diviner is about to shake the basket full of divining objects: the person's voice changes and the person doesn't use the Lunda language anymore, but speaks hoarsely in another tongue. Diviners sometimes make a deep wheezing noise in the course of ordinary conversation. I can't help doing it myself when I talk. It's the voice of the Kayong'u spirit inside me.

Faced with the rooster I saw its color was red, the color of the shedding of blood. My mother used it in her women's rituals. It came to me. Blood!

I sprang forward in a sudden spasm, in trance. My teeth snapped, and the rooster's head lay apart from its body. What had I done? I had beheaded it. I seemed crazy. Blood was pouring out of the head, so I took it up as it bled and beat it on my heart to quiet my mind. Then the big doctor ordered a goat to be beheaded. Its blood poured on the ground—and the blood was also for the spirit in me. I lapped it up where it puddled.

They took the rooster's head and put it on a pole made from the tree of the ancestor's tears. My dead rooster was up there in contact with the ancestors, with the spirits. All was opened, now that the rooster was killed. The openings of my body that had been stopped up, my nostrils, ears, and eyes, were released and became supersensitive. From the killed animal I obtained wakefulness and heightened sensitivity, necessary for a diviner who would need to seek out hidden things.

Now the sun was rising. The doctors kept me quietly waiting while they went on some strange business in the bush. This is what they were doing: the old doctor took a hoe, a cupful of the goat's blood, the hearts of the rooster and goat, and a collection of special sharp objects. The old doctor led a procession of men and women doctors out of the village into the bush. Soon the path forked. Usually people make a choice which fork to take because they know the way. But these people were diviners. They didn't take either of the forks but went straight on into wild bush. They were seeking a certain path to a secret place. They knew more than other people, they had secret knowledge. That's how they found a *kapwipu* tree, a hard wood, a sign of misfortune to begin with followed by success. They hunkered down and prayed to the spirits who were burdening me, then started to hoe up a mound of earth at the foot of the tree roughly in the shape of a crocodile, with legs and a tail. Next they took the hearts of the rooster and goat and used some of the special sharp objects, a needle and razor, to prick the hearts. The pricking was the pain that sick people feel before they're healed. Now that the hearts were pricked, the sick person wouldn't feel it again because it was already done. They hid all these objects, including a knife, a bracelet, and a string of beads, in various places under the soil of the crocodile mound. Then they brought the drums and beat out the Kayong'u drum rhythm. They were ready.

They came for me. They led me to the crocodile in the bush and seated me on its neck.

"Okay," said the old doctor. "What have you come here for, eh? Speak up."

"To look for divination," I said. "To be healed. To be a healer. I'm looking for my spirit."

"Now, *divine! Find the objects.*"

A great power came upon me. My hands went out over the mound and a fierce pricking entered my fingers. My fingers plunged in, pushed by the spirit, and in a flash I found everything except the needle, and I snatched up the needle an instant later. I could divine. Now, whenever I work at divining the sense of that pricking returns. It's the thing that tells the diviner how to scan the objects tossed in the basket and see the cause of the client's illness or bad luck, or see whether someone's death was brought about by a witch or sorcerer. The diviner will gain the sharpness of the needle, and the cutting power of the knife and of the sharp teeth of a human or crocodile. The diviner goes straight to

the point in hidden matters. He sees the right ritual to use by shaking the basket, and his fingers see by the sharpness of the needle. The divining objects
and sharpness help one another.

Because I found all the objects the doctors praised me and the women trilled
aloud. I was extraordinarily happy. We danced home. I was cured of my illness—which disappeared instantly—and I was protected. The very spirit that
had made me sick cured me and immediately entered my body to aid me in
making correct decisions. As the saying goes: making a new healer starts by
the healer getting sick. *Kutachika wakata.*

Shortly after the ritual I sought out an experienced diviner and apprenticed
myself to him. Now I could learn the difficult craft operations and interpreta-
tions needed for the profession. I learned all the herbs; I even learned how to
cure a woman who was suffering from delusions as a result of puerperal fever.
For that cure I had to venture alone into the graveyard, full of ghosts and far
from the firelight. Only there could I exorcize the agencies of evil at work on
the poor woman, making her writhe and babble nonsense. I had to subdue my
fear to my curative vocation.[21]

The stories of Umigluk, Bhirendra, and Muchona are especially significant. The basic features of spontaneous spirit initiation are all here,
represented by the three regions of the world, arctic America, Nepal, and
Africa. The stories from cultures so distant from each other are touching, and their significance cannot be denied. One has to accept that humans anywhere go through the same processes, and they are spiritual
ones. It dawns on one that this tendency toward religion is inborn, an
endowment, existing for the purpose of just such communication with
spirits, and that the only common human process to which it can be compared is childbirth, a biological event. The religious process tops that of
childbirth because it is the most generally benign activity in which anyone can engage, a matter of full consciousness and the expansion of being.

CONCLUDING OBSERVATIONS: SPIRIT HEALING

This book is not a regular anthropology, nor does it follow the complex philosophy that plumbs the mystery of the individual, a separate soli-
tary being who creates his or her own imaginary life. What it does do is
to release the facts about the profound mystery of human permeability.
Humans are permeated by each other and by spirits. As Willis says, he
made the bridge to this discovery among the Lungu when he was experiencing communitas, the prime, natural, unstructured social sense. This

is the sense felt among the Pentecostals and in all the sacred communities of our examples. Within the glow of communitas—as with the sweet saints appearing in the light at Knock—the spirits appear. At Knock, the Lady Creatrix herself was there, "the Mother of the Creator" as the litany says, creator of the creator and of everything—which is a dazzling illumination. Further on in the chapter, the reader becomes familiar with a quite different scene—the multitudes of colorful humans whose personalities have come adrift, float as spirits, and get into Sudanese women; also the *ngulu* spirits, so attracted by music, who heal as they dance, and who gave great peace to Willis the anthropologist; then the mission of those who were dead, to come back as visible spirits to Umigluk and give him eight songs of power. The Iñupiat tribe, in order to survive in their fearsome land, needed that battery of power from their ancestors. They surely needed to know how to switch it on more than they would need to know in later years how to switch on the furnace in their prefabricated houses.

Peters documented how the good grandfather of Bhirendra came back from his grave in Tibet, the man who had been a shaman. But a dead shaman is no dead shaman, but a shaman all the more powerful over time and space—in the grandfather's case, a matter of the passing of ten years and a distance of 1,000 miles. In the same way my own mother-in-law (in her lifetime, a Scottish spiritualist) came back to me twenty-nine years after her death and 5,000 miles over the Atlantic from her ashy grave in England, to help her errant daughter-in-law when she was lost in Miami, Florida—an interesting spiritual experience indeed. Time and space are minor problems to a dead shaman.

So Bhirendra was to learn. The spirit of his grandfather entered into his body and rooted itself there, in all benevolence, giving the young shaman its own powers that could overcome the illnesses and fears of his patients and point them to the beauty of the healing that comes from heaven.

Lastly came the story by my old friend Muchona, now dead, whom I remember well as one of three black heads bent together around a table in a grass hut in central Africa, lost in writing down the mysteries of Ndembu spirituality—these three, Windson Kashinakaji the schoolteacher, Victor Turner, and Muchona. I remember the laughter, the amazed voices of discovery, and Vic in exaltation as he learnt to "read" a new spiritual world and discern its own kind of speaking in tongues.

Muchona is dead, and his son now stands as elder in the Christian Fellowship church—a church related to the Apostles of Maranke, the

Assemblies of God, and the Pentecostals. There Muchona the younger gives healing through the Holy Spirit, and the brethren also fall in the spirit and remember nothing.

So the threads weave back and forth. Muchona still lives. The Pentecostals draw down the power. Healers throughout America—little by little—learn the power. That peculiar language of the spiritual world is heard. Healers of different persuasions stare at each other in conferences, suddenly recognizing they are talking about the same thing, something very hard to put into words. The hands of the healers can feel it. Is the spirit pricking? The truthful accounts from all over the world—accounts of actual experiences—do succeed in saying it, just as William James found when he took on a similar task when assembling *The Varieties of Religious Experience*.[22] He let the spirit flow in his words about many religious conversions. He did not adopt a cold objective style, and his book has never been equaled.

As for talking about what spirits *are*, I have found this cannot be done without "listening," a kind of prayer or "invocation" to the spirits, as it is grandly called. It is more like pleading, "C'mon, give, give. *Please*." Could people—*possibly*—know what spirits are? One gets the sense that the drive for the ordinary type of knowledge will never make contact with such matters, and has never been able to. But through stories, for some reason, one does make contact. This is a very serious business, this matter of stories. One asks, "Why does the inquiry work through stories?" It is because of human permeability, because other people's experiences may become actually "one's own." One sees through such a story—as Victor Turner said of the spontaneous social drama—right into the experience of the person who told it, and it becomes one's own, "whole cloth." Stories touch a very spiritual matter. They slip under one's skin, so to speak; they cause one spirit to slide into another in the same way that healing works, by the coming-into-concrete-reality of sympathy—*sympathy*, which has the literal meaning of "feeling with."

This very sympathy is needed in order to grasp the idea that humans are contacting other entities and are in active relationship with them, and that there is a spiritual world "out there" that has its own patterns and its own ways of acting. In the stories about spirits, that world appears to be not so hard to describe, because the spirits come visually, unlike energy or power, which is not visually experienced. People experience possession by spirits, incorporation by them. (All this makes the psyche look much simpler than what many of the psychologists and psychiatrists have concluded when they say that "spirits" are some condition of the mind.) Furthermore, up comes in 3D an understanding of the soul, very much a spirit, wedded deep in the human body and spreading to an aura outside, creating it, the permeable organ itself, everything that shakti says it is, and that Jacob Levy Moreno says it is, and just as Lévi-Bruhl put it, even Jung: it is the unlimited psyche, connected with everything else in mystical participation.

CHAPTER 6

———❊———

The Idea of Communitas

The communitas element is present in religious healing wherever there is human contact between a healer and a sufferer. *Communitas* is the general term for love, community, fellow feeling, compassion, sympathy, and the search for the benefit and response of another soul. In this volume it has appeared notably at the moment of healing in Ihamba in Zambia, among the bushmen healing each other in the Kung dance, in the *vimbuza* drumming in Malawi that heats up communitas, and in the Yuwipi ritual among the Oglula. It is implicit in the Maori act of *aroha*; and the spirits taught it to Umigluk in Alaska as he taught his people how to drum. This chapter depicts situations showing the milieu of communitas, either anchored into the ritual as in the Dhikr chant and uttered in a circle of prayer taking place within the comity of Islam, or, as we see, developing in the African ritual of Chihamba, prescribed by divination and unfolding courtesy of an irascible, unpredictable grandfather spirit. Both have their names for communitas. The Muslims have their word, which translates as *comity*, "social harmony," and, in Chihamba, comradeship has a name, *wubwambu*, "friendship of the bosom."

I had heard tell of the prayers of the Sufis, and rumors of their healing. I was glad to discover that actual Sufis have given a running commentary of their own prayer scene, in Shaykh Hakim Chishti's *Book of Sufi Healing*. Shaykh Hakim describes a circle of especially focused people, a circle of trust, in which the members become so strongly aware of their spiritual interrelationship that they have changed into something different, that they are even humbly joining the angels in their praise of God. How the reader may come to understand this is to join in sympathy with them—again, through the written story. Islam is the most focused religion of all, so passionately monotheistic that all other deities or even hints of them are cast aside before the prime mystery of God. This Islamic circle is a group of Dhikr-praying Sufis seeking healing for their humble gathering of mystics.

SUFI HEALING: THE DHIKR CEREMONY OF DIVINE REMEMBRANCE

In the foreword of *The Book of Sufi Healing*, these words occur:

Not even the highest degree of dedication to worship may earn anybody the claim of divine forgiveness or recompense in any other form, yet there is one thing that everybody should make sure of, which shall not go unrequited under any circumstances by Allah the Almighty, and that is selfless service to ailing humanity.[1]

The humility of the Muslim's "unconditional submission to God's pleasure" is seen in these words, with the trusting proviso that if one heals the sick, that at least will be requited. Nothing else has that assurance. The writer of *The Book of Sufi Healing*, Shaykh Hakim Chishti of New York and Lahore, Pakistan—a man also familiar with Sufism in India and Afghanistan—says that Sufism, the mystical branch of Islam, is the very core of Islam itself; it is the love of God. Chishti gives the following description of Sufi Muslims outside the headquarters of the Sufi mystic order in Ajmer, India.

There is one street (more like an alleyway) that runs alongside the shrine. Along that street are sitting perhaps three dozen men and women at any given time, and from all outward appearances they are outcasts and the most despicable beggars in the world. But one look in their eyes reveals a countenance of supreme joy and peace, of contentment, of complete reliance and trust in Allah to provide all that they may need. Whether they eat or do not eat does not matter to them. They do not even know whether they are clean or dirty. Every person who crosses their path, be he criminal or saint, is given the same greeting—an expression of unrestricted love for that person and the deepest prayer that the person may receive the mercies and blessings of Allah. Once this condition sets in, there is no end. Praise Allah![2]

The story that follows is Chishti's description of the ceremony in which Sufis sit in a circle uttering the remembrance of Allah. Such an act may drive out serious diseases.

The Dhikr Ceremony Described by Shaykh Hakim Chishti

Allah said, "If you remember Me, I will remember you."[3] Therefore, the words of remembrance are continually recited: "There is nothing. There is God."

Men and women of piety once approached the prophet Muhammad after these verses were descended and asked for a clarification of the term *dhikr*, remembrance. He said that the end of the world would not arrive so long as there was one person left alive reciting the line, "There is nothing. There is God."

One of the great Shaykhs has said, "The ecstasy produced in the heart of the dervishes in their remembrance is a kind of turbulence, which is the cause of the waves foaming and breaking upon the shore." The prophet Muhammad said that the gates of heaven would open for anyone who recited it even once in a lifetime with true sincerity.

The Sufis evolved certain congregational practices for remembrance, which have come to mean sitting in the circle of Dhikr. The Holy Prophet has said that a group of angels is given a special duty by Allah to perform a patrol of the entire earth, looking for those who are engaged in remembrance of Allah the Almighty, chanting His name. When such assemblies are discovered, the angels are so amazed and pleased that they call more angels to join them and, placing their wings together in embrace, they make a column that reaches up into the Heavens.

When the assembly of remembrance has ended, these angels return to Heaven, and Allah asks them where they have been.

The angels tell Him that they are returning from an assembly of persons engaged in remembrance of Him and that they were glorifying and praising Him. Allah asks of the angels, "Have they seen Me?"

The angels reply, "No Lord, they have not."

Allah the Almighty asks them more about their worship and their need of protection. Then He commands each of the angels present that He has forgiven all of those engaged in remembrance of Him. One angel says to Allah, "But lord, there was one among them who only accidentally sat down and did not belong there" (that is, he was insincere).

Allah the Almighty replies, "Even that one have I forgiven, so exalted is the assembly that even one on the edge is not deprived of My reward."

Generally, the remembrance ceremony is held on Thursday evening. Usually the dervishes (mystical mendicants) will arrive for dinner and pray the final night prayer together. Then they await the signal from the shaykh to begin.

First one must have ablution. The dervishes sit on the ground in a circle in the posture of prayer, the legs folded under the body. The shaykh leads the group in intoning the sacred formula of *La ilāha illā Llāhū*, "There is nothing. There is God," continually for perhaps four hours. When reciting, the head is moved in an arc, starting with the left cheek resting on the left shoulder. Then the head is swung down across the chest, around to the right and up. A pause is made with the face looking upward. In one action the *La ilāha* is uttered and the head is thrown rather forcefully downward in the direction of the heart. The recitation concludes by raising the head again, looking upward as *illā Llāhū* is uttered. The real object of the Dhikr—intense as it may be—is not to get "high" or to become disoriented; rather, it is to ascend the ladder of stations of the soul, so that one may arrive at the Threshold and attain a glimpse of the Divine. When this happens (which is by no means uniformly achieved), the person may fall into a state of ecstasy. As a mark of respect, all present rise until this condition departs from the dervish.

Whenever making recitation of formulas to treat disease, it is important that the number of recitations ends in zero (e.g., 30, 60, 100, 300). This is so because the desire is for the result to end with nothing.

The reason the Dhikr is so effective is that the long vowel sounds of the words *La ilāha illā Llāhū* are primarily resonating in the heart, causing a tremendous dissemination of divine attributes in a very short time. Moreover, the breath is compressed and condensed in a manner that generates a high degree of heat, which itself burns out many physical impurities in the body. It is common to see dervishes drenched in sweat at the conclusion of the ceremony.

I once attended a Dhikr in the northern part of Afghanistan. About forty men were present. This particular Sufi order had conducted Dhikr ceremonies every Thursday evening for almost 1,200 years without one interruption.

As we were seated and beginning the initial recitations, the shaykh paused for a few seconds, and a loud grinding and shooshing sound roared through the adobe room. As I looked up, I perceived that a cleft had appeared in the far wall of the room, which sealed up in an instant. Later, at the end of the Dhikr, the shaykh spent almost an hour reciting "*Salāms*" of greeting to all of the pious souls who had slipped in through that cleft.

I have seen many serious diseases driven out from those who sat among the circle of Dhikr—and those people attempted no other treatment. The nature of Allah is not one of limitations or sickness, and one who fills the mind and heart with thought and consciousness of Allah will find that all things other than Allah are vanquished. When one arrives at the state of performance of Dhikr with sincerity, one is at the famous stage when knowledge gleaned from books is of no further use. Allowed to flourish and unfold, the Dhikr leads one, as He may decide, to the highest stages of human evolution, and one gains access to the origin of miracles.[4]

The *Sufi Book* contains several consecutive illustrations of a young dhikr suppliant, wearing a simple turban and beard, going through the turns of the head that one should perform while saying the *La ilāha illā Llāhū*, ending with the head bowed forward in humility and then raised. This circle of poor people sitting in their adobe room, totally devoted, engaged in a religion that has been associated with rulers and tyrants, causes one to draw back in awe. It is the true circle of love, no different from the Holiness church in that respect, patient and self-abnegating, a circle of people knowing just a little bit about the nature of spirituality. It puts one in mind of the old Christian Jansenists and their self-abnegation, their endless words of worship, and their lives of bliss, with miracles rising around them unceasingly; or perhaps of the Quakers in their heyday, each struck by the spirit on frequent occasions, with a kind of egalitarian holiness, bowing to the holiness in each other. The relationship of the Sufis to one another is communitas, Victor Turner's word for love between many, a form of the "social" not often described in anthropology. As he described it, this love is of a different order from the "social" implied in, for example, the "socializing" that children are supposed to receive. One is aware of this different social sense, communitas, in liminal situations, in times of change and creativity, and during sacred events. One can recognize these differences as religious. Communitas is in no way society governed. Government and opinion are never in the picture of communitas. The following pairs of terms represent the differences:

Humility (the Muslim word being *submission*), compared with pride.
Equality, compared with inequality.
Absence of property, compared with having possessions.
Disregard for personal appearance, compared with signs of wealth.
Transition, compared with state.

Much prayer to the spirit, compared with business speech.
Totality, compared with partisanship.
Sacredness, compared with secularity.
Simplicity, as opposed to complexity.[5]

The marvelous beneficence of communitas comes into many of the doings of our own society, markedly in the joining of voices, or when the players of instruments "get in the groove," or in great disasters when all the public is at one in giving help, or at those times when the scene suddenly lifts—the wall opens, as it were—and revelation occurs.

For the last story of all, at the end of this series of stories, I present a ritual of healing from our early fieldwork in which the power of communitas was paramount. The story starts with a notable ongoing feud between an able man who was a sorcerer and the village respectables. Vic liked the sorcerer personally. He liked him better than the others.

THE RAIN GOD AND COMMUNITAS: THE HEALING OF THE SORCERER'S WIFE

Let us look with emotional sympathy at the story of the sorcerer and his wife, Zuliyana, set in the time I was doing fieldwork in Zambia in the 1950s. Samutamba was a man who had real charisma. Way back in the past he began to exploit the attraction of his own particular personality. He was handsome, with a kind of thrawn Humphrey Bogart or Han Solo charm, a propensity to grin and to show a bit of extra power, to fix things for his friends, to rollick around and get things done. As several decades passed he became accustomed to using these gifts for the sake of power. Anything but a shy man, he was ebullient, a leader. He went to the Copperbelt and got a job, succeeded, and enjoyed his beer. Anything went, on the Copperbelt, so he took up with a woman he did not know. Then he found he had developed gonorrhea, a disease of yellow pus in the semen. He must have endured this trouble for thirty years. He came home after a decade on the Copperbelt, now well experienced in the white man's world, and at Mwinilunga township walked into the chief road man's job, called *capitaõ*. He married two wives from his local major lineage, one of whom was linked to the power structure of the village of Kajima. She was the headman's daughter. Samutamba, whom we ourselves loved and in whom, somehow, we felt no evil, used to get drunk and bad-mouth the whole village. The most human of Ndembu, he was the worst. He killed by witchcraft, by the power of his anger. I know this is possible. I have been ill through people's anger, and have myself caused bad things to happen by my own anger, which I truly regret. It should be stated that these contradictory feelings were the facts of our relationship with Samutamba, for better or for worse, a mystery in the tangle of morality and love.

The Africans said Samutamba bewitched his favorite aunt to death, so they drove him out of the village. The shouting must have been terrible—the gathering of men, the positive danger from blows and thrown weapons. He must have rushed home and grabbed his hunting gun, his ax, his knife, and one or two oddments—medicine horns, it was thought—in a shoulder basket. He went raging north up the road to the trading chief at Ikeleng'e.

Nevertheless, the village performed a reconciliation for Samutamba. I now find the reconciliation episode much more interesting than I did formerly. The dead aunt was now an ancestor spirit; she had been a good woman. Her name, Nyamwaha, literally meant "good woman"—just that. What the people felt was this: that the spirit of this dead person, Nyamwaha, wanted to "come out" in another person. So people watched for it. Whoever felt that something of the kind was going on inside them was beginning to take notice. It was close to the idea of reincarnation; it was the metempsychosis of a spirit into an already living adult person. The Ndembu called it "inheriting the name" or "becoming the dead person," *ku-swanika ijina.*

It was my dear spiritually minded friend Manyosa, the daughter of Nyamwaha, who was affected by this compelling spirit. Manyosa felt that her mother was near, asking again and again for her spirit to be taken into the younger living body of her daughter. Now, much later, I can see the contrast with the earlier interpretation made by Victor and myself, which was that the ritual was merely a renaming. Much later I realized from more careful study of the fieldnotes and my own various experiences of the dead that the Africans were right about these intimations: one can indeed sense the ancestors around us. Back in the 1950s, even without much insight at that era, when I saw the ritual of naming I particularly saw its beauty. Its main physical feature was a section of a tree sapling planted as a shrine, its bark stripped at the top like a circumcised penis, glistening white, its wood running with clear sap like semen or like tears; while the two principal women, Manyosa and her cousin Yana, sat near the shrine-tree wearing white cloth headbands. Drumming and a keening chant broke forth; then the medicine man poured white maize beer on the ground at the foot of the planted tree in honor of the spirits. This

Bringing back the spirit of one of the sorcerer's victims.

kind of tree was the ancestor tree itself, able to quicken and send out shoots when planted, even though it had been brutally cut off at both ends. *Muyombu* was its name, a holy thing that one might call the "tear tree" because it wept.

Now that the songs had called the spirit, the two women drank the white beer and were sprinkled with medicine; and forthwith the spirit jumped over from the ancestor into them. In a few weeks the muyombu sprouted. The tree was Nyamwaha-Manyosa-Yana.

All felt happier, even though Samutamba was absent and not able to be the principal figure in the rite. Nyamwaha was now back with them, empowering the fertility of the village, spreading goodness as when she was alive. Vic and I wrote down notes on the rite as an ethnographic exercise of close observation, and we were never able to forget it. However, it took me forty-eight years to even partially understand it.

The story of Samutamba did not come to an end after the name inheritance but continued in a way typical of him. He was back in the village, and trouble began again. It was to do with Samutamba's wife Zuliyana, the daughter of the headman. The worst effect of being abandoned by the ancestors is sterility, and Zuliyana was not giving birth. Samutamba could not give healthy semen because of his gonorrhea, and that only made him drink more. Both Zuliyana and her mother, Nyamukola, the headman's wife, were in deep misfortune, Zuliyana because of childlessness, and Nyamukola from leprosy. It was December, the time of high storms, terrible heat, and malaria-inducing chills. Bad times had come again. In the swamp-like miasma of the people's depression, could anyone find hope?

At night we could hear Samutamba's bellowing voice cursing the village because of his sterility, "*Wa-a-a-anza wey-ey-yi!* DIRT under your foreskin!"

The story of Samutamba portrayed a people on its own path—the Ndembu in their own saga, a saga we should treat with deepest sympathy. This was no mere story, but their own pitifully destined path, down from conflict, from anomaly, from the rift in the system that arose between descent through a woman and marriage in the husband's house, down, down, down, step by step.

It was *their* path. For Samutamba it was a helpless social fall, fate itself, becoming transformed into a dreaded path, down to the terrors that form when many things go wrong, caused by who knows what witchcraft and what disgust and abandonment by the ancestors. One may well ask, "What spirit was it in reality that finally took up Kajima Village in its misery and fears and set it going once more to perform the ancient healing ritual of Chihamba, a word taken from *ku-hambwisha*, the defecating of a baby?" The name was enough to make you laugh. But in this service to the spirit, the village was to venture along a woodland path to the *isoli* revelation shrine of the thunder god himself. There, the villagers were going to have to "kill" the thunder god to reverse the whole process of degradation, for this is what he himself, the thunder god, commanded them to do.

There were medicine men living in the vicinity whose job it was to lay an ear to the people's troubles, not as a doctor might begin to combat measles, but more like the way the prophets in the Old Testament received messages from their spiritual entity and started listening to the people floundering in their mess, finally leading them out of it. The growth of healing would be for everyone, in this case a kind of simultaneous stirring by those of the Kajima lineage who had been given spirit help before, by the spirit master Lambakasa, Itota the beeman, and a diviner from far away, all of whom were gifted to hear the spirits plainly. The villagers met with the diviner and asked him to toss the objects in his basket so that he could read in them the spirit's instructions. The diviner said, "Go to Chihamba. Go to the Grandfather, the Storm. He will help you."

So the greatest of the Ndembu rituals was set afoot, with Vic and me like little mirrored buzz flies with cameras, hovering around everywhere and taking things in. Additional patients volunteered from the outlying villages. I lined up among the patients, and Vic joined the medicine men. The rituals began.

The old beeman and mead-maker, Itota, a hunter with a deep gravelly voice, had always been the central personage of the ritual. When the rites began, we saw that a curious identification with him and the Grandfather seemed to flash into being, for Itota was a shaman. Then the power that was afoot everywhere would take over the white-haired old man and narrow him into the lightning flash, and the same power would contrive, along with the medicine men, to bring everyone together into the presence of the Grandfather. The Grandfather's own name, Storm, from ancient times must never be told to the patients.

Throughout the village the cult revived quickly, and its message soon became known: "Never despair." The ritual the god desired was a four-day stratagem that combined an initiation, a revelation, a sacrifice, a healing rite, and, after the killing, a rebirth. Quickly, Samutamba came to see Vic, wearing his road captain's fez and military shirt, and the frown of sorcery power was in his eye.

"I'd have you know I'm the principal doctor," he told Vic. He bustled out into the rain to take control. Vic and I followed at a discreet distance and found a noisy group of doctors gesticulating in front of Nyamukola's hut. Samutamba's voice had a cantankerous edge. It appeared he intended to run Chihamba like a shaking ceremony, in which the patient goes into a trance.

"But Samutamba, there's the chasing, the Voice, and . . ."

"It's a night drum, ninnies." His arm sawed up and down. "You're not going to drag in that old crap about the Grandfather, are you?"

Lambakasa pushed to the fore, his face glittering with serious intent. "The diviner gave us the words. 'Seek the Grandfather,'" he said, "and he is found with Chihamba. That cannot be modern, don't you understand? Look, my friend, we're making this drum ritual for Zuliyana and her mother, Nyamukola. We know how to cure them."

Samutamba's brow lowered. "Zuliyana's my wife, not yours. I ought to know what's best for her."

Samutamba preferred the trance ritual for Zuliyana, for by its means a woman could become an important doctor, especially if she were childless. Samutamba tried to avoid the true shit ritual, which demeaned a person and then blessed, whose principal medicine was from the tree of the "revelation of secret things." Samutamba did not want too many secrets revealed. He was an individualist and liked to plan his own life.

"Samutamba." Lambakasa's voice was low. "Come over here a moment. Now we all know what the trouble is. Come to Chihamba with us. Strange things can happen, for Grandfather has many powers. How can you be expected to remember him? You were only a small boy when you were caught by him the first time."

Truth was written all over Lambakasa's shining face. Samutamba felt his shoulders relax, and a longing for the wild bush come over him, a memory before the days of road making. He gazed at the trees. A force seemed to draw him into the bush, seducing his will.

"I'll come," he said, "but I'll be doctor—"

"You can be doctor in charge of candidates, okay," they told him, and they got on with the job of assigning positions. There were many positions and many patients. The two principal patients, Zuliyana and Nyamukola, would undergo primary initiation. I myself went to join the party of patients, and was immediately included in their growing comradely feeling. My friend Manyosa smiled at the thoughtful expression on my face.

"What's this? You're a patient now, are you, Edie?"

"Yes." I had a reason. "Are you one, too?"

"No, no. I entered the cult a long time ago. I'm in an advanced grade now. But you and I can be friends of the bosom, *mabwambu*, the way people pair up in Chihamba."

"Sure." I started to give her an enthusiastic handshake.

"Wait a minute. Don't do that. I'll teach you the special handshake for Chihamba. You have to remember to put the power, *ngovu*, into it." She seized my hand and pulled. "Pull back," she told me. There was quite a tussle before we let go. "That's right. It gives power to Chihamba."

Old Nyaluwema, the doctor of medicines, provided each of us candidates with a new African rattle with a carved handle. This was the special musical instrument of Chihamba. We played it that day while singing around the fire, when Nyaluwema washed us with her herbal medicine and especially when we heard the terrible hoarse sound of the Grandfather, who was at the same time the one with the gravelly voice.

Early next morning Nyaluwema came to our hut door with a rhythmic rattling. "Cho-kokoko choko-o!" she cried. It was the sound of a rooster's crow. As we put out our heads, Nyaluwema scattered red rooster's feathers all over us.

"Hey, steady, Nyaluwema," we spluttered, picking feathers out of the corners of our mouths. She led us into the woods where the group of patients was collecting. The forest was alive with movement and the shrieks of children. It appeared that the doctors were out catching additional patients.

Two small boys, Samuwika and my Bobby, skipped down the trail leading to the stream.

"A doctor," warned Samuwika, and they scuttled into the bushes. They watched as an elder went by. Strange; he was advancing backward through the forest dragging a red rooster along the ground between his legs. After him followed a line of doctors.

"Sho, sho, sho-sho-o!" came a rasping shout. They had been observed. A man came crashing through the bush.

"Aka-ah!" cried Samuwika. The doctor had him by the hair and grabbed Bobby with his other hand. Samuwika and Bobby were laughing so much they were caught and included with the patients.

The doctors lined up our group to the sound of rattles and harmonized singing, then to our surprise they turned each one around facing home and set us walking backward into the bush, away from home. What we were walking toward no one rightly knew. Suddenly, at an arbitrary signal, the doctors shouted and chased us back to the village. Without a pause they came at us and chased us into the forest again, where we once more performed our backward walk. That took us just a little further. And so it went for twelve hours, further and further in each time, and always out again, while the rain poured down. We were bored, patient, delighted, giggling, and horrified by turns. The older patients sang themselves hoarse. Nevertheless, at every backward approach we were drawing nearer to our goal.

We watched as the doctors caught Spider, the government odd-job man, and put him in the line. The others broke out trilling with delight because Spider had shown disrespect for the people's celebration.

I sighed and went back into the line, ready for more. Running with the others to and fro, I wondered, "Is this some kind of profound loosening-up, an experience we have to go through, like girl's initiation?"

I was becoming so accustomed to finding my place in the line that toward the end the chasing did not seem to matter. What mattered was that at every backward approach, the group drew nearer its goal. The wonder that was growing inside of me was reflected in the eyes of my companions. No one spoke; we were restive, but the doctors made us sit down in the line, where I now felt at home, with Yana in front and Masondi behind.

Suddenly, at the back end of the line, deepest into the forest, Nyamukola, the mother of Zuliyana, stopped. She had been very patient but now found that she could go no further. There was an obstruction. We peeped around and saw a high jumble of twigs closing off our path. "The hedge of mystery, *chipangu*," murmured Nyamukola. "To hide the *isoli*, the revelation."

I held my breath. I could see down the line the shoulders pant, though the heads were still; through the silence nothing could be heard but the dim rolling of the thunder. Rain began to pour again, and now the doctors came up behind us, fierce and relentless, and drove us back to the village. Then immediately they drove us out of it again to the hedge of mystery. We did not know where Vic and the other doctors had gone.

The hour had come. The doctors marshaled us facing the hedge. Nyamukola was in front, full of forgetful happiness. Zuliyana came next, very beautiful with her swaying body, yearning to bear children. Then Yana, of the women's troubles. I followed, restlessly peering; then Masondi, suffering from a burn; and all the others. Manyosa and Samutamba stood beside us as our teachers.

"Keep still," they said.

Suddenly the hoarse voice we all knew was heard.

"What's this rabble doing here?"

"We've come to do our shit ritual, sir."

A crack of thunder sounded. We crept forward. There was a gap in the hedge. Beyond it glimmered something white. It moved. There was a hubbub of sound—music, drums, a keening harmony, syncopation, and we could see something risen up from the ground, dazzling in its whiteness in the dim forest light. Ah, it was the *Isoli*, the Sighting, something unexpected, quite strange. It was moving back and forth, dancing to the off-beat rhythm, a round dome rising from the earth, vibrating voluptuously to the rhythm of the drums, filling our eyes with whiteness.

"It is the spirit! *Diyi mukishi*. It is the Grandfather," chanted Lambakasa the medicine man beside us, sussurating loud on his two-chambered rattle.

I knew we had reached the crossing point. Zuliyana's eyes were a marvel. All our toes were twitching with the rhythm—we trembled and sang as the drums tore out sound. The ancient one seemed about to break loose in the rising syncopation of his dance and walk all over his grandchildren. The aggressive rhythm surged through us and I was muttering, "You're great, you're great."

Each patient in turn went forward, crouched to the ground, and hailed him, "*Karombo vrai*, Chief!" and the women milked their naked breasts before him. Even I felt my breasts tingle and harden. I did not understand why until much later.

But it was time for the killing: it had to be done.

Lambakasa placed the rattle in Nyamukola's hand. "Strike," he said. "You must kill your Grandfather."

She looked at him with fear and awe.

"Go on. Kill him."

She took the rattle by the handle and, with the butt down, struck hard on the white solid object before her; and so did all of us, in turn, setting our teeth and giving mallet blows fit to crack a skull. Thereupon a huge convulsion shook the thing, and it stilled, its ribs gradually caving in. There was silence.

"You have killed the Grandfather," chanted Lambakasa.

The fact sank in right down the line, faces were amazed; all of us smiled—we smiled. This was the revelation; we got it.

But how? I had only just learned to love the Grandfather when I had to kill him. Somehow the blow seemed to cause things to jump a notch. I knew I had a foolish grin on my face. Every one of us came alight—we were full of glee, in fact we were all goggling with happiness. Why was this? Why? It was this. We had set the spirit free from what was a white cloth with a wooden mortar underneath, and the spirit was with us. "Now all of you are innocent," came the words of Lambakasa. We had performed a sacrifice in fear and humility, and somehow we had been released from our troubles.

I did not have time to puzzle about it, for the finale was coming. Everyone rose and formed a triumphal procession. We saw that it was evening, for the pale orange light was seen half around the earth, far between the trees. We set off walking on the long trail back home; everyone was smiling like a brother, like a mother, like a sweetheart. The narrow path was broad, somehow; everyone walked abreast, cheerfully strolling. Manyosa and I were together, friends of the bosom, Vic and Samutamba also, all the others in company with their bosom friends, two by two. All our heads were held high and we sang. It is a fact that I have never been so happy before or since. We had come down the woodland path, *njila*. In Chindembu, *chinjila* means holiness. We were innocent and free.

Back at the central fire, Lambakasa picked up a firebrand and struck it on the ground. He shouted, "It's done!"

Vic and I talked for a long time that night. "There are all sorts of puzzles in this . . . performance," I said. "To begin with, why weren't we told his name?"

"It's not just an Ndembu problem, Edie. It's a common one throughout the world. They're trying to express what can't be named, and can't be thought of rationally. Artists and poets try to break into that domain; they try to express it by various strange means."

"It's the same 'it,'" I said. "But you never actually see it."

"No. It's like Yahweh. When you open the ark of the covenant it's empty."

"And when we strike the Grandfather—the point of destruction—that's the crossing place. I love that. The Grandfather wants us to go up as far as we can to the spirit with those contraptions; we use all those odd means, as you say. The spirit comes close and listens to this material fabric they've got ready for him; how can he resist it when it roars and grunts and twitches? It *is* him. He takes it over and just coalesces with it."

"Yes," said Vic, "and they immediately sacrifice him. That's what he wants. We can't grasp this."

"No. Zuliyana was dumbfounded. I'm dumbfounded."

"Grandfather Storm is formless energy," said Vic, sitting up. "like the lightning flash. He keeps everything going, the crops in the field, the people and their interactions. . . ."

"Yet he's a person."

"Yes. It's strange how important that is. He's unpredictable. He threatens. Frightens people. And then gives people benefits. It's just the opposite of reasonable behavior. It's . . . antistructure. You have to be loosened up to understand him."

The next day, each patient was going to be given her own shrine. The medicine people collected many leafy branches from their favorite herb trees and made them up into bundles, one for each patient. In the middle of each bundle was a live cutting from a cassava plant, a stick that would actually sprout. The whole was called, literally, a "thought bundle," *kantonga*. They planted one of the bundles in the ground before Nyamukola's hut door, and sowed around it a scatter of bean and corn seeds, making a little shrine. They made a similar shrine in front of our own hut door, for us. When Zuliyana's shrine was finished and the doctors had gone away, Samutamba squatted brooding by the little construction. The exuberantly leafy column of the thought bundle stared him in the face while he pondered.

In a couple of weeks the thought bundles were alive with bean shoots, and big hand-shaped fronds projected from the top of the cassava cuttings. They had taken root. Moreover, their healing power was beginning to take effect. Shortly after the ritual Nyamukola forgot her previous reaction to the idea of hospital and found the courage to go to the leprosy sanitarium in the capital city, where she was easily cured. The second was Yana's healing. She looked rested, and her period pains entirely vanished. What was really strange was that when I came to change the dressing on Masondi's burn and lifted off the gauze, time seemed to have jumped. There was nothing but a healthy scar. Zuliyana seemed happy enough to wait indefinitely; Samutamba was busy repairing road drains, so she had peace.

In the village, people once again laughed at jokes. Now was the time to wind up Chihamba and switch back to normal life. The Thunder Friends gathered in a circle around Nyamukola's thought bundle, and Lambakasa gave everyone a cassava food pellet. Vic and I watched Lambakasa's face for a signal.

"Yipu!" he said, and we all flung our pellets into the shrine and burst into laughter. The ground was whitened with pellets. Our band of Thunder Friends went off to bathe, we cut our hair, put on our best clothes, and gathered for a beer party. Chihamba was over.

Two more things happened after a long interval. One was the birth of Zuliyana's two sons by Samutamba, fine boys whom I met as teenagers thirty years later. Zuliyana told me that Samutamba never did take clinic medicine for his gonorrhea; the disease simply left him after the Grandfather ritual. The other was my own healing. My request had been for the healing of my uncertainty and self-deprecation, a trouble as nagging as stomach ulcers. Again, it took decades, but in the end old Grandfather came through and gave me the cure for those troubles of the soul. Furthermore, my secret desire for more children was fulfilled. A decade after the ritual, I gave birth to a couple more babies. Often, during those early days of motherhood and breast-feeding, when I regarded the determined chin of the elder and stroked the wafting auburn hair of the younger I recalled the savagery and power of the Grandfather.

"Babyshitters! Bring me my love beans, and I shall heal you." In return we had killed him.

COMMENTS

Vic tried to explain this ritual in three books, and I tried in one.[6] I do not think we have gotten near to it. We could see that Grandfather was a person-spirit, and yet, as Vic said, he was formless energy. The energy-power-spirit conundrum has dogged us all through this book. With which of these entities are we dealing at different times? However, it is here in Chihamba where one can see the change from one to the other, after the killing of the Grandfather. The Grandfather's spirit, after being released from those blows of wood on wood, rayed out to all of us. This was palpable, and was rather like the blessing of a spurting, milk-laden human breast coming out in multiple sprays, just as in the style of blessing the women had given him. Here we are not talking about symbolism but about some real actions and a strong experience of extraordinary happiness.

The Grandfather made himself known as soon as we began Chihamba; he was using the hoarse voice of the old beeman, and he was a person. He loved tenderly cooked red beans. At the culmination of that crazy forest scene, we came to know that the way he would heal us was through our killing him. The healing process was turning back onto itself, and the Grandfather, to our surprise, was telling us to prevent the very thing we wanted, telling us to kill him. We never thought about it but just went and did it. It was just as if we had released the catch on a treasure box, or scratched open an egg whose chick could not get out.

During later years I came across many examples of the ritual destruction of sacred objects: meticulously created sand paintings (Native American and Buddhist), the Native American potlatch, the Bemba African destruction of a huge clay serpent during girls' initiation, and others. The desire of the caribou or seal in the Arctic to come to a virtuous hunter and lay down its life is similar. The spirit of the animal can then endow the human hunter with spiritual power. And so it goes.

Thus, as we saw the strange white mound in the woods shudder and die, the character of the event dissolved—like some movie scene into another scene—into a different state of affairs. The effect migrated into the people and also into the growing plants, the cassava, the corn seedlings, and the beans. This thing—so-called formless energy—was now with us, and since then has hardly ever left us. What we had seen was a close-up view of the change that can happen between a personal spirit and energy and power. People catch a glimpse of this change from time to time.

Back before 1953, how could I know that the Africans were right and did heal? These were "pagans," "animists." No one in the West believed in African animism, no one. Yet as our fieldwork progressed, as the scene in Africa rose for us more and more, in ritual after ritual, I realized not only that I had escaped the old cruel hypocrisies that had gotten into Christianity, but also that even the positivist "means-of-production" determinism of Marxism was falling behind—we had eaten it up, it was a thing of the past.

CONCLUDING OBSERVATIONS: COMMUNITAS

At last we have in front of us Dhikr and Chihamba, two major examples of communitas that show it in action, and we will be able to recognize its workings in those rituals, such as the themes of equality and comradeship. The word *communitas* originally came from Paul Goodman in the 1960s. Then, Goodman was using it in his suggestions for planning towns on community lines. Vic Turner adapted the word for the friendship found in Chihamba and among Ndembu teenagers who were initiated together. He saw it as a relationship of full, unmediated communication between people, and he saw that it could arise spontaneously in all kinds of groups, situations, and circumstances.[7]

Vic had experienced this thing many times, in work gangs in the army, in sport, and in various endeavors, before ever he realized quite what it was. He and I both became conscious of it as a pleasure in Chihamba; and, indeed, it can arise anywhere, for example, between patients going through the same troubles or old people laughing about their disabilities. It is classically found among novices changing from childhood to adulthood; it is also, in our time, found in band groups started by teenagers for the pleasure of it. Teenagers tell me that being in a band is an initiation for them—they now have a reason to live, and they can become adult. These teenage years are the betwixt-and-between years of liminality, when much change goes on. Communitas cannot be imposed on groups from the authorities above, because it defies deliberate planning and purely intellectual understanding.[8]

People feel their joining in communitas as something going on in its own right, and even as hard to describe. All are equal, the experience is right here on the spot, and everyone is a full person and a friend. And they remember such occasions because the communitas is so palpable. Communitas strains toward including everybody in the world; it does not take sides.

Communitas, like our own biology, is not a specialized gift. It remains open and unspecialized, a spring of pure possibility. It has something magical about it. Those who experience communitas feel the presence of spiritual power, and it comes unexpectedly like the wind and warms everyone to each other. It can arise when people hold to negative capability, that is, a sense of openness to each other, of readiness and sensitivity without preconceived ideas. There exists a democracy and humility about communitas: no one can claim it as their own. In the group, what is sought and what can happen is unity, seamless unity, so that even joshing is cause for delight and there is often much laughter.

The benefits of communitas are joy, healing, mutual help, collective religious experience, long-term ties with others, a humanistic conscience, and the human rights ideal. Communitas is found in the rituals of preindustrial cultures and also in the humbler churches, temples, mosques, and shrines all over the world, existing, consciously or unconsciously, in collective prayer and music. Pentecostal and Charismatic churches seek and find those moments of universal love, praying for the sick. Such a sense grows between pilgrims, especially when they come in sight of their goal. Sufi brotherhoods in India, Pakistan, and Afghanistan, in their intense, collective, and submissive chants to Allah, find that sense of unity. It is very real in Jewish funerals. Communitas is sought in the world of sport and Olympic games, where the finely tuned human body is the common factor, an achievement democratically possible for all humankind. But the communitas spirit is not always present.

The implications follow that if one responds to communitas, one can no longer treat another human being as an object, because each soul is too much part of other people's souls. We find ourselves, as in the Copernican revolution, smaller than we thought, even on a par with the animals and not above them. We exist in a vast interchange of spirit personality—often glimpsed, sometimes seen clearly in the acts of spirit sociality. The social itself can become a matter of intuitions passed between people and a joyous sense of bonding, sometimes providing the power of collective healing and of acting in visionary harmony.

CHAPTER 7

——— ✠ ———

Patterns of Healing

Stories of healing have indeed been the basis of this book. Now at this vantage point one may discern how spiritual experiences can be distinguished from energy experiences. Once I made a shaman journey. I found myself on a high cloud speaking with a monk. For some reason he showed me a large TV set on a wall. In the TV was a picture of animal internal organs—a quite unexpected sight. However, four months later during new fieldwork, I witnessed with my own eyes the actual internal organs of a seal. They were what I had seen on the TV. The same. It was curious. Now, I would not have called those organs in the TV picture *energy*; they had form and definition, oddly elongated and dark red. On another occasion I saw in a waking dream the face of my Iñupiat shaman friend, Tigluk, alive, on a bone mask. But why? Then I saw Tigluk himself, by coincidence, a few minutes afterwards, and he was also laughing. I would not term that laughing mask face *energy*; it was not in the least abstract. The old-fashioned term *spirit manifestation* was a truer description. What I had seen in both instances was a purposeful visitation of a discernable form, connected with some mysterious consciousness intent on communicating something to me, and claiming importance in my life.

Healing is felt to be central at the depth of human consciousness—at the depth of its human pole; and healing can happen just there, where the consciousness latches onto the conscious spirits and powers that dwell around and through a person. Along with creating a new life, healing is the best physical act a human being can do. As I have said, broadly speaking, acts of religion are what people most love and respect, and of all religious acts, healing is the most is earnestly desired—and that desire has led humanity to explore the fruitful paths to healing. Those paths open before the hopeful healers, not merely in practical ways such as in their training, but they also open of themselves when a new healer is first wandering bewildered. Those first paths showed them the mystic way, just as the paths opened in the wilds for Bhirendra and in their own way for Roy Willis, Umigluk, and Muchona. The healers took the paths offered and came through to that most strange other world, the other state of consciousness. Because healers found the healing that best applied to their own people in the various cultures of the world, each society cherishes to its heart its own secret healing gift, and very often, as among the Iñupiat, healing—*healing*—is said to be what expresses the people most. "What do we Iñupiat people have that's most important to us? What is really, really *Iñupiat?*"—it is healing. The Chinese will say Tai Chi and acupuncture. And the Swedes, the sauna. And the Africans, *ngoma*, the drum. *Ngoma* always means a healing ritual. As for Christians who read the New Testament, it is the healing events they really love, though the priests say that that is not what Christianity is all about. But the people themselves know that healing is "this-worldly," "human-friendly," beloved. No one goes to war about it. No one deprives anybody of it as a punishment. When people experience this kind of power, they have a sense that it exists all the time, that it is part and parcel of the whole universe.

So powers of mystical participation, the creative winds, are working through humankind, and humans perceive their trail, sense the connections like threads that easily leap the gaps between souls. Claire could feel with her hands through the skin of the sufferer what that person was feeling; she was connected. Thérèse O'Mahony felt through to the trouble with her hands. Something like an electric current was connecting her healing hands to the painful back. Messages fly back and forth. The Maori who is in connection with his people can restore the connection to someone in spiritual shock just by his human touch. Even the stalking lines of chi, awakened in the body by needles and growing out from point to point along a limb, show the location of major threads of power, the energy lines, the ineffable chi. The lines can be felt. Furthermore, we have mentioned the existence of an orbit or aura around the body that can be felt, extending about four inches out. It is echoed as in a rainbow by a further orbit about six feet out, detectible with divining rods. This whole psychic field is permeable to other people's auras; the

auras are all the time in connection with each other—mostly unconsciously. Busy people in a house or building will not stop to analyze their
impressions of everybody they are with, but the soul-signals from those
others register on that curious brain-soul that can do far more than is
generally thought. Moreno saw this organ as interwoven with the psyches of others; and Jung had a telling vision of us all dwelling in a collective unconscious that we can sometimes access for marvelous
purposes—such as building a cathedral or a new grand shrine of everything that is Native American, a staggeringly beautiful building that has
actually appeared on the Washington Mall.[1]

The psyche, the field, then, spreads and connects in a vast collective
unconscious that can well be actually conscious. Through this gossamer-
thin and almost imperceptible medium, healing can pass, just as the air
carries voices and music. Love travels on these roads too, such as Sachin's
love for his guru and the guru for him; this is how the Sufi Dhikr men
felt their astonishing unity, and teenage American students become
awakened to the mysteries of communitas at the moment when their
band music reaches the zone—and then they know what their biology
was made for, spiritual communion.

A singularly recognizable phenomenon is that of the "opening." It occurs repeatedly in the stories. My own vivid sense of the climax in
Ihamba, when I felt that the healing was being "born" and everything
suddenly became all right—was an "opening" phenomenon. The opening also flared into existence at the end of Chihamba, when a spirit transfer took place from out of a dancing string-and-sticks-and-cloth
contraption and was caught in the act of migrating into all of us, and this
was after we had struck it with our rattles. Megan, the acupuncture patient, described being under the needles like this: "Something is lifting
up and up out of my body and I begin to feel very light, although my
mind is somewhat shaken by the experience." The opening can come in
trance, as Friedson found among the Tumbuka, the sense of equiprimordiality—a long word meaning that everything was, is, and evermore shall
be: that is, equal to the primordial. Friedson, who experienced it, put it
like this: "The body space feels strangely elastic, with the front part of
one's body/spirit stretching outward and upward. The energy of the
vimbuza spirit causes one's 'self' to expand, creating a space within one,
an opening, a clearing. Along with the expansion of one's body, one feels
a tremendous exhilaration."

The suburban American patient expressed it well: "It feels like a total
surrender, a total letting go, a total opening, a heightened degree of

awareness of every cell of your body, and a connectedness between your body and your mind and your spirituality, an incredible, incredible connectedness there. Just wonderful! You know a healing has occurred because there's a freeing in your body and your mind. There's more space. There's more energy. And your mind has let go of whatever it was you were tenaciously clinging to. That's the only way I can describe it. I mean, I just know." Bhirendra the Nepali achieved a breakthrough at last when he had a vision of Ghesar Gyalpo, the god of the shamans, at the head of the great staircase. Muchona of the Ndembu described how he felt the opening up at the moment of release from his illness: "All was opened now that the rooster was killed. The openings of my body that had been stopped up, my nostrils, ears, and eyes, were released and became supersensitive. I obtained wakefulness and heightened sensitivity, necessary for a diviner who would seek out hidden things. I was extraordinarily happy." The humble saints of the Dhikr prayer saw the wall open and imprisoned souls emerge. The way spirits work includes this phenomenon—the opening, or revealing, or release.

An opening? Where from, and where to? Victor Turner spoke of the limen, the threshold, the doorway, telling of a deep sense of difference between the mundane world and a sacred, liminal time.[2] A person is often aware of the change-over. Entering a sacred place causes one to take a deep breath. There is a point at which the change takes place, the entrance point. So with the opening experiences I have related. Our friends in the various experiences tell it straight: there is an opening. Some anthropologists have gone through it. Many more stories like this exist, and this book will elicit many as-yet-untold stories from the readers.

The experiences of the many healers in this book are spontaneous and immediate. The fact that the cases cited are drawn from such a variety of cultures shows that every religious form is capable of producing a perfect, innocent, real, and coherent mystical experience. They can all do it. Thus, no one religion has the monopoly of God or spirituality—which is a sobering thought. Nonmedical healing has tended to remain among nonofficial levels of society, part of the people's second life, as Mikhail Bakhtin would have said. The craft survives well, and at the same time it does not seem amenable to regulation and mass production.

In this book I have been endeavoring to return the ownership of religion to the ordinary people, away from its expropriation by philosophers and its mutation into theologies, abstractions, generalizations, flights of holiness, and the kind of rule-bound moral teachings found in holiness books. Here instead we have Kinachau tripping and falling into trance; we have Singleton hot and bothered because the spirit will not come. We have Thérèse all of a shiver and happy, having just done a healing; we have the humble Sachin, his eyes shining with his vision of light. These are people you and I might have known—the boy Bhirendra scared to death—the tales go on and on. I remember my friend Irimoto coming to a halt by a lamppost in the main street of Sapporo, just past the gambling halls, telling me—telling me—it began about his dad who came back to him after he had died, and this was Irimoto speaking, the Japanese rationalist. He went on to write a wonderful book about the spirituality of the Russian far east. So many have the experience. I have asked you to meet these people and honor them as I honor them, and I hope that our *communitas* will flood out and obliterate all the differences—those of "station of life," those that are nothing but petty quibbles, and all the other messy points of difference long ingrained in the great religions.

I have found that this can be done through the understanding of healing—maybe only that way, as the good Chishti said. Allah *does* recognize healing. I am immensely relieved by that. And it can be done by the telling of a story, as the Dene Tha of northern Alberta,[3] the Apache,[4] the Hasidim, and many other peoples have said.

The reader may still be trying to make a single philosophical system out of these stories. But the stories are too down-to-earth to be transmuted into something abstract. They are too particular: "general forms have their vitality in particulars, and every particular is a human being. And that human being is spirit"—to slightly paraphrase William Blake in *Jerusalem*.[5] Yet, through recognition, the innate sharing of nonverbal knowledge, the reader is able to catch at the hints that come up, then actually grasp what has happened in an event of healing. This is how religion tends to be conveyed, by recognition, not, when it comes to practicalities, by a mass of inert definitions and generalizations.

The book has been doing certain things: it has been giving credit to healing experiences as true, centering on accounts in the context of a variety of religions or sects of religions; it has been favoring a particular type of story, deliberately selecting those that have managed to surface as running events—live experiences of ordinary people, happening at a particular time and in a particular place; and it has been giving readers the "I was there" sense and thus including them in the experience. I have been taking special note of all bodily responses, cold chills, shivering, shaking, and falling down, regarding these phenomena as biological salutes to the divine and signs of oneness and grace, and of highest value as acts of religion; I have been particularly marking the experience of great heat, or a sudden clearing of the eyes, or the sensing of music as sacred, therapeutic, and effective in breaking barriers into the spiritual world. I have been endeavoring to create a communitas of exploration with the reader, counting as primary the story and event, not the generalizations and abstractions to be obtained from them; and I have been taking the reader—presumptuously, I am afraid, for such a great task— taking the reader in poetic sympathy to heavenly regions, to the land of quiet in Megan's experience of chi, to the gods of the Kung, to the "equiprimordiality" of Stephen Friedson, to the goddess Shakti, to the Christian sense of a God person with his gift of charism or anointing, to the suburbanite healers' "letting go" and "opening" and finding an "incredible connectedness there," to the power of Wakantanka in the earth below our feet, to the arms of the Blessed Mother, to the high seat of Ghesar Gyalpo of Nepal, to the throne of Allah, and even to the irascible Ndembu Grandfather.

It only remains to give my apologies to all whom I may have offended through my ignorance or, just as likely, through the unworthiness of my praise.

Charlottesville, Virginia, 2005

Notes

CHAPTER 1. BREAKTHROUGH TO HEALING: THE SIGHTING OF AN AFRICAN SPIRIT

1. Victor Turner (1957, 1967, 1968, 1969, 1975).
2. Harner (1980), 113–134.
3. Ibid., 115–117.
4. Ibid., 127–128.

CHAPTER 2. ENERGY HEALING

1. *Chi* is sounded by the Japanese as "ki."
2. Julia Megan Webb, personal communication, April 2002.
3. Eisenberg (1985), 43, 65, 66–67, 108–110, 126, 141, 167, 211–212, 217, 218–219.
4. Ibid., 43.
5. Ibid., 65.
6. Ibid., 66–67.
7. Ibid., 108–110.
8. Ibid., 211–212.
9. Ibid., 141.
10. Ibid., 218–219.
11. Eisenberg's statement to Bill Moyers (1993), 297.
12. Moreno (1943), 3.

13. Katz (1982).

14. Ibid., 64–65.

15. Ibid., 108.

16. Ibid., 70.

17. Ibid., 84.

18. Ibid., 105.

19. Ibid., 82, 83.

20. Ibid., 110.

21. Ibid., 100.

22. Ibid., 100.

23. Ibid., 113–114.

24. Ibid., 44.

25. Ibid., 105.

26. Video recording from *Num Tchai: The Ceremonial Dance of the Kalahari Kung*.

27. The passage on the Tumbuka's comparison of spirit energy with radio was taken from Steven Friedson, *Dancing Prophets: Musical Experience in Tumbuka Healing* (1996), 74–99. Also see 5, 32, 101, 149–150, 158.

28. Friedson (1996). I pieced together events and discussions from Friedson's "In the Vintage Mode" in *Dancing Prophets*, to make a consecutive story showing how a patient in Tumbuka culture would go into trance and later become a healer herself.

29. Friedson (1996), 134.

30. Ibid., 136–137, 149–150.

31. Ibid., 134, 156–158.

32. Ibid., 158, 161.

33. Ibid., 62.

34. Deren (1953), 242.

35. These passages are taken from McGuire (1988), 95–183.

36. Ibid., 4–9.

37. Ibid., 175.

38. Ibid., 100.

39. Ibid., 113.

40. Ibid., 114, 116.

41. Passages on therapeutic touch are paraphrased from Karen Johnson, personal communication, June 1998.

CHAPTER 3. THE EXPERIENCE OF POWER

1. Neihardt (1988).

2. Teilhard de Chardin (1957).

3. This account is based on Samanta's article, "The Powers of the Guru: Shakti, 'Mind,' and Miracles in Narratives of Bengali Religious Experience" (1998).

4. Ibid., 34–35.

5. Ibid., 35.

6. Ibid., 35.

7. Ibid., 36–38.

8. Ibid., 39.

9. Ibid., 39–40.

10. Ibid., 46.

11. Thomas ([1939] 1996), 1460.

12. Excerpted and paraphrased from Csordas (1994), 248, 250.

13. Ibid., 60–61.

14. Paraphrased story from Ibid., 232, 239, 242.

15. MacNutt (1974), 304.

16. Ibid., 304.

17. Csordas (1994), 235.

18. Ibid., 236–237.

19. It has become the custom among social scientists and psychologists to use the word *self* in a very broad way, practically equating it with the old meaning of the word *soul*. This usage came into being when Jung proposed the concept of "the Self" with a capital S, which, he said, was not just the mere conscious "ego" of Freud but included the unconscious—even the collective unconscious (the "collective" here referring to the more mystical range of knowledge of an individual whose "Self" extends into wider space and time dimensions). Recent social anthropologists might wish that he had meant here the connections of person to person in a kind of communitas or communion, but no, this was not within Jung's range of study, which was *the individual.* Jung did not study groups of people in communitas with each other. So the "Self" it had to be. Thus we see that the term *Self* does not rightly replace *soul* or *psyche,* the meaning of which implies other powers beyond ourselves and often a oneness with a communion of beings. Here, *soul* is better and *Self* gives the wrong impression.

20. Lame Deer and Erdoes (1972), 172–189.

21. Powers (1982), 38–68.

22. Lame Deer and Erdoes (1972), 265.

23. Ibid., 39–40.

24. Ibid., 188–189.

25. Powers (1982), 47.

26. Ibid., 56.

27. Ibid., 193–194.

28. Ibid., 55.

29. Ibid., 66.

30. Lame Deer and Erdoes (1972), 172–189; and Powers (1982), 38–68.

31. I Kings, 12, 19.

CHAPTER 4. SCENES OF THE IMPARTING OF POWER

1. Edith Turner (1996), passages from chs. 6 and 12.

2. The material is taken from Joan Metge (1986), passim. Metge, who is the anthropological authority on *whakamaa*, did not give the phenomenon any mystical explanation.

3. Ibid., 15.

4. Ibid., 101.

5. Ibid., 26.

6. Ibid., 26.

7. Ibid., 28–30.

8. Ibid., 33–36.

9. Ibid., 75–76.

10. Ibid., 94.

11. Ibid., 99.

12. Ibid., 101.

13. Reid (1983), 67.

14. Quoted in Dow (1986), 107–110.

15. Excerpted from Niehardt (1961), 96–203.

16. Bilu ([1993] 2000), 100–102.

17. Ibid., 100–102.

CHAPTER 5. THE PRESENCE OF SPIRITS IN HEALING

1. John 1:18.

2. From Reinhardt's article (1988), 126–142, which was adapted from his Ph.D. dissertation in anthropology, University of North Carolina, Chapel Hill.

3. Ibid., 130–132.

4. Acts 1:8.

5. Reinhardt (1988), 130.

6. Quoted from Tyson (professor of religious studies and anthropology; 1988), 107–110.

7. Milingo (1984).

8. Taken from the fieldnotes of Turner and Turner, August 1971 and August 1972; also Cadhain (1945), 20–37; and Walsh (1959), 108–112.

9. Derived from Boddy (1989), 125–237.

10. Ibid., 350.

11. Willis (1989), 11.

12. Willis (1985), 1–2.

13. Extracted from various accounts given by Willis dealing with different episodes and facets of his healing history (1985), 1–2; (1989), 11–12; (1992), 14–15.

14. Derived from Willis et al. (1999), 78–123.
15. Ibid., 94–96, 122.
16. Turner and Turner (1978), 250–251.
17. Taken from Rainey (1947), 275–277.
18. Taken from Edith Turner (1996), 204–207.
19. From Peters (1998), 79–110; adapted to make a story.
20. Harner (1980), 76–91.
21. Derived from Victor Turner (1967), 143–145.
22. James ([1902] 1958).

CHAPTER 6. THE IDEA OF COMMUNITAS

1. Barkat Ali (1985), ix.
2. Chishti (1985), 3–4.
3. Qur'an 2:152.
4. Ibid., 141–147, abridged.
5. Adapted from Victor Turner (1969), 106–107.
6. Victor Turner (1957; 1962; 1975); and Edith Turner (1987).
7. Victor Turner (1992), 58–59.
8. Passages in this section are paraphrased, passim, from Victor Turner (1969; 1974a; 1974b; 1982; 1992); Victor Turner and Edith Turner (1978); and Edith Turner (2004).

CHAPTER 7. PATTERNS OF HEALING

1. The National Museum of the American Indian, opened September 21, 2004.
2. Victor Turner (1699), 94–130.
3. Basso (1996).
4. Goulet (1994).
5. Blake ([1804] 1970), 249, plate 91, lines 29–30. Original: "But General Forms have their vitality in Particulars: and every Particular is a Man, a Divine Member of the Divine Jesus."

Bibliography

Barkat Ali, Abu Anees Muhammad. 1985. Foreword to *The Sufi Book of Healing*, by Shaykh Hakim Moinuddin Chishti. New York: Inner Traditions International.

Basso, Keith. 1996. *Wisdom Sits in Places: Landscape and Language among the Western Apache*. Albuquerque: University of New Mexico Press.

Bilu, Yoram. [1993] 2000. *Without Bounds: The Life and Death of Rabbi Ya'aqov Wazana*. Detroit: Wayne State University Press.

Blake, William. [1804] 1970. "Jerusalem." In *The Poetry and Prose of William Blake*, edited by David Erdman, 143–256. Garden City, NY: Doubleday.

Boddy, Janice. 1989. *Wombs and Alien Spirits: Women, Men, and the Zār Cult in Northern Sudan*. Madison: University of Wisconsin Press.

Cadhain, Liam Ua (William D. Coyne). 1945. *Cnoc Muire in Picture and Story*. Tuam, Ireland: St. Jarlath's College.

Chishti, Shaykh Hakim Moinuddin. 1985. *The Book of Sufi Healing*. New York: Inner Traditions International.

Csordas, Thomas. 1994. *The Sacred Self: A Cultural Phenomenology of Charismatic Healing*. Berkeley: University of California Press.

Deren, Maya. 1953. *Divine Horsemen: The Living Gods of Haiti*. London: Thames and Hudson.

Dow, James. 1986. *The Shaman's Touch: Otomi Indian Symbolic Healing*. Salt Lake City: University of Utah Press.

Eisenberg, David. 1985. *Encounters with Qi: Exploring Chinese Medicine*. New York: Norton.

Eliade, Mircea. 1972. *Shamanism: Archaic Techniques of Ecstasy.* Princeton, NJ: Princeton University Press.

Friedson, Stephen. 1996. *Dancing Prophets: Musical Experiences in Tumbuka Healing.* Chicago: University of Chicago Press.

Goulet, Jean-Guy. 1994. "Ways of Knowing: Towards a Narrative Ethography of Experiences among the Dene Tha." *Journal of Anthropological Research* 50, no. 2: 113–139.

Harner, Michael. 1980. *The Way of the Shaman: A Guide to Power and Healing.* San Francisco: Harper and Row.

Huxley, Thomas. 1860. "Letter to Charles Kingsley." In *The Great Quotations*, compiled by George Seldes, 338. New York: Pocket Books.

James, William. [1902] 1958. *The Varieties of Religious Experience.* New York: Mentor.

Katz, Richard. 1982. *Boiling Energy: Community Healing among the Kalahari Kung.* Cambridge, MA: Harvard University Press.

Lame Deer, John (Fire), and Richard Erdoes. 1972. *Lame Deer, Seeker of Visions.* New York: Washington Square Press.

Lévy-Bruhl, Lucien. [1910] 1985. *How Natives Think.* Princeton, NJ: Princeton University Press.

MacNutt, Francis. 1974. *Healing.* Notre Dame, IN: Ave Maria Press.

McGuire, Meredith. 1988. *Ritual Healing in Suburban America.* New Brunswick, NJ: Rutgers University Press.

Metge, Joan. 1986. *In and Out of Touch: Whakamaa in Cross-Cultural Context.* Wellington, New Zealand: Victoria University Press.

Milingo, Emmanuel. 1984. *The World in Between: Christian Healing and the Struggle for Spiritual Survival.* New York: Urbis, Maryknoll.

Moreno, Jacob L. 1943. "Sociometry and the Cultural Order." *Sociometry: A Journal of Interpersonal Relations* 3, no. 3.

Moyers, Bill. 1993. *Healing and the Mind.* New York: Doubleday.

Neihardt, John G. 1988. *Black Elk Speaks: Being the Life Story of a Holy Man of the Oglala Sioux.* Lincoln: University of Nebraska Press.

Peters, Larry. 1998. *Tamang Shamans: An Ethnopsychiatric Study of Ecstasy and Healing in Nepal.* New Delhi: Nirala.

Powers, William. 1982. *Yuwipi: Vision and Experience in Oglala Ritual.* Lincoln: University of Nebraska Press.

Rainey, Froelich G. 1947. "The Whale Hunters of Tigara." *Anthropological Papers of the American Museum of Natural History* 41, no. 2: 231–283.

Reid, Janice. 1983. *Sorcerers and Healing Spirits.* Canberra: Australian National University Press.

Reinhardt, Douglas. 1988. "With His Stripes We Are Healed: White Pentecostals and Faith Healing." In *Diversities of Gifts: Field Studies in Southern Religion*, edited by Ruel W. Tyson, Jr., James L. Peacock, and Daniel Patterson, 126–142. Urbana: University of Illinois Press.

Samanta, Suchitra. 1998. "The Powers of the Guru: Sakti, 'Mind,' and Miracle in Narratives of Bengali Religious Experience." *Anthropology and Humanism* 23, no. 1: 30–50.

Teilhard de Chardin, Pierre. 1957. *Le Milieu Divin*. London: Collins.

Thomas, Dylan. 1996. "The Force That through the Green Fuse Drives the Flower." In *The Norton Anthology of Poetry*, 4th ed., edited by Margaret Ferguson, Mary Jo Salter, and Jon Stallworthy, 1460. New York: Norton.

Turner, Edith. 1987. *The Spirit and the Drum*. Tucson: University of Arizona Press.

———. 1992. *Experiencing Ritual: A New Interpretation of African Healing*. Philadelphia: University of Pennsylvania Press.

———. 1996. *The Hands Feel It: Healing and Spirit Presence among a Northern Alaskan People*. DeKalb: Northern Illinois University Press.

———. 2004. "Communitas." S.v. In *The Encyclopedia of Religious Rituals*, edited by Frank Salamone, 97–101. Great Barrington, MA: Berkshire/Routledge Religion and Society Series.

Turner, Victor. 1957. *Schism and Continuity in an African Society: A Study of Ndembu Village Life*. Manchester: Manchester University Press.

———.1962. *Chihamba, the White Spirit: A Ritual Drama of the Ndembu*. Manchester, UK: Rhodes-Manchester University Press.

———. 1967. *The Forest of Symbols: Aspects of Ndembu Ritual*. Ithaca, NY: Cornell University Press.

———. 1968. *The Drums of Affliction: A Study of Religious Processes among the Ndembu of Zambia*. Oxford: Clarendon.

———. 1969. *The Ritual Process: Structure and Anti-Structure*. Chicago: Aldine.

———. 1974a. *Dramas, Fields, and Metaphors*. Ithaca, NY: Cornell University Press.

———. 1974b. "Pilgrimage and Communitas." *Studia Missionalia* 23: 305–327.

———. 1975. *Revelation and Divination*. Ithaca, NY: Cornell University Press.

———. 1982. "Liminal to Liminoid in Play, Flow, and Ritual." In *From Ritual to Theatre: The Human Seriousness of Play*, edited by Victor Turner, 20–60. New York: Performing Arts Journal Publications.

———. 1992. "Variations on a Theme of Liminality." In *Blazing the Trail*, edited by Victor Turner, 49–65. Tucson: University of Arizona Press.

Turner, Victor, and Edith Turner. 1978. "Appendix A: Notes on Processual Symbolic Analysis." In *Image and Pilgrimage in Christian Culture: Anthropological Perspectives*, edited by Victor Turner and Edith Turner, 243–255. New York: Columbia University Press.

Tyson, Ruel. 1988. "The Testimony of Annie Mae." In *Diversities of Gifts: Field Studies in Southern Religion*, edited by Ruel W. Tyson, James L. Peacock, and Daniel W. Patterson, 105–125. Urbana: University of Illinois Press.

Walsh, Michael. 1959. *The Shrine of the Pilgrim People of God*. Tuam, Ireland: St. Jarlath's College.

Willis, Roy. 1985. "Personal Experience Supplement." *The Aquarian Group (In-*

dependent Special Interest Group of British Mensa Newsletter) 8 (August): 1–2.

———. 1989. "A Healer's Personal Experience." *New Paradigms Newsletter* 7 (June): 11–12.

———. 1992. "Encounter with Healing." *International Journal of Alternative and Complementary Healing* (April): 14–15.

Willis, Roy, with K.B.S. Chisanga, H.M.K. Sikazwe, Kapembwa B. Sikazwe, and Sylvia Nanyangwe. 1999. *Some Spirits Heal, Others Only Dance: A Journey into Human Selfhood in an African Village*. Oxford: Berg.

Index

About the Author

EDITH TURNER is a renowned anthropologist and editor of the journal *Anthropology and Humanism*. Her books include: *The Hands Feel It: Healing and Spirit Presence among a Northern Alaskan People* (2003), *Image and Pilgrimage in Christian Culture: Lectures on the History of Religions* (1995), and *Blazing the Trail: Way Marks in the Exploration of Symbols* (1992).